Housewise

Housewise

The Smart Woman's
Guide to Buying and Renovating
Real Estate for Profit

by

SUZANNE BRANGHAM

PERENNIAL LIBRARY

Harper & Row, Publishers, New York

Cambridge, Philadelphia, San Francisco, Washington
London, Mexico City, São Paulo, Singapore, Sydney

HOUSEWISE. Copyright © 1987 by Suzanne Brangham. All rights reserved. Printed in the United States of America. No part of this book may be used or reproduced in any manner whatsoever without written permission except in the case of brief quotations embodied in critical articles and reviews. For information address Harper & Row, Publishers, Inc., 10 East 53rd Street, New York, N.Y. 10022. Published simultaneously in Canada by Fitzhenry & Whiteside Limited, Toronto.

First PERENNIAL LIBRARY edition published 1988.

LIBRARY OF CONGRESS CATALOG CARD NUMBER: 87-46122

ISBN: 0-06-097164-9 (pbk.)

88   89   90   91   92   FG   10   9   8   7   6   5   4   3   2

If moving as often as we did
can produce a son like William,
I highly recommend it.
To him,
I dedicate this book.

Many thanks to Liza Mundy, who first helped me get all my ideas and enthusiasm on paper. Christine Tomasino, who guided and steered me through the exciting world of publishing. Judith Sachs, who organized, added to, and doctored all my material to make it a book. Nancy Novogrod, who skillfully edited, polished, and fine-tuned the manuscript. Raymond Brown, John De Martini, and M. Butterfield-Brown for their direction and corrections.

Contents

Photographs appear after page 148

Housewise

Introduction

Not long ago, at a lovely dinner party, I was seated beside an investment banker, an amusing man who regaled me with stories of the marketplace. Eventually, he asked me, "How do you spend your time? Do you work, or are you a housewife?"

In the spirit of the evening, I said, "No, I'm actually a homewrecker!"

He blushed and blinked, taking me at my word. "I beg your pardon," he said.

"Seriously, I tear homes apart and put them back together again," I explained.

My dinner partner sipped at his glass of Cabernet, peered at me over his glasses, and said, "You're not a housewife, you're *housewise*."

The man was right. In the past fifteen years, I've bought, renovated, and sold 71 houses and apartments. I've seen my work featured in newspapers and magazines, and have participated in television shows and seminars, sharing with millions what I've learned about the field I adore.

In my other lives, I've been a teacher, an interior designer, an advertising executive, and a publicist, but home-wrecking—a term I coined for home renovation—suits me best. Call it a short attention span if you like, but I'm a firm believer in changing either jobs or cities every five years. There's a lot to experience in this world, so why stand still?

My story began in San Francisco in 1972. When I couldn't find a job I liked, I decided to create my own career. I agreed to purchase a dilapidated apartment with very little cash, then renovated and resold it in six months for an enormous profit. After a few more successes like this one, I formed a California corporation with two friends in order to renovate homes. Three years later, I bought my partners out, returning four times their original investment. I kept rolling real estate, buying more and more property with the profits from houses I sold. I was making money on every single house I renovated.

The biggest lesson I learned in the property business is that there are no absolutes except yourself. Prices fluctuate; products change. Markets move up and down. Tax laws are rewritten every year. Interest rates are as predictable as unwired champagne corks. But there is one stable element in all this: the person who renovates for profit.

That person can be *you*. Whether you know it or not, you are innately blessed with most of the abilities you need to go into this business. Few women realize the marketability of their decorating and management skills—acquired strictly by taking care of their own homes.

Property renovation is for everyone but this book is, in particular, directed to the woman who wants to be creative and productive and is eager to have an income of her own.

I'm about to provide you with invaluable information on every aspect of real estate: looking for property, negotiating a contract, financing a purchase, redesigning a house, hiring the right crew, supervising the work, participating in the renovation, selling the finished product, then rolling the profits and starting all over again. I will introduce you to the people who play an essential role—the agents, buyers, sellers, bankers, accountants, lawyers, business partners, architects, and contractors.

This is not an interior decorating book or a real estate

get-rich-quick manual. I provide no secret recipes for wheat paste or how to buy a fifty-unit building with no money down. Rather than telling you precisely how to stipple your walls or finesse the finer points of accounting, I will paint a big picture of the house and its market in broad, bold, money-making strokes. I'll lead you step by step along the way in choosing what property to buy and how to finance it, then I'll take the whole house apart, room by room, and make practical recommendations on what to eliminate, what to install, and most important, what will *sell*. I will provide you with the confidence and know-how to create a job for yourself—perhaps a career. The biggest requirement for entering the field of home renovation is a positive attitude. The rewards, both financial and emotional, are tremendous.

Having been a wife, a mother, and then a single parent during my fifteen years in this business, I can attest to the fact that this career accommodates all life-styles and schedules. There's no reason why you can't be a homemaker and a homewrecker at the same time. You can put all your acquired homemaking skills to good use and turn these talents into a sizable income.

If you're a housewife, you're an expert at making a home work. If you have children, you're undoubtedly a manager, a budgeter, a scheduler, a referee. If you're divorced, home renovation is the perfect way for you to start a new life, find a new job, generate your very own income. If you're single, home renovation is an ideal career. You're free, flexible, and mobile. You can move when, where, and as often as you like. You can be your own boss, work long hours or short as you see fit. You can gamble and take risks.

Being married is a wonderful way of life. Being single is a wonderful way of life. But being independently wealthy is the most wonderful way of all. If I can do it, so can you—you can turn your instincts and talents into a career. You are eminently qualified to become a success in real estate, just as I have.

Now, I'm going to show you how.

1

Turning Your Talents into Profit

Virginia Woolf said it beautifully: "Every woman must have a room of her own." I like to carry this one step further. To my way of thinking, every woman must be financially independent, with a nice bank account of her own. Then she can have as many rooms as she likes.

Financial independence means that you have the freedom to do what you want, go where you want, buy what you want, give away what you want—depending on no one else for support. You're free to make yourself a richer, more exciting life.

How I Gained My Independence

I got started on the road to financial independence by going into the business of renovating residential property. It happened purely by accident.

In the past, when I was looking for a job, I'd let my fingers do the walking through the classifieds until I saw something I thought I'd like to do. Then I'd whip off a telegram to my potential boss, saying, "URGENT! YOU NEED ME!" It had always worked before; it took employers utterly by surprise. By the time I got to an office for a personal interview, I was pretty confident that I could talk him or her into hiring me.

But this time, the tactic wouldn't have worked even if I'd found something worth pursuing. This was San Francisco, in 1972. The city was teeming with qualified job hunters, and there were twenty-five people competing for each available position. They were all willing to work for peanuts just for the privilege of having a view of the Golden Gate Bridge.

I wasn't interested in peanuts; I wanted to do something lucrative, and something wonderful. I knocked on every conceivable door, but they were all slammed in my face. I was beginning to think I'd never find anything really appealing that someone would pay me to do. And then it fell into my lap.

While I was searching for the ideal career, I was also looking for a place to live. I located a lovely but dilapidated old apartment house on Nob Hill, a posh neighborhood where you pay four times the price for four times the view. Built before the 1906 earthquake, the building hadn't been touched since it was constructed. It was now making the painful transition from rentals to condominiums and advertising apartments for sale or rent.

Sales were very slow. Slow? They were practically nonexistent. Only two of the fourteen units had sold, both to older tenants who had lived in the building. The "condo concept" was still pretty new, which kept potential buyers at a distance. To compound the problem, the building's owner had made a tactical error with the model unit. It was terrific, streamlined, complete with a magnificent kitchen of Italian-modern design. But the contrast between the model and the other unrenovated units—the apartments actually for sale—was scary. In fact, you wouldn't dream of putting money down on one of these losers unless you had degrees in architecture, interior design, and sanitary engineering.

Or unless, like me, you were bored and unemployed.

I made an appointment with the building's sales manager, armed with an irresistible proposition. He was reading the paper when I walked into his office. Probably scanning the classifieds himself.

I was wearing my business-meeting best, and had rehearsed my persuasive speech until I could say it in my sleep. With my head held high, preliminary plans and a budget tucked under my arm, I was about to make the manager an offer he couldn't refuse.

I told him that in lieu of paying the $800-a-month rent that was being asked for a two-bedroom, two-bath unit, I would renovate the entire apartment, spending the equivalent of one year's rent, or $9,600, in labor and materials.

Basically, I was selling myself. I wanted to show him that my personal taste reflected the way I lived and the environment I would create. I didn't really know what I was getting myself into, but I've always enjoyed making deals. I had been complimented on my taste in interior design in the past. I knew what I liked, and had an ability to transform an empty space into attractive living quarters.

I told the manager exactly what was wrong with the apartments and what should be done to make them livable. I also told him what *I* would do to make one of them salable, and worth a great deal more money. He looked surprised at first, but admitted that the place needed a lot of work. I promised him that I would finish the renovations within twelve months, and show him the receipts for $9,600. I also requested a year's lease-option, an agreement to rent with an exclusive option to buy at anytime during or at the end of the year. The asking price was $45,000, and by signing a lease-option agreement, I would be investing in something I could buy tomorrow at yesterday's price.

The manager's face brightened. At the end of a year, he would either make an easy sale to me or he would have a deluxe apartment to sell at a higher price. He decided to gamble on me. We had a deal.

Unemployment was becoming a lot more fun. I stopped pounding the pavements and started on the walls. Anyone who saw the place would have agreed that the $9,600 renovation budget I'd set myself was very low for the amount of work that had to be done. So I got as many contractor's estimates as I could in a city where I knew no one, using the Yellow Pages as my trusty companion and guide.

I ran around town looking at renovations and inquiring about contractors. I decided to hire not the highest-priced and not the lowest-priced contracting firm, but the one whose work I had seen and admired, the one run by a man who had no objections to my participation in the job. Overalls became my daily attire and the workmen my closest friends.

We removed the wall between the kitchen and dining room to make an open kitchen—family room, kept the walk-in pantry, and replaced all the old cabinets, countertops, and appliances. We installed a 6-foot center island for extra storage and eat-in space. I took the old brass chandelier from the dining room, polished it to within an inch of its life, and hung it in the kitchen. A new vanity in the master bathroom, some wallpaper in the kitchen and baths, and paint throughout completed the job. When all the workmen were gone, I called in a professional floor man to scrape and wax the hardwood floors. The job was done in four months, on budget and way ahead of schedule. It looked terrific.

Two months after I'd moved in, I had some friends over for cocktails. One of my guests, a real estate agent, brought along a client of his—a gentleman who was moving to San Francisco because of a job transfer. He thought my apartment was fantastic. So fantastic that he wanted to buy it.

At 10:00 A.M. the following day my friend the agent

handed me an offer from his client. He wanted to purchase the apartment for $85,000.

I gulped, glanced quickly at my calculator, and shook hands on the deal.

REAPING THE BENEFITS: A $23,000 PROFIT

*O*f course, I had to purchase the apartment before I could pass title to someone else. So I exercised my option and signed an agreement to buy it for $45,000. I signed a second contract with the new buyer, took his 10% down payment ($8,500), and opened a double escrow account at the title company. Both purchases would occur simultaneously.

An escrow is a deposit of agreements between buyer and seller, held by a third neutral party (generally a title company or a lawyer), who sees to it that the terms of the deal are carried out to the letter.

On closing day, when title to a property passes from seller to buyer, I went to the title company and signed all the closing documents to exercise my option and purchase the apartment. Then I signed another set of papers to sell. I owned the condominium for a matter of minutes—just long enough to collect a $23,000 profit.

Unemployment was the best-paying job I ever had.

My First Deal

Sales price for the new buyer	$ 85,000
My option price	−45,000
	40,000
Renovation costs (my only cash in the deal)	− 9,600
	30,400
Real estate commission (6% of $85,000)	− 5,100
	25,300
Closing costs (buyer pays for some in a double-escrow deal)	− 2,300
PROFIT	$ 23,000

ROLLING THE PROFITS

I didn't stop there. Nothing speaks like performance, and I had performed admirably. So I contracted to buy a second apartment from the manager. Maybe the only thing that speaks louder than performance is cash—and now I had much more cash, thanks to my first sale.

The asking price on a four-bedroom, three-bath luxury unit was $100,000, but after I explained in detail all the work that had to be done, the manager agreed to a sales price of $90,000. After all, it meant another "Sold" sticker on his condo map. Because I was rolling the profits from my primary residence into a second, more expensive purchase, I didn't have to pay the government any tax on the profit I'd made.

I didn't want to sink all of my recent earnings into this new apartment, so I told the manager I would give him only a 10% down payment ($9,000). Then, armed with the contract as proof of my first sale, I went to a savings-and-loan and secured a mortgage for 90% of the purchase price ($81,000). I would be paying about $3,000 for closing costs (title insurance, recording fees, prorations, and loan fees). This left me $11,000 from the first sale for renovations and monthly debt service—my mortgage payments, property taxes, and insurance.

I had learned from my first experience that I had to budget in all costs of homewrecking when making a purchase. That includes monthly carrying costs as well as renovation plans.

This second property needed a new kitchen, a master bathroom, and painting and polishing throughout. It took two and a half months of full-time work for me and a crew of four to complete the major part of the job. In order to bring the renovation in on schedule, they agreed to work weekends and nights. Not only did the workmen become my best friends, they became my roommates as well.

When the renovation was completed, the place was, I must modestly confess, a knockout. Before I had a chance to

operate the new self-cleaning oven, I had an offer for
$140,000! Closing day couldn't come soon enough for me. It
was beginning to feel like going to the winners' window at
the Kentucky Derby.

Turning Your Skills
into Dollars

*A*s I accumulated my real estate successes, I real-
ized what a natural choice homewrecking is for
anyone who wants to begin marching down a de-
lightful path toward security strewn with appreciating assets. Well, you say, that sounds great, but how do I know *I*
can do it?

It requires initiative and some risk-taking to start a
new business. But the time and money are worth the gamble, especially since you are starting out in a profession
where you already have some experience—creating a comfortable home environment. You know that a well-equipped
kitchen works and how a three-bedroom house with only
one bath doesn't. Whether you want to sow the seeds of an
empire or simply start a little venture of your own, what
could be more natural than buying, renovating, and selling
houses?

There are women for whom buying a million-dollar
mansion is both a goal and a real possibility. There are
those for whom an extra $10,000 or $20,000 a year would
more than suffice. Both have the key to either type of success.

A woman today can hold an executive position inside as
well as outside the house. Whether she manages a company, serves as an executive secretary, or argues legal
cases, she also has the job of running her own home. She is
generally in charge of all decisions about household money,
maintenance, and interior design. She may also organize
the lives of the other family members.

Even career women living with men who share the load

can shop, cook, clean, budget, schedule, entertain, and put together a household routine. Who hasn't hired repairmen, negotiated estimates for the jobs to be done, and paid the bills? Every woman has probably pounded a nail or two in her time—maybe even painted or papered a wall.

There's not a reason in the world why you can't turn your natural and acquired skills of organization in the home or at the office to professional advantage. You are eminently qualified to become a success in real estate, just as I did.

GETTING STARTED

*A*ll you have to do to get started is to take your talents and your experience to market.

Where do you begin? You don't have to fill out an application form or have a college degree. There are no want ads for this job, no interviews, no preparatory courses. It doesn't require a lot of capital or a Harvard MBA. You are the boss, relying on your own instincts and ideas, capable of handling a dozen different aspects of each job, from money to Masonite, from terms of agreement to termites.

What do you need to get started? Something you already have—*an ability to ask questions and to get along with others*. Homewrecking is a people profession, involving bankers, realtors, accountants, lawyers, architects, contractors, designers, and the sellers and buyers of houses you will own. It's a profession all about seeking advice, dealing with people, and knowing how to treat them well. You will be in the driver's seat, listening carefully to all the suggestions your colleagues will be giving you, and then making the final decisions. You will be pitching in yourself and supervising the work of others, transforming a diamond in the rough into a sparkling gem.

So What's Stopping You?

*F*or some reason, buying property for the first time stops a lot of people in their tracks. They've bought cars and financed college educations, they've splurged on a trip to Europe or an expensive computer, but the idea of purchasing a home fills them with dread. It used to do the same thing to me.

Making an offer on your first piece of real estate is nothing compared to getting on a roller coaster or a pair of skis for the first time. It's easier than having four wisdom teeth pulled, and it's a piece of cake compared to getting married! The wonderful thing about buying property is that after you make an offer, you have time to consider and investigate your decision thoroughly. If it doesn't feel right, you can change your mind and walk away.

Here are the most common fears people have about getting into the real estate market:

1. FEAR OF KNOWING NOTHING ABOUT BUYING property. You can conquer this one by educating yourself. My book and many others (see the recommended reading list at the end of this book) will give you a good start. Talk with real estate agents, bankers, lawyers, accountants, contractors, architects, designers, and friends and relatives who have just bought homes. Make a habit of reading the real estate section in your local newspaper. Check out the interest rates, fees, and mortgage conditions of local banks and savings and loan associations. Take a sample loan application—they're free!

2. FEAR OF KNOWING NOTHING ABOUT CON-struction. All right, you don't have a carpenter's or plumber's license. But you don't *need* to know about channel locks, hose bibs, or plumb lines. All you have to know is that every system must run smoothly—plumbing, electrical, gas, heating, and cooling—and that you need a good foundation and a leakproof roof. The contractor or the engineering inspector who examines your house will show you where all the shut-off valves are, so you'll be able to turn off the water and power in case of an emergency and get to a phone to call an expert to repair it.

Once you start remodeling, it's incredible what you pick up by just being on-site and watching the pros at work. Suddenly you'll find yourself able to fix a leaky faucet, stop a running toilet, install a dimmer switch. That's if you want to. If you don't, you can always pay someone else to do it.

3. FEAR OF NOT BEING ABLE TO PUT A DEAL TO-gether. If you can add, subtract, multiply, and divide, you're halfway there. You deal with numbers all the time—shopping for food and clothing, balancing the checkbook, figuring out the monthly household budget. You negotiate terms every day, whether it's discussing an issue with a colleague at the office or the curfew hour with your teenager. Your real estate agent, accountant, or lawyer will help you with any heavy or technical wheeling and dealing. An appraiser will make sure that you're not spending a lot more than a property is worth, and a banker won't lend you money if he feels you can't afford to pay it back.

4. FEAR OF NOT BEING ABLE TO COME UP WITH the down payment. You may not have a huge chunk of money stashed away, but you undoubtedly have some assets you can rely on. You can do without a new car for a while; you can postpone your deluxe vacation one year. You can beg or borrow money from a variety of sources; and, perhaps the seller himself will go for some creative financing, if he's eager to move his property.

5. FEAR OF NOT BEING ABLE TO MEET YOUR monthly mortgage payment. You already make monthly payments, don't you? If you are currently paying your bills on time and satisfying your outstanding financial commitments, there's no reason to assume that you shouldn't be able to manage the costs of running the house you own—whether it's your residence or an investment property. And because you are going to do all your figuring beforehand, you won't be buying a house you can't afford. There are properties available for every income bracket—I'll show you how to be a creative buyer and select the right one for you.

6. FEAR OF BUYING AT THE WRONG TIME. THERE *is* no wrong time to buy real estate, regardless of the market, regardless of the interest rates. I've turned a profit on my properties through good times and bad, every year for the past fifteen years.

An advantageous time to purchase is in a buyer's market when mortgage money is hard to get, interest rates are high, and sellers are having a difficult time moving their homes. If a seller is motivated to move his house quickly, you can usually bargain effectively on price and persuade him to finance a large part of the deal. A seller's market occurs when there's plenty of money for new homebuyers at competitive interest rates and a seller can sit back and choose the best offer.

But if you're patient and careful in your selection of residential property, you can find a good buy and sell at a profit. You must, of course, remodel your house beautifully, but if you've got quality, you'll sell. It makes absolutely no difference what day, month, or year it is.

7. FEAR OF HAVING TO MANAGE PEOPLE. IF YOU treat your workmen as you treat anyone else, if you have respect for others' opinions and are a good listener, you'll get along fine. You can draw on your executive qualities as you make decisions and supervise the direction of the remodeling. As long as you maintain your own standards and are firm but flexible about your expectations, you can manage any staff.

8. FEAR OF BEING LABELED A SPECULATOR. Speculators are investors who pick up a piece of property, give the place a new coat of paint (if that), and sell again to turn a profit. I've never taken this approach. Instead, I push my profit upward by making a lot more out of the properties I buy and renovate.

What I do—investing creative time, energy, and a substantial sum of money to improve property—is not speculating. It's hard work and a labor of love, and everyone benefits from it. You almost guarantee yourself a profit because of the quality work you do, and at the same time, you make the new buyers happy, improve the neighborhood, and brighten a corner of the town or city. You don't have to split your profits with anyone, but you share all the rewards.

9. FEAR OF NEGLECTING FAMILY COMMITMENTS. You may think you can't go into this field because:

- You're single and alone.

- You're divorced and unsure.

- You're married, living with a husband.

- You have children to care for.

Excuses, excuses! Remodeling houses is completely adaptable to any life-style. If you're single or divorced, your time is your own. You can take your money and do what you please with it.

If, however, you are married to someone who feels that you should be a full-time homemaker instead of a full-time homewrecker, you can make your own hours, quitting at noon, 2:00 P.M., or 5:00 P.M. to tend to the needs of your household. This is a perfect career for the married woman who wants a lucrative part-time job. And as for taking care of children at the same time, their school hours become your work hours.

Home ownership and renovation is to be enjoyed, not feared. What more satisfying field could you find than one that earns you a good salary, is flexible enough to adapt to your schedule, and puts a roof over your head, all at the same time?

You Can Be
a Homewrecker
Anywhere

*W*herever there are people, there are houses. This means that homewrecking is a profession that can be practiced almost anywhere in the world. If you live in a small town, the pickings may be slimmer than in a major city or a bustling suburb, but there are always houses crying out for attention. Housing is likely to be more affordable in rural, residential communities where salaries and the cost of living are lower than in more densely populated areas.

Getting started may also be easier in a suburb or a small city. Basic trust still cements deals in small towns, and a loan officer at a local bank may be more reliant on his impression of you than on impersonal financial statements, and therefore easier to deal with.

On the other hand, your opportunities for real estate investment widen with the size of the city you live in. In addition to houses, there are condominiums and cooperative apartments available, and you will find a greater variety of architectural styles, sizes, locations, and prices. If you are moving to a new area, do some research about the real estate possibilities before you relocate.

Start Small, Think Big

*Y*our first homewrecking job will be your hardest— and it may also be your cheapest. Budget it carefully. You should spend the least amount of money you can, so that if you make a few mistakes, it won't spell catastrophe for your checkbook or the property.

Never get in over your head. Don't expect to transform a

rambling wreck into a magnificent castle your first time out. That comes later.

A small house is a great place to start, because it's doable, and its flaws won't overwhelm your abilities. The same goes for a studio or one-bedroom apartment—either a condo or a co-op. Obviously, the smaller the property, the less expensive it will be. And the more remodeling it needs, the greater your ability to bargain the purchase price down even lower.

You may be able to get something for little or no money down, or, as I did, a lease-option, where all you have to pay is the cost of the renovation. You're looking for a "fixer-upper," or a "handyman's special," a single-family house that's been on the market a little too long, or a unit in a multiple dwelling that's in disrepair.

Once you've turned this first property around—perhaps by tearing down some walls, replumbing old pipes, adding a brand-new kitchen and bath, and covering the floor with a carpet plush enough to swim in—you'll take it to market so that you can quickly experience the joy of making a profit. And that profit may motivate you to start looking for property number two.

A NEW WAY TO THINK ABOUT REAL ESTATE

*T*he field of home remodeling changed the way I looked at the world, and will probably do the same to you. It engulfs you in the way a new job, marriage, or parenthood does. Before you know it:

- *Your sense of sight will change.* You'll become aware of colors, shapes, patterns, materials, lighting—what works and what doesn't. That means you may buy an eggplant at the grocery store and try to duplicate the rich, dark sheen on your dining-room walls.

- *Your sense of hearing will change.* You'll be aware of traffic sounds, and whether they're too close for comfort to the property you want to bid on. You'll learn to know the hum of a properly functioning boiler and the sickening grind of a busted dishwasher.

- *Your sense of smell will change.* You'll know that a purchase near a sewage-treatment plant is out, and that the bouquet of freshly cut lumber is in.

- *Your way of thinking will change.* You'll start to think like a homewrecker, viewing houses for their investment potential and resalability. Don't be surprised if on the third day of vacation, you start looking at property.

When your way of looking at real estate changes, your own city will take on new dimensions. You'll start observing housing trends, changing neighborhoods, newly painted facades, terrific landscaping. You'll drive down a street and realize that "For Sale" signs are as important to you as STOP signs.

You're about to dress up and go shopping. I will show you where to look, whom to call, how to recognize the right property, when to buy it, and what to spend. Then I'll explain what goes into that crucial transformation from "a nice house" to "a knockout."

Any woman can take a house and turn it into a home. Now you're going to learn how to turn it into a bonanza.

Checkpoints

You can be a home renovator if at least half of these statements apply to you:

- ▶   You can sell yourself to others.

- You can listen well and take advice.

- You are handy around the house.

- You know how to get things done.

- You have a flair for home decorating.

- You are willing to work with a budget.

- You can manage a schedule.

- You enjoy the challenge of negotiating terms.

- You are in the market for an exciting full- or part-time job.

- You want to gain financial independence.

2
Real Estate: A Guaranteed Investment

here is simply no better asset than owning your own home. It's the only investment you can see, touch, stand on, live in, develop, and control completely. When you own property, you can watch your asset appreciate and, at the same time, deduct from your taxable income almost everything it costs to maintain it.

Real estate is *real*. It's real land, real appreciation, real tangible, and real profitable.

Our legislators confirmed with the tax reform bill of 1986 the great advantage to taxpayers of owning the property they live in. Deductions of all the interest paid on your home loan and real estate property taxes make the purchase of owner-occupied property and second homes one of the best investments in America.

REAL ESTATE
SURROUNDS US

*E*verywhere we look, there's real estate—parks, playgrounds, factories, freeways, farms, schools, libraries, churches, houses, high-rises, hotels, restaurants, refineries, theaters, sidewalks, and shopping centers.

You can explore other investment opportunities, but you'll be hard pressed to find another commodity that's as permanent and profitable as real estate. Stocks can go bust and even in the best of times provide mostly paper profits, oil wells dry up or the price per barrel can plummet, metals rust, gold and silver values fluctuate, and diamonds, at today's astronomical prices, are rarely in the comfort range of the average investor. Savings accounts, money market accounts, and certificates of deposit are safe, but after you pay taxes on the income they generate, they aren't very lucrative. They can never provide the kind of return on investment or the tax deductions that property offers.

Real estate lasts forever and is worth more every day. Why? Because there's only a finite amount of land—we can't manufacture any more of it. Our land growth is at zero; our population growth is not.

The baby boom of the late forties and early fifties has sent an enormous number of eager buyers into the real estate offices of the eighties. Housing prices, however high they may appear today, will never be any lower in almost every part of the country. The average one-family home in 1970 cost $25,000. By 1976, the price had nearly doubled, and by 1980, it had nearly tripled. According to a January 1986 survey conducted by savings and loan associations in 420 urban areas across the country, the average homebuyer is thirty-eight years old, married, with a family income of $42,000. The typical price of a first house is $75,000, with a down payment of $14,000. A survey done by the National Association of Realtors at year end, in December of 1987, found that the median-priced American home was $87,900. In the biggest cities, the scale is thrown off completely. The median sales price for a single-family home in the metropolitan New York area in December 1987 was $180,800. In the San Francisco Bay area it was $176,000. In Boston, it was $178,000; in Los Angeles, $145,200; in San Diego, $131,800; and in Washington, D.C., $122,400.

Real estate is an active industry. Houses never stop selling. The housing market may have slowed at times in the past, but it has never—nor will it ever—stand still. Supply and demand is the name of the game, which means that *you can't lose if you invest in well-located residential property— urban or suburban.* Next to food and love, shelter is our most basic need. Prince or pauper, count or caveman, we all need a place to bed down.

BUY! DON'T RENT

*I*f you are currently paying out a monthly fee to live in someone else's property, you're throwing money out your window—or, actually, your landlord's window. If you are writing a rent check every month, at the end of the year you have twelve canceled checks to show for your investment. Your landlord, on the other hand, gets to use *your* money to cover his mortgage payments, property taxes, and the insurance on his building.

Your rent should be going for an investment in your future. If you buy a house, a condominium, or a cooperative apartment and put your monthly rent toward a mortgage, you will be building equity in a piece of property as well as building yourself a nest. Since we all need a place to live and we all like a good return on our hard-earned money, it only makes sense to buy property, not lease it!

Why are you still renting? Is it because your parents did it? Or because you feel you can't afford to buy? Is it because you can't bear the idea of being responsible for the heat going off or the toilet overflowing? In most cases, it's you, the tenant, who suffers when something goes wrong with your rental unit, because you're on-site and have to deal with the problem immediately. You get reimbursed for expenses but not for your time and inconvenience.

Perhaps the persistence of the rental market has something to do with the notion that we should pay today for what we use today. A ten-, fifteen-, or thirty-year mortgage seems staggering if you're the type of person who pays her bills on the first of the month and never owes anyone a dime.

But consider your use of credit cards. If you charge items with a piece of plastic, you are, in effect, buying into the "on-time" system. You figure you don't have the money today for that new desk or the terrific coat you found on sale, but you'll have it by the time the credit-card company bills you for it. If you can tolerate the "credit-card mentality" to this extent, you can live with a mortgage. And if you become a dedicated homewrecker, you won't be holding on to a mortgage for long anyway. You'll be paying off your existing loan and making a lovely profit before assuming your next one.

Let's look at what happens when you buy a house or apartment and finance it with a long-term (fifteen to thirty year) mortgage. Each month, you'll be sending your checks —the ones you would have sent to your landlord—to a lending institution. These payments, your **debt service,** go to reduce the amount of money you owe on your house. Each month, you are paying the lender a certain amount of interest (at whatever the prevailing rate was when you obtained the loan) and a portion of the principal. At the beginning, you'll be paying more interest than principal. It reverses about two-thirds of the way through your mortgage term. But remember, *the interest is deductible from your federal taxable income.*

Not only are you benefiting from paying a monthly check into your own account instead of a landlord's, you are also gaining immeasurably every year as your home appreciates and you build more equity by slowly paying off your loan. And every improvement you make increases the value and offers a variety of benefits:

- A proven hedge against inflation

- Tax write-offs

- A sound, low-risk investment

- An appreciating asset

- Increased value through improvements

- More control of your environment (you don't
  need to check with your landlord)

- Generally, more space—indoors and out

- More privacy

- More personal stability

- Pride of ownership

Many incentives for homeownership are built into our
economy. The government *wants* you to own property:

1. When you own a home, you can deduct your
   expenses (interest and property taxes) from
   your federal income tax.

2. When you want to sell and buy again, you
   can defer all your taxes from each home sale
   as long as your new home costs as much or
   more than the sale price of the last. The government allows you two years (during which
   time you can do whatever you like with the
   proceeds of your house sale) to purchase a
   new home.

3. When you're over fifty-five, you can take a
   one-time profit from Uncle Sam of $125,000
   on the sale of your principal residence, tax-
   free, as long as you've lived in it for three out
   of the past five years.

The only time you want to handle a rent check again is when you're on the receiving end—collecting money on a residential property you may be leasing out to someone else . . . someone who's still paying rent!

WHICH NEIGHBORHOODS ARE BEST?

*S*ome areas appreciate faster than others. Some questionable neighborhoods are coming back with a vengeance. And some boom towns, once the capitals of steel or fabric production, have turned to ghost towns as factories close down. You have to do your research thoroughly each time you buy in a new area, but it's generally safe to say that if you stick to residential property near bustling population centers, you can't go wrong.

Under no circumstances should you begin with recreational, agricultural, or raw undeveloped property. You want all those nice amenities like water, streets, and sewers built into your first purchase. You want to buy and be where the action is, and that's where people live and work.

Established neighborhoods are a safe investment, if you can afford them. They will have a high percentage of schools, churches, recreational facilities, and good shopping. "Changing" neighborhoods—those undergoing development and gentrification—appreciate more slowly, but you'll get a better buy for your money. You may notice interesting properties in an older section of town where formerly grand houses that have fallen on hard times are being given a face-lift. If at least 25% of the houses in a neighborhood are in the process of renovation, and if you have a little bit of the pioneer spirit, then this may be a perfect place to begin your homewrecking career.

If you plan to hold on to your first house for two to five years, then you can wait for an up-and-coming neighborhood to up and come. But "iffy" neighborhoods, where no movement or renovation is going on, are a bigger gamble. It costs just as much to do the plumbing in a questionable neighborhood as it does on the best block in town. My advice is to *pay more for location,* because you'll get more out of your investment in the long run. A higher mortgage is worth the monthly expense when it means a quick resale.

WHAT KIND OF HOUSING IS AVAILABLE?

*W*hen you start looking for your first **home-wrecking** project, you'll have a variety of options to consider:

1. SINGLE-FAMILY DETACHED HOUSES. NEW OR used, this is by far the most popular housing alternative available today. The houses are separated from others and sit on a piece of land. About three out of five American homeowners buy single-family detached homes.

2. SINGLE-FAMILY ATTACHED HOUSES. YOU OWN your own home, but share common walls. **Row houses** in New York, Baltimore, Boston, and San Francisco are one example; another is the **duplex** or **mother-daughter** home with one unit built on top or beside the other. This housing style can be more economical and easier to maintain than a detached house, but it does not offer the same benefit of privacy.

3. MULTIPLE-FAMILY DWELLINGS. APARTMENT houses sprang up at the turn of the century and were most often used as income-producing properties by absentee landlords. These buildings range in size from two- or three-story walk-ups to high-rise buildings. Many developers are converting multiple-dwelling apartment houses into condominiums or cooperatives, at great profit.

4. CONDOMINIUMS. ALL THE RESIDENTS OWN the interior of their particular unit, which may be in a multiple-unit dwelling or an attached townhouse in a develop-

ment, but not the exterior or the land it sits on. They also own an undivided interest in the common elements of the property. The homeowners are responsible for maintaining the interior of their own units; in the common area, they are in charge of deciding on work that needs to be done, and they share the costs—for example, of a new lobby or roof. The owners pay a monthly maintenance fee which goes toward the care and feeding of the property. A condo can be financed like a house.

5. COOPERATIVE APARTMENTS. RESIDENTS IN A co-op building do not own their apartment, but rather own shares in the building which entitle them to occupy a unit. As shareholders, the residents are jointly responsible for all debts incurred by the building. A board, made up of shareholders, controls the purse strings and decides on all maintenance and repair work, and also approves all prospective homebuyers. Financing a co-op with a standard mortgage is possible in most cities, but in some buildings you are required to pay all cash because this is one way the board can be sure that you can "afford" to live in the building. As in condos, there's a monthly maintenance fee.

6. MOBILE HOMES AND HOUSEBOATS. IT'S TRUE you can live almost anywhere, in anything that provides you with shelter from the elements. But because mobile homes and houseboats are valuable only in and of themselves and not for the land or water space they occupy, they are not generally good candidates for renovation.

WHERE TO BEGIN YOUR HOMEWRECKING CAREER

*R*eal estate investment is enormously flexible, which is one of the reasons it's so exciting and challenging. Depending on your life-style, you can choose the approach that will work for you.

Think about the following ways to begin your first homewrecking project:

1. RENOVATING SOMEONE ELSE'S PROPERTY TO earn a down payment. Susan has been paying $300 a month rent in an old apartment house in Jersey City. She has only about $500 in savings, hardly enough for a down payment and renovation budget on anything at all. But for the past six months, she's been noticing a small attached single-family house for sale on a nice block in her neighborhood.

Susan phones the owner and makes an appointment. That afternoon, she makes a tour of the premises and discovers that the house had been leased to some uncaring tenants who'd painted the rooms purple and left holes in the walls. The carpets are stained, and the smell of used kitty litter fills the air, but Susan can see that the place has potential. She asks the owner what he'd take for the house, as is. He says $47,000.

Susan, who is very handy, suggests to the desperate owner that she could make his house worth more than $47,000. She offers to take her own $500 (if the owner absolutely refuses to pay for the materials himself) and fix the walls (plaster and tools, $10) and repaint the interior ($100 worth of paint, rollers, and brushes). Then she'll shampoo the stained carpets ($70), wallpaper the bathroom and kitchen (eight rolls, $60), change all the kitchen hardware to brass knobs ($35), replace the kitchen countertop ($150), and add flower boxes to the exterior ($75). The total of those renovations equals $500. She says she can do the work in three weeks.

Susan assures the owner that after the work is done, the house should sell within the next two or three months for around $50,000 to $53,000. What she wants out of the deal is for the owner to give her any profit he makes over $48,000. This is $1,000 more than he'd take today.

The owner accepts her offer, and Susan asks a lawyer friend to put everything in writing. She has the owner sign the letter of agreement, and then she gets to work. After the job is done, the house goes back on the market and sells one month later for $52,000. The owner gets his $48,000, and after Susan's expenses, she nets $3,500 on the deal. For three weeks of work, she's earned herself a hefty chunk of a down payment on a house. She won't be renting much longer.

Another possibility for Susan in this particular situation would have been a lease-option, similar to the one I negotiated on my first apartment. She could make a deal to rent with an option to buy, then fix up the house and sell it for more than her option price.

2. DOING MINOR RENOVATIONS TO THE HOUSE you live in. You can stop looking at your house as just a shelter and begin thinking of it as a business. You're in it now for a profit. Maybe there's money to be made if you fix it up and sell it.

Ask a few real estate agents over to give you their opinion of its fair market value. They will offer you a very good idea of your house's current market value, and suggest improvements that might increase its worth. If there's no difference in what you paid for the property when you bought it and what you'd get for it today, you could stand a little home renovation—fresh paint, new carpeting, general cleanup.

Make the job as easy on yourself and your family as possible. Confine your remodeling to one area at a time so that you won't completely disrupt your life.

3. DOING MAJOR RENOVATIONS TO THE HOUSE you live in. If you are really serious about doing a bang-up job on your own home to increase its value, and you know yourself well enough to realize that you would go mad living in a demolition site, then clear out and temporarily make your home somewhere else. Renting another place or staying with relatives for a month or so will allow you to renovate without risking your sanity or your marriage.

You *can* consolidate your necessities and live out of a suitcase for a while. The wonderful thing about vacating the premises while you're homewrecking is that the job gets done faster and you and your crew don't have to work around your family.

4. PURCHASING YOUR APARTMENT WHEN YOUR building goes co-op or condo and renovating it. If you're presently renting in a building whose owner is planning to convert the apartments to co-ops or condominiums, you may be sitting pretty. The owner is required by law in many states to offer a tenant in residence a unit at a substantial discount. A certain percentage of the tenants must sign an intent-to-purchase form in order for the conversion to go through.

Buying an apartment in a converted building at a discount price is making an investment with a built-in profit. Be sure to get several real estate agents' opinions of value to be certain you're getting a good deal.

5. BUYING, RENOVATING, AND THEN LEASING A property. If you've already begun thinking of your own house as a source of profit, the next logical step is to consider a second piece of property. In most states, you can take a second mortgage on your present home and use the money for a down payment on a new house or apartment, which you'll own strictly for investment purposes. Check with your accountant, because the new tax law states you can only deduct the interest on a loan amount that totals the price you paid for the property plus any improvements you've made.

If you have trouble selling your property once it's remodeled or you decide you want a long-term investment, you can rent it out to cover all or part of your carrying costs. When you finally sell, you will see the financial rewards of being a landlord—and real estate appreciation.

THE BONUS
OF REAL ESTATE:
A GUARANTEED
SAVINGS PLAN

*I*f you are one of those people who, like me, find it difficult or impossible to put away a little something every month, real estate is the ideal investment for you. Without lifting a finger, you are, in fact, earning additional assets.

Each month, as you write out your mortgage check, your house is appreciating in value. This means that you are gaining **equity** (the difference between your outstanding loan and what the house is worth). You own more than you did when you started. If that's not savings, what is it? The four walls around you and the roof over your head are better than money in the bank. They are your guaranteed tickets to financial independence.

Checkpoints

You can be successful in real estate if you:

► Keep abreast of local and national real estate activity.

► Investigate all the neighborhoods in your area.

► Understand the various benefits of home-ownership. How much are you spending for housing as a renter? Are you getting your money's worth?

▸ Recognize how our government assists the homeowner.

▸ Examine different kinds of residential properties—condominiums and cooperative apartments as well as houses.

▸ Consider the financial potential of your present house or apartment.

▸ Understand that you are saving money while gaining equity in the property you own.

▸ Believe that owning your own home is the best investment of a lifetime.

———

3
What Can You Afford?

 house will probably be the priciest item you will ever buy. The wonderful thing is that you can own it without paying for all of it yourself.

How is this possible? Just ask some homeowners. Unless they're exceptionally wealthy, they've probably bought their own house, as you will, with a small down payment and a loan—or mortgage—for the rest. This procedure, using a small amount of your money and a large amount of someone else's to get something you want, is called **leveraging.**

Leveraging: Spending a Little to Make a Lot

*M*aybe you've been reading the real estate section of your local paper and have seen a few properties in the $80,000-to-$100,000 range that look appealing. You'd probably need at least $10,000 to $15,000 for a down payment, closing costs, and minor repairs. You have $5,000 socked away. Should you wait until you've managed to save $15,000? If you do, those $100,000 houses will have turned into someone else's $125,000 homes! Now is the time to start. Even if the price seems staggering to you, and the idea of getting anything near what you want seems impossible, let me assure you that *property ownership is within your reach*. All you have to do is understand how to leverage.

If you buy a $100,000 house with a $10,000 down payment and plan to finance through a lending institution, you will need a $90,000 mortgage. We'll assume you want a long-term (thirty-year) mortgage, because you pay less when you amortize over the longest period of time. Let's say you qualify for the mortgage and get a 10% interest rate on this loan.

How does a $90,000 mortgage amortized over thirty years at a 10% interest rate translate into the dollars and cents you have to pay out per month? There's a manual of comprehensive mortgage tables available at any bookstore or lending institution that will give you the answer at a glance. The monthly rate would be $789.82, or $9,477.84 a year.

If you did the house up beautifully, sold it a year later, and netted a $15,000 profit, for example, you would have an excellent return on your investment.

Down payment	**$10,000**
One year's carrying costs	**9,500**
Minor renovation, taxes, insurance	**5,500**
Total investment	**$25,000**

A $15,000 profit on $25,000 equals a 60% return on your money. Not bad.

$15,000 profit ÷ $25,000 investment = 60% return

If you didn't leverage at all and instead paid cash ($100,000) for the house plus $5,500 for the renovation costs (there are no mortgage payments, just taxes and insurance), you'd have a 14% return on your money.

$15,000 profit ÷ $105,500 investment = 14.2% return

The guiding principle of leveraging is: *Fewer dollars invested mean more dollars returned.*

But suppose it takes much longer to sell. That's another $800 every month coming off your profit. Herein lies the cautionary note about leveraging. If your house is highly leveraged, your debt service will be high. Granted, you will be able to deduct these interest payments from your taxable income, but that refund or deduction can be a year away.

If you're thinking about a highly leveraged property, you must go into it with your eyes wide open!

AN INVESTMENT
YOU CAN LIVE IN

*O*ne of the great advantages of buying and renovating a property, though, is that you can also live in it. If it doesn't sell right away, you can just stay where you are, enjoying the house you slaved so hard to remodel. Your investment is appreciating annually and at the same time is providing you with a home and a tax benefit. In effect, you're paying yourself rent plus deducting your monthly interest from your income taxes. Sometimes you may have to wait out a slow real estate season, but lows are *always* followed by highs in this business.

If you don't want to live in your renovated house or apartment, you can lease it for six months to a year to help cover your monthly debt service. There aren't many investments like residential real estate that offer you the versatility of high usage, rental income, tax benefits, and continued appreciation.

DETERMINING YOUR HOUSING EXPENSES

*J*ust because you don't have to *pay* for a house outright doesn't mean it's a good idea to get in way over your head. It is important, as I said before, to *start small and think big*. Your first time out, you must select a house that's low in price and fixable, too—one that you can work your remodeling magic on without incurring too large a monetary burden. Your reasonable, small investment is going to turn into a large profit, as long as you keep your costs within targets that are reasonable *for you*.

One of your first considerations is to calculate how long you intend to hold on to your property. If you've found a house in a fantastic location and you're sure you can renovate and sell it in a year, it's relatively safe to budget a healthy monthly mortgage payment into your costs. But if you intend to stay two to five years, you may have to consider a lower-priced house, a smaller mortgage, or a less upscale neighborhood.

Suppose you're still renting and you want to get into your first property. You have some cash in the bank, but you're afraid that your monthly mortgage payment will be higher than your present rent. The simple formula to translate renting into buying is: *Multiply your present monthly rent by 100, and you can safely look for property in that price range.*

If you are paying $425–$500 a month in rent, you can purchase a property that costs around $50,000. If you're paying $850–$1,000 a month, you can purchase a property that costs around $100,000. How is that possible? Assuming that you have saved enough for a 10% down payment, you can probably convince your seller to finance the balance for a short-term (1- or 2-year) interest-only loan at 10% interest. The seller doesn't get his principal loan amount back until you resell the house and repay him—but he only has to wait a year or so.

Monthly Payments Formula

Purchase price:	$50,000	Purchase price:	$100,000	
10% down	−5,000	10% down	−10,000	
Loan	45,000	Loan	90,000	
10% interest	4,500	10% interest	9,000	
Per month (4,500 ÷ 12)	375	Per month (9,000 ÷ 12)	750	
Plus approximate property tax and insurance per month	125	Plus approximate property tax and insurance per month	250	
Monthly payment	500	Monthly payment	1,000	

If you buy a house, you won't be taking anything out of your pocket that's not coming out already in rent, except for your down payment. You will, on the other hand, be accumulating assets and increasing your potential to earn large profits in the future.

WHERE DOES THE MONEY COME FROM?

*W*ell, you may say, this all looks very nice and neat, but what about that money for a down payment? What will the renovations cost me? Suppose the seller won't finance the deal, and I have to pay **points** (a fee) to a lending institution? And what about all the other closing costs? Don't I need some extra cash for that? Yes, you do. You really do. It's very difficult today to buy real estate without *any* money, despite the number of books on the market that urge you to try it. My belief—and personal experience—shows that you must have some cash of your own.

My first deal—that condominium apartment in San Francisco—was a lease-option in which I used my rent money for renovation. That was as close to "no money down" as I ever got. I certainly would never have been able to renovate dozens of properties if I'd had to work a "nothing down" transaction each time. The way I got my homewrecking business off the ground was by using some of the cash that I'd made in one deal to finance the next.

When you have some capital of your own, it's just plain easier to purchase property. With a little cash in hand—especially when you're starting out in this field—you're more likely to get financial support from a seller, partner, friend, family member, and, most important, your neighborhood banker. These people will be likely to match the amount you put down, or lend even more money, if you've invested something yourself. When you've put *your* money in the deal, you're showing a serious commitment; this will make others more comfortable about committing themselves as well.

When you find the perfect house, you will want to act quickly, because someone else may have found it too. For this reason, you must know where your money's going to come from *before* it's time to make an offer.

NINE WAYS TO GET UP-FRONT MONEY

*L*et's explore some of the ways you can secure the up-front capital you need to get started.

1. YOURSELF. IF YOU'RE REALLY SERIOUS about buying a home, you may have to make some changes in your life-style. When you're married, you have to persuade someone else to make sacrifices; when you're single, deprivation is easier. In either case, you can probably do without a few luxuries like a new car, a fancy computer, another two speakers on your stereo system, expensive meals in restaurants, or a big vacation.

You want to start saving *now* for the thing that really counts—a home. Open a savings account specifically entitled "My House" and put something into it *every* month. Wear last year's coat. Stop smoking. The pack-a-day smoker can save a "Kool" $500 a year.

2. YOUR FAMILY. PARENTS OR SIBLINGS MAY BE your best source of additional income. They'll treat you more leniently than a bank on a personal loan, without requiring loan fees or applications. They may also offer lower interest rates. Most mothers and fathers have already financed their children through school, have taken care of doctor's and dentist's bills, paid for clothing, weekly allowances, and maybe a car or two. But that doesn't mean they won't grant one more financial favor—particularly since this time they're going to get their money back, with interest.

When you approach your family for a loan, type up an organized proposal, with photos if you have a specific property in mind. Outline in detail:

- The kind of property you want to buy and renovate

- Needed capital

- Renovation budget

- Carrying costs

- Scheduled completion date for work

- Projected sales date

- Expected return on investment

- Interest you intend to pay

Your family will be impressed if you present your package in a businesslike manner. And don't stop at your parents or siblings. You might ask your husband to offer "spousal support" that might improve your marriage, instead of paying for it when it's over—or ask *his* parents. A lot of down-payment money comes from "GI financing, not a government program . . . but 'good in-laws,'" according to George Sternlieb from Rutgers University. "People are getting loans from their parents; they are drawing on multigenerational wealth."

3. FRIENDS. DON'T BE SHY, JUST ASK. TALK TO all of them. Everyone, you'll find, is interested in real estate. Everyone is looking for a good investment. You should approach friends, as you would your family, with a complete dossier of costs and plans. To earn their trust, you should agree to pay them a generous interest rate. It will preserve the deal as well as the relationship.

4. YOUR ASSETS. YOU CAN TAKE A SECURED loan on your possessions, like your antique furniture, paintings, oriental rugs, stocks and bonds, boat or trailer, stamp collection, or old Peggy Lee records.

A secured loan is safer than a personal loan made on just you and your signature, because it's secured—by the seller, by a lending institution, or by a friend of yours—against something of value, some collateral that the lender can take back should you default on the loan.

5. YOUR CURRENT RESIDENCE. IN MOST STATES, you can use the house or apartment you own as collateral for a second mortgage. Second mortgages suffer from a bad rap, although there's nothing dangerous or negative about them. Taking a second mortgage does not imply that your finances are shaky or that your house is leveraged to the chimneys. Instead, it means that you've made a wise investment. Your house has appreciated in value since you bought it, and the amount of appreciation (the equity) can be used as collateral so that you can secure a secondary loan.

If you purchased your house several years ago, improved

it, and had a first mortgage of $50,000 and the house is now worth $100,000, then you have $50,000 worth of equity to secure a second mortgage. Nothing wrong with this.

With the enactment of the 1986 tax reform bill, you can continue to take the equity out of your home but you can only deduct the interest on a loan that totals your original purchase price and any improvements you've made—unless the money is used for further home improvements, medical bills, or education. If the house you bought cost $75,000 and you put in $25,000 in improvements over five years (totaling a value of $100,000) and you have a $50,000 mortgage, you can borrow up to $50,000 and write off 100% of the interest you pay to borrow it. Always check with your accountant for the correct rules of the game.

6. A PARTNER. A PARTNERSHIP IS A WONDERFUL way to get started in the real estate business. A partner can be a friend or a colleague, someone who's willing to finance you and possibly work with you on the renovations.

A joint-venture real estate partnership is an arrangement whereby two or more parties with plans, projections, and a budget invest jointly in a property. Upon sale of the improved property, profits are split in a prearranged proportion among the partners. A written agreement, approved by a lawyer, is essential.

Partnerships are great in a homewrecking career. You have someone to share the trials and tribulations, someone to take over if you have the flu and can't get out of bed, someone to knock heads with over a budget or the latest hardware catalogue.

Another possibility is that you find a partner to be your financial backer. He or she puts up the initial investment while you do all the work. This is an excellent way to get off the ground as a homewrecker.

After one or two successful projects, you and your partner may want to rethink your original financial arrangement. Whoever does more work should get a bigger return—a larger percentage of the profits.

7. THE REAL ESTATE AGENT. USING YOUR REAL estate agent's commission is in no way an under-the-table

money scheme. The real estate brokerage commission is a percentage of the purchase price of the property—usually around 6% in residential sales. This percentage, although it comes out of the sale of the house, is actually paid by you, not the seller, since you are paying for the property.

An agent who's a friend, and would like to see you get started in the business, may agree to credit his or her commission to you at the close of the escrow and wait a year to be paid.

It's important to understand that you're not milking the agent on this deal. The agent *will* get the commission, with interest, at the end of a year, but if he or she doesn't sell the house to you because you can't supply all the up-front money, the agent will lose the sale entirely. Also, when you're ready to sell the renovated property, you will return the listing to this same agent, who will then have two commissions evolving from one property.

8. THE SELLER. THIS IS ABSOLUTELY THE BEST way to get started in the real estate business! I always ask for seller financing, and I get it about a quarter of the time. When funds are tight and banks have minimum mortgage money, sellers often come through with at least partial financing. If you're a qualified buyer, a seller may agree to total financing for a year or two, until money loosens up and it's easier to get a mortgage.

Owner financing can be mutually beneficial for both buyer and seller. The buyer avoids the application procedure, loan fees, and waiting time that come with a mortgage from a lending institution. The seller, who signs a paper stating that he will "take back" (finance) a mortgage, may not be getting all the cash he wanted up front, but he will get a nice interest check every month for the length of his short-term loan. We'll discuss seller financing at great length when we get to the deal itself.

9. YOUR LIFE INSURANCE OR PENSION COMPANY. You can borrow against your life insurance policy or pension plan. The money is loaned at surprisingly low interest (as little as 5% in some states), and the amount you can obtain is based on how much "cash value" is in your insurance policy or how long you've been under the pension plan. In both cases, you're receiving the interest on your money and getting it to work for you at the same time.

ROMANCING
THE BIG LENDERS

*T*he two biggest lenders for residential real estate in America are savings and loan associations and banks. An S&L is not a bank—it's a place to "save" your money while earning interest and a place to get a "loan" from all the other depositors' savings. Although S&Ls were originally created to handle mortgages (long-term loans), and banks previously were set up to be full-service institutions offering checking accounts, savings accounts, short-term car loans, personal loans, and new-business loans, the two have grown closer in their services.

Today, because banking is as competitive a marketplace as the automobile or computer industry, S&Ls are offering full banking services and banks are well into the home-mortgage business. A commercial bank may be very helpful to you if you intend to do a lot of homewrecking. Its short-term loans (usually one year, but renewable) are available at competitive interest rates.

If you're over eighteen and plan to invest in anything in your life, start cultivating your local banker. The big lenders are very accessible, and their staff is ready to help you get the highest return possible on your hard-earned cash.

Many married women feel it's easier to manage the family's finances with a joint checking account they cosign with their husband and credit cards in their husband's name. But just a second! "Easier" does not pay off in the long run! You need to build some credit of your own.

One of the first questions you'll be asked when you apply for a loan is whether you hold accounts *in your own name.* You cannot begin any financial transaction unless the lender is entirely confident that you are capable of handling money *by yourself.*

One way to get a credit rating is to acquire your own set of plastic—Visa, MasterCard, American Express. If you don't qualify for a big credit-card company because you've never had a job or your income level is too low, start with a department store. Charge a few items and pay your bills promptly to get an "A" rating from the credit bureau when you apply for a mortgage.

If you have never had a bank account of your own, *open one today*. Get to know your banker and establish credit as soon as you can. Why? Because being a good credit risk is your ticket to borrowing money—and to owning a home of your own.

If you are opening an account in a new bank, call first and make an appointment with the manager. Dress in an attractive and businesslike fashion. Your first meeting with the manager should impress on him the fact that you're a serious person, seriously interested in finding the right financial home. When the time comes for you to request a loan, you'll be a familiar face.

Do not stop at one lending institution. If you have the cash, establish credit at a number of different places. It's a prudent idea to romance several lenders at once, because you never know when you'll need a backup.

I worked with one commercial bank for ten years. Then suddenly it was bought out by a foreign investment group whose board of directors decided to wind down the bank's real estate loan portfolios. Within a year, I knew no one there. But fortunately, I had cultivated two other banks at the same time, so I moved the majority of my business to new financial homes.

To establish credit with a lending institution, borrow $1,000 from one bank and deposit it in another to earn interest, then pay it back within six months or a year. If you borrow at 12% at one bank and earn 8% interest on deposit in another, it costs you only 4%, or $40, to demonstrate that you are a good credit risk.

Many people—I used to be one of them—are struck with terror at the idea of sitting down with a loan officer and requesting a home loan. When your financial history is totally exposed, you're as vulnerable as you are at the doctor's office when you go in for a thorough physical exam. But bankers are people, after all, and even in this computerized world, deals are still made by people.

When you need to borrow big money—for part of a down payment, for your renovation budget, or for the mortgage itself—sit down with your banker and ask for financing suggestions. What is the existing interest rate? What kinds of mortgages are being offered, and which would be the most advantageous for you?

Not only are bankers valuable support for a loan request, they are also a warehouse of information. After all, it's their job to help you get money.

HOW WILL I QUALIFY
FOR A MORTGAGE
AT A BANK?

*T*he bank, understandably, wants to know that you will be financially capable of assuming your monthly debts. If you couldn't afford the house you've bought and were unable to make your monthly payments, the bank would be taking a loss by giving you a loan. Believe me, the bank is going to make sure its investment is safe before it signs over a large loan amount.

Obviously, if you are making $50,000 a year and have $40,000 equity in your present home, the bank will look more kindly on you than if you have no equity and earn only $15,000. It will also be more impressed with the woman who has a stable, high-paying job than with the one who is unemployed and depends on a spouse's income, or perhaps on alimony and child support.

You should find out what will make you qualify *before* you apply. Take home a loan application to see just what the lender wants to know about you.

A lending institution wants to know:

- Who you are and where you're presently living

- Whether you own or rent

- How many dependents you have

- What your assets are (stock portfolio, paid-up car, life insurance policies, the amount in your checking and savings accounts, a parcel of raw land)

- What your liabilities are (student loans, car payments, installment payments due, unpaid balances on credit cards)

- Your employment (where you work, length of time employed, salary, bonuses)

- Additional income (trust funds, stock dividends, alimony, rental income paid to you)

- Address of the property you are buying

- Amount of your down payment (and where it's coming from)

From this information, the lender will figure out your **net worth**—what's left after you've subtracted your liabilities (all the money you owe) from your assets—to see what you can afford. It's a good idea for you to work the figures yourself, to see if you qualify, and to see what you can spend on a house, before you go to a bank and apply for your mortgage.

Here are some formulas lenders use to qualify an applicant:

1. The house should cost no more than 2½ times your gross annual income. If you make $40,000 a year, you shouldn't spend more than $100,000 on a house.

2. Your housing expenses (mortgage plus insurance plus property taxes) should not equal

more than 30–38% of your gross monthly income.

3. Your total monthly payment of all housing costs and long-term debts (car payments, credit-card bills, student loans, your children's tuition) should not exceed 35–40% of your gross annual income.

Lenders may be willing to stretch these figures a bit if they feel you are a good credit risk or if you have extra assets.

A NEW WAY TO THINK ABOUT MONEY

*B*uying power is not predicated on what you have in your pocket at any particular time, nor does it depend on the amount you can pay today with the funds available in your checking account. Money is a bargaining tool, even when you can't see it or touch it.

As you learn more about real estate and the ability to leverage, you will understand that a little can buy a lot—*if* you know how to pick the right house, bargain properly, and roll your profits from one sale into another.

And by continually trading up, you can turn today's dreams into tomorrow's reality. Once, at the beginning of my homewrecking career, I asked a real estate agent if I could tag along when he showed a client a fabulous San Francisco mansion that was on the market. I gasped when we drove up to 10,000 square feet of gorgeous gothic. I simply *knew* that only in my wildest fantasy could I ever own anything like this. Well, I was wrong. In less than five years, that mansion was one of my million-dollar deals.

Anything is possible for a real estate entrepreneur; the sky is never the limit (look at the World Trade Center!), nor is your current bank account. With enough time and energy, with a grasp of leveraging and a good nose for the right, well-located property, you can spin straw into gold, turn wood-frame houses and brick condominiums into a personal fortune.

Now about that search for the right property . . . let's get started.

Checkpoints

Property ownership is within your reach if you:

▸ Do a thorough check of your assets and liabilities.

▸ Canvas all available sources—family, friends, and potential business partners—for loans.

▸ Apply for credit cards.

▸ Start a bank account.

▸ Develop a good credit rating.

▸ Understand how to leverage.

▸ Start thinking about money as a bargaining tool instead of cash on hand.

You are going to apply the "worst in the best" formula—
to find the worst house on the best block, the *least expensive
home in the finest neighborhood.* If you are certain that all
you can afford is a "handyman's special," then you've got to
buy the very best handyman's special you can get your
hands on.

But first things first. Let's start with the community.
Whether you are thinking about a single-family house, a
co-op or a condo, or a summer house at the shore, you've got
to know the territory. Before you can even begin to sift for
the needle, make sure you're looking in the right haystack.

A LOCATION PRIMER:
LEARNING WHAT
TO LOOK FOR

*A*s a budding renovator, you will be relying on your
ability to notice details, and that starts right here,
when you begin narrowing your sights on one
community. You will, of course, be guided by your personal
situation. If you're being transferred for work reasons to a
new city or state, you may want to live near your office. If
you have young children, you want a good school system. If
you're not planning to live in the property you purchase,
you'll want to buy something near your home so you can get
to the construction site each day.

Do some legwork and see what's available that meets
your needs. The greatest buy in town may be right around
the corner, or four communities away.

The best way to start your market research is to find out
as much as you can about the town you're investigating.
Even if you've lived there all your life, you still may have
blind spots. You want to look at it with fresh eyes now, because you're about to consider it, not just as a home, but as
the beginning, perhaps, of a new career.

Where do you start? Well, crazy as it might sound, I al-

4
*Checking Out
the Territory*

hen a real estate agent calls to say that
the perfect piece of property has just come
on the market, there are only three questions that you need to ask right off the
bat: Where is it? Where is it? Where is it?

No other single element is more important in the selection of residential property than its *location*. If you're buying with the intention of renovating and selling within a
year, it's crucial that you put your money in a prime residential area. If you intend to stay awhile in the neighborhood you select, you want to be certain that the relative
property values around you are growing.

Don't worry if you can't afford a prime residential area
right now. Even if you can't afford to *start* there, I will show
you how to get there. I will outline the intermediary
moves—the stepping-stones—so that you can eventually
wind up in the best part of town.

ways start looking at property with an immediate thought of resale, because my houses aren't always my homes. If you plan to turn over properties quickly, you can't just examine neighborhoods (and eventually houses) with a thought to your own future. You must also consider the person who will eventually buy the property from you. This means that your criterion should not just be personal taste, but rather what the next person is apt to like.

- Your property should be where the action is, in a flourishing city or suburb, close to thriving businesses.

- It should be in a stable community, close to shopping, schools, churches, parks, recreational centers.

- It should be in a growing area, where there are plans on the books for expansion and development (but not excavations on every block in sight with no evident city master plan).

- It should be in an area where people are getting a lot of municipal services for the tax money they are paying.

- It should be in an area with an excellent school system, with a good pupil-to-teacher ratio, where the average SAT scores are high compared to others in the state, and where a reasonable percentage of the students go on to college. (This information is generally available from a qualified real estate agent, or you can query the state board of education.)

- It should be in a low-crime area.

If you're new to a town, you can collect a huge amount of information from the local Chamber of Commerce. A good real estate agent will also be well informed, as will the local shopkeepers, restaurant owners, and bank officers.

Try to get every bit of information available about

what's ahead before you pick one block or one house. It would be an awful shame—not to mention a financial disaster—to find out too late that a high-rise that will cut off your river view is going up right across the street.

It should take you a few weeks or a month, depending on how assiduously you devote yourself to this preliminary research, to discover that one or two communities keep coming up again and again as outstanding in most of the areas that interest you.

UNDERSTANDING WHAT YOU SEE

*T*he next stage of your market research is done on the scene, driving or walking slowly through the streets. That's the only successful way to canvas a neighborhood.

What, exactly, defines "a neighborhood"? It may be a grouping of houses around a physical landmark, such as a park, marina, valley, or hill. It can be as small as one block or large enough to surround a fashionable shopping area.

When you start looking for a neighborhood, think about what you want in terms of proximity to people and goods and services. Do you want to be close enough to stores so that you can get there on foot or by bicycle? Do you want a closely knit community where everybody knows everybody else, or a more impersonal place? A huge apartment house can be a neighborhood all by itself, where you nod to people in the elevator for years without ever knowing their names.

Drive around and investigate neighborhoods in the car, then get out and walk around those that really interest you. You learn a lot on foot! Ideally, you shouldn't tackle more than three neighborhoods in one day, because no matter how good an observer you are, communities will start to blend together in your mind.

If you see a "For Sale by Owner" sign as you walk, go into the house and look around. If you see a place under

renovation, stop and speak to the contractor. Or if you notice an ad about a neighborhood block association meeting
or a house tour, take advantage of it. You want to educate
yourself as much as possible about the community before
you even begin to think of buying there. It's like marriage—you've got to know the man before you make the big
decision.

What are you looking for as you scout around an area?

- Are yards well landscaped? Or are they filled
  with weeds? Are there broken-down cars and
  bikes in the yards? That's a sign of sloppy
  homeowners and lack of community concern.

- If you're looking in a city, are there vacant
  lots? Boarded-up stores? How long have they
  been that way? The neighborhood may be in a
  state of deterioration.

- Do children play in the streets? This could be
  good or bad. It might be a sign of a safe community, or it could indicate that there are no
  playgrounds or parks available. Cul-de-sacs or
  dead-end streets are very desirable for kids,
  since they mean no speeding traffic.

- Do you see older people sitting on porches as
  well as children outside? A sign of good balance in the population.

- Are the residential neighborhoods sprinkled
  with commercial establishments? Many homeowners like having a corner grocer, a few bou-
  tiques, and some popular restaurants nearby.
  Of course, the encroachment of shopping malls
  or industry with large parking lots would be a
  different story.

- How close is the nearest highway? Do you hear
  a lot of traffic as you walk the streets? Is it safe
  for kids?

- How's the public transportation? Is it near

enough to be convenient but distant enough
not to be noisy?

- Are you too close to the airport or a railroad?
  An all-night disco? Noise pollution could be a
  problem.

- If you're looking in a city, are there iron bars
  on *all* the windows? This sign is self-explana-
  tory—who wants to live in a prison?

Make yourself a list of pros and cons. No one neighborhood will be perfect, but there will be some whose faults
you can overlook because their positive qualities overcome
their liabilities.

BORDERLINE AREAS

*I*n many U.S. cities, the up-and-coming neighborhoods are not always established or stable. But
many have proved to be bonanzas for adventuresome
buyers. Long-neglected urban areas that are going through
a renaissance can be very advantageous for the conscien-
tious homewrecker who buys at the right time.

But sometimes it's difficult to tell when a "bad" neighborhood is turning around. My barometer, as I mentioned
earlier, is seeing some kind of renovation going on in at
least 25% of the area's houses. And even then, the rewards
of homewrecking will come much slower, although the profits can be quite extraordinary if the community changes
just as you decide to sell.

If you intend to live in a changing neighborhood, you
will have to be the sort of person who:

- Feels comfortable in an ethnically and racially
  mixed setting where perhaps half the population is not exactly like you.

- Doesn't mind traveling to go to nice shops,
  movies, or parks.

- Enjoys the street life—people congregating on stoops or porches on summer evenings, for example.
- Can live with disruptions in municipal services, such as an occcasional lack of garbage collection.
- Can wait an indefinite period of time before making a profit.

You will spend considerably less to get a nice house in an iffy neighborhood, which means that you can put considerably more into your renovation. But you must be exceptionally careful of overimproving. If you turn one of the very ordinary houses on the block into a palace, you will have a lot of trouble selling unless the other houses are going in the same direction. Few buyers want the most expensive house on the block in a changing neighborhood. And if a bank has trouble finding houses of comparable worth to use as a yardstick, your buyer won't be able to get a mortgage.

Another possible investment is rural property. Buy it if you want it as a getaway for yourself, but not if you're interested in going into homewrecking in a big way. Rural property never appreciates as fast as urban or suburban locations unless all the land is being eaten up by developers for what often results in high-density construction.

My final word on this subject is that you should buy in a borderline area only if you are something of a pioneer and feel it's a good, safe gamble. Think of it as a long-term commitment, not as an easy homewrecking turnover.

A FEW SUCCESSES; A FEW FAILURES

Why do some cities' housing prices skyrocket while others remain flat as a pancake? There are a number of explanations. Many industrial states have suffered gravely from major plant closings and, consequently, major job layoffs. In the Pacific Northwest, the airline and lumber industries have fallen off, and the slump in oil and gas production has contributed to sales declines in many other states. Another cause, affecting Florida in particular, has been the decrease in demand for second homes and vacation condominiums.

These particular successes and failures can be temporary. Tomorrow, the flat places could be hot and the hot ones dead as doornails. My philosophy has always been that you can be a successful homewrecker *anywhere* if you buy right and remodel with quality. But you still will have a better chance if you do your research thoroughly so that you know where the action is, or where it's going to be very, very soon.

HOUSE, CONDO, OR CO-OP?

*I*f your first homewrecking project is going to be a residence you'd like to live in—as it is for most people —there are three housing possibilities for you to explore: houses, condominiums, and cooperative apartments.

When you own a single-family house, be it a rambling mansion on an eighteen-acre estate or an attached row house in a major city, you have title to the land and the building on it. A house, particularly an old one, offers incredible challenges to the remodeler. It's very often architecturally unique—unlike many condominium townhouses, built uniformly to look alike.

If, on the other hand, you're a city person and hate commuting, you probably want to buy an apartment. In most cities, that means a co-op or a condominium.

Cooperative apartments are available only in the largest U.S. cities, with New York leading the way. If you decide to buy one, you should be looking at apartment houses in established neighborhoods that have been well maintained during their lives as rental units. It's never wise to purchase a co-op in a building undergoing complete renovation. Major structural changes mean astronomical bills—which all the owners will have to share. Be sure conventional financing is available. Savings and loan associations and banks are frequently unwilling to make loans to finance co-ops.

Condos will generally be in converted buildings or in suburban developments that offer residents common ownership in the land and responsibility for its maintenance. Many suburban communities have a large percentage of condominium townhouses, and some are quite elegant, offering the privacy of a house with the amenities of a good security system, a community pool, tennis courts, and clubhouse.

Suppose you're interested in a brand-new condo. Some terrific deals can be found on the drawing board, before the units or townhouses are even built and the only proof you have of the builder's work is the model unit. However, I would be wary of buying something I couldn't see. If possible, examine other finished projects by the developer.

WHAT A REAL ESTATE AGENT CAN DO FOR YOU

*R*eal estate agents are invaluable. You need them as much as they need you, particularly if you are a first-time homebuyer. After you have narrowed your choice to one or two neighborhoods or towns, you should enlist the aid of an expert. The real estate agent will be your guide and chauffeur, so that you can sit back, take out your notebook, ask questions, and learn.

Frequently—about once a day—someone asks me why I don't get a real estate license and avoid paying someone else the commission on each property I handle. My answer to this is that I don't want to sell real estate—I want to invest in it, renovate it, and resell it.

More important, if I did try to sell my own properties, I'd lose some of the most valuable assets in this business—the agents I work with. Good agents know what properties are selling for, which areas are strong, and which neighborhoods are getting hot. They know what's gone up in value in a year and which areas may be coming down.

How do you find a great agent? When I'm new in a place, I ask around for the best agency in town. And I often choose the largest or the oldest one with the strongest reputation. I figure if it's respected in the community, it must be doing something right.

When I call, I ask to speak with the manager and get him to recommend an agent who is sophisticated, hardworking, fun, fast, and smart—a person who knows the town inside out and makes a lot of deals. Why is this important? If you are taking the trouble to search out the best, I feel you deserve to get it. Your time is valuable—don't waste it.

Make an appointment and schedule several hours with the agent on your first time out. Make it clear when you meet that you may be buying and selling property as a business, that you may well buy several properties, and that you will always return the listing on the renovated house or apartment to the individual who sold it to you. Even if you eventually decide to stay put, this tactic is going to get you the finest service you can buy.

Good, experienced agents, of course, are salespeople who want to make deals, but the successful ones care about making the right deals for the right people. They're not going to get any repeat business or referrals from you if they put you in the wrong home.

In addition to showing property, agents:

- Suggest sources of financing.

- Research current interest rates for clients.

- Provide "comps"—other houses that have sold recently in the area.

- Get sellers to offer total or partial financing.

- Run interference between buyer and seller.

- Write contracts (if no lawyer is in the deal).

- Do all necessary paperwork.

- Recommend contractors.

- Run all over town with loan applications, contingency removals, needed signatures, and, occasionally, the odd briefcase full of cash!

An agent will work hard for the serious buyer. After all, there's a 6% commission on every sale, of which he gets a large portion. His boss, the broker, gets the balance.

For every easy sale, an agent has to deal with countless tire-kickers—people who make a hobby of looking at houses with no intention whatsoever of buying, or who, when they do buy, feel no obligation to purchase through the agent who squired them around town in the first place. This means that you, a determined buyer who is also loyal to one special agent, are a very desirable client.

Before you start looking at properties, your agent will want to make sure you qualify financially for the house that interests you, which means that he'll be asking pointed questions about your work and income. Don't be embarrassed; just answer honestly. Together you'll be able to figure out an accurate price range by examining your current housing costs and your particular financial and employment situation. If you already own a house or apartment and are considering the purchase of residential property as an investment, let the agent know. He can advise you of the best locations and potential rental income on a renovated building.

As in any other field, there are bad apples and good apples. Some real estate agents only want to make a sale— they'll drag you around to anything that happens to be available and try to get your signature on an offer before you've seen the second bathroom. When I meet agents like this, I thank them for their time at the end of our appointment and politely mention that I'll be in touch. If they phone me back, I say no thank you. You're not going to hurt the feelings of an agent with the hide of a rhinoceros, but you will be wasting a lot of your precious time if you go out with him or her again just to be kind.

Once you've found an agent you really like, and you feel a good working relationship is developing, by all means stop playing the field. Allegiance is terribly important in the real estate community, especially to one who has contributed a lot of time to your early explorations of a city. If, in your travels on your own, at an open house or co-op or condo showing, you find a property you want to make an offer on, have the courtesy to submit it through your own agent. If you're loyal to your agent, you'll get the same kind of loyalty back.

If you let your agent know that you plan to purchase and sell a couple of properties over the next few years, he will do everything short of breaking and entering to show you the properties that are available.

Of all the properties I've bought, at least a quarter are houses and apartments I spotted during my own early explorations. One of these was a beautiful two-unit building that I'd been lusting after for years. But it had never been up for sale. My agent called me the minute it was listed, and I bought it in less than an hour. In fact, I soon became notorious for signing offer forms on the roof of her car. When there's a race to get in your bid on a particularly juicy piece of property, a faithful agent who knows exactly what you want can make all the difference.

SEEING PROPERTIES WITH YOUR AGENT

*O*n your first day out with your agent, request a tour of the city or suburb you're interested in before you start looking at houses. Yes, you've driven around by yourself, but now you're going to get a new perspective. Even if you've done your research and think you know the answers, you'll learn even more. An agent offers an insider's view of a community, since agents generally live in the town they work in. You're going to get an education without paying tuition, and at the end of the day, you'll feel as though you've been through a semester of Real Estate 101, covering everything from financing to fire escapes.

Now sit back, listen to your chauffeur's running commentary, and ask questions.

- Is this neighborhood appreciating? What are some recent house prices? What's high and what's low for the neighborhood?

- Have property taxes gone up markedly in the past year or two? Why? Is there a new school? An influx of big business? How have these changes affected the town?

- Where are the local banks you deal with? How easy or difficult has it been to get mortgages lately? How long does the procedure take?

- How far is the nearest school (church, market, cleaner's)? Can I walk or must I drive?

- Why is that Victorian priced $10,000 lower than the one next to it? Why has that brick brownstone been on the market for eight months? Is the owner being unreasonable about pricing?

- Are there zoning ordinances that will restrict the building of a filling station or a fast-food restaurant right across the street?

- How quiet is the area? How friendly?

As the two of you explore the community, you should be working to home in on what *you* want—which neighborhoods and properties appeal to you aesthetically and which ones you can afford. You must make it clear to your agent that you're looking for a property in a good location but not necessarily in pristine condition, one that has excellent potential but perhaps has been on the market for a while. If your agent is sharp and savvy, he should start seeing with your eyes after a few trial runs around town.

You'll receive **statements** on many properties. A statement is a fact sheet, distributed by the listing agency. It can be a simple sheet of paper with all the pertinent data and a photo, or a handsome, full-color brochure. These statements tell you:

- Address (location first, remember!)

- Age and price of house

- Available financing, if any

- Number of bedrooms and baths and approximate measurements of each

- Type of heating

- Whether there's a garage and driveway—and whether you have to share it with the neighbor

- Extras like fireplaces, built-in bookshelves, eat-in kitchen, skylights, landscaped garden, or a balcony with a view

- Whether the carpets, draperies, or appliances are included in the purchase price

During these first few days, you'll want to see as many properties as possible in the neighborhoods you've selected. A picture of a house may be worth a thousand words, but a walk-through is worth a thousand pictures. No matter how descriptive an agent is by phone, no matter how glitzy the written statement, no matter how smashing the photograph, I still can't appreciate a property until I've seen it.

After viewing a lot of properties, if you still haven't found a winner, you might want to go through the Bible of the industry—the Multiple Listing Book. This is a compilation of nearly all the properties on the market, represented by the agencies in town. It's the Yellow Pages of real estate.

You can go to see any house that's for sale, regardless of who the listing agency may be. And a very good way to get a wider view of the community and its comparative prices is to sit down with the book and have your agent go through all the listings with you. You can learn a lot by looking at the book with someone who can read between the lines.

Recognizing what neighborhoods appeal to you, what areas are appreciating, and what community you'd like to buy in is all pretty easy if you've done your research properly. As for finding the right house, well, that's a little harder. Now it's time to target that perfect property.

Checkpoints

You can learn to recognize a potentially good area if you:

- ▸ Do research at the Chamber of Commerce, the local bank, and at realtors' offices.

- ▸ Drive and walk around, learning to see negative as well as positive characteristics.

- ▸ Decide whether you will be more comfortable living in a house, condo, or co-op.

- ▸ Enlist the aid of an experienced real estate agent who knows the city intimately and will share all this information with you.

5

The Right House

Lovelyland, U.S.A. Spectac. house on 1.3 acre. Pogen Pohl ktchn, 20x30 liv. rm. w/fplc, frmal DR, 14x25 fam. rm overlks gdn, sunrm w/redwood deck. 1st flr mstr bdrm suite, sep bath w/Jacuzzi, plus 3 bdrms 2 baths on 2nd flr. 4-car gar. Decorator's dream. Won't last long!

*Y*ou've seen hundreds of ads like this. They are written by real estate agents or homeowners to entice prospective buyers to view their "decorator's dream," the very best house that ever existed.

If you're smart, you'll read right through this purple prose and ignore most of it. Because *you don't want to buy the best house on the block*—you want to *create* it.

Reading the classifieds can be a great way to find property, but some of the best homewrecker houses aren't advertised at all, because they aren't on the market long enough. Some of the most terrific finds aren't in the paper because they don't have any of those exclusive selling elements—the fancy kitchen, the Jacuzzi, the four-car garage. This is where you come in. You're going to come upon a shabby but promising Cinderella of a house, and get her dressed to go to the ball.

LOOK FOR THE WORST IN THE BEST PART OF TOWN

*Y*ou have already picked one or two neighborhoods that seem appealing, where homeowners care about their property, where physical charm, proximity to stores and schools, and excellent services indicate a solid, established place to live.

You can always find a buyer for a good house in a good location.

Let's say there are two houses for sale in a great neighborhood that really interest you. One's in good shape, the other bad. They're asking a considerable amount for the house that's in respectable condition, but you think it's a fair price for what you'd be getting. If you don't feel up to a really big renovation job your first time out as a home-wrecker, you may want to spend a little more and buy the nicer house. Especially if you intend to live there yourself as you're fixing it up, you may find it more convenient to select a property that's in pretty good condition—one that might just need some new carpeting, interior painting, and maybe a new stove. You can invest in the "nice" house, turn it into a "spectacular" house with a great decorating job, and still make a substantial profit when you sell in one or two years. It will also ease you gently into the process of turning houses around.

But suppose, in this same neighborhood, there's a house tucked away in the middle of a block that hasn't been tended to for years. It's potentially attractive and appears to be structurally sound, but it's crying out for some major help. The stone steps are broken and there's moss growing up the side of the garage, the kitchen floor tiles have curled up because of a leaking dishwasher, and the bathroom fixtures are permanently stained with rust. And the owner wants to sell. Badly.

If you're eager to throw yourself into homewrecking with a vengeance, this is the house for you. You'll be able to keep your purchase price at a reasonable level, saving most of your money for renovation. And if the seller has had no luck at all for some length of time, you may be able to bargain the price down even further.

Both houses in this neighborhood—the one that's in good shape and the one that needs work—will appreciate each year because of their location. But the run-down one will appreciate more.

The same is true of apartments. It's always a good idea to buy property at one of the best addresses in town. Many people will pay for a fancy address, just because it's considered chic to be there. If you are considering a co-op or condo as your first remodeling job, you should always begin by selecting a building on a terrific block and looking at the lowest-priced units for sale. You are looking for the *worst unit in the best building*.

A one-bedroom or even a studio apartment in a great building is a good way to begin as a real-estate investor. I personally like units on the ground or first floor in a multiple-unit building or high-rise. They are usually the least expensive, because most people feel safer on upper floors. But lower units have less of an apartment feeling, the front doorman becomes your personal doorman, the entrance lobby (which all the residents pay to furnish) becomes your foyer, you're never dependent on an elevator, and there's a chance that you might have a garden.

Remember, you are going to *start small and think big*. A tiny living space can be made into a perfect, cozy home in very little time with minimal expenditure on your part. Newlyweds, double-income couples, and highly salaried single people are attracted to small houses and apartments in major cities. Although good small houses are relatively rare and usually sell quickly, there are still many excellent buys to be found in condominiums and cooperatives.

THE HOUSE YOU LIVE IN

*I*f you already own your residence, you may be sitting on a nice profit. Unless you're living in a house that's been in your family for generations and you have sentimental reasons for not selling, you should think about what you can earn by putting your home on the market. Ask yourself:

- Is my house in a good location?

- Is it in good condition?

- Has it appreciated in value considerably since I bought it?

- Could I be living better in a nicer house?

- Am I sitting on a lot of equity?

If you've answered yes to all of these questions, it may be time to sell. If you're not certain about the value of your home, you should get an opinion of its worth from two or three reputable real estate agents or a professional appraiser. (The appraiser will charge for this service, somewhere around $100 to $200 in most parts of the country. The agent's opinion of value costs nothing—he hopes you'll let him sell the house so he can collect a commission.) You may be dumbfounded to learn that the dull brownstone in the up-and-coming neighborhood that you bought four years ago for $75,000 is now worth $150,000. You played "double or nothing" and won!

Let's say there *is* a handsome profit in your present home and the thought of moving to a better neighborhood has got your adrenaline flowing. If there's little or no difference between what you originally paid for the property and what you can get for it today, ask the agents who gave you an estimate of the fair market value if they would recommend any improvements to make your home more valuable.

If they suggest *major* changes (new kitchen and bathrooms, for instance) and you have the ability to finance these home improvements, move out of the house and do them. I believe every dollar spent on quality improvements equals two or more dollars earned when it comes time to resell your home. But I can't recommend that you and your family live at home during the renovations.

What's so bad about turning your own home into a construction site? It is a major—repeat, *major*—disruption in your life. If you have to clear away debris before you can make a cup of coffee, if you must sweep plaster dust off every table and desktop before you can use it, you may grow to dislike this profession.

And then, after you've endured months of dirt, dust, and paint fumes, and it all looks wonderful, you'll be damned if you're going to move. What's so bad about staying put? What has happened is that you've spent a lot of time and money without making a cent. You haven't sampled that real taste of success that comes when you sell your house at an enormous profit.

Unless you are truly a superwoman with a superfamily, I advise you not to disrupt your lives by living on a renovation site. Maybe you should consider, instead, a little sprucing up. A minor investment in some new carpeting, a paint job, new wallpaper in the bathrooms, or new kitchen flooring may be all that's required. A house that's considered in "move-in condition" always sells faster than one that needs work. It goes without saying that getting rid of accumulated junk—like the empty aquarium, the three-legged chair, and piles of old magazines—can really affect the appearance of your house. Disposing of the old clothes you never wear will make your closets look larger, and therefore more desirable, to a prospective buyer.

If you can sell your house and net enough profit to buy another one at equal or greater cost, take out a mortgage and pay for renovations, and still have sufficient cash to live comfortably (i.e., have the money to cover debt service, property taxes, utilities, insurance, and living expenses for two to three years, until you might wish to consider selling again), then it's time to roll the dice. In my book, this is a low-risk gamble, not a high-risk investment. And the winnings can be phenomenal!

There's still one more option when you're thinking about taking a profit out of the house you live in. Suppose you don't really want to move. After all, you made a smart purchase a few years back, you love your home, and the neighborhood is great. To find anything just as nice or nicer would mean spending a fortune with maybe less favorable financing than your current mortgage. All right then—don't budge.

But in most states, you can still borrow against the equity you have in that house and begin homewrecking a new property. And the cash you pull out of your equity is completely tax-free.

Well, you ask, won't the monthly debt service on my own residence jump when I take out a second mortgage? Yes, it will, but not for long. When you've bought, remodeled, and sold your home renovation project in a year or so, you can pay the loan off and use your profits to buy yet another property.

The "right house" to get your homewrecking career started may be no farther than your own backyard!

OPEN HOUSES

*O*pen houses—viewing of properties for sale that are held for the public—take place every weekend in towns all over the country. Their hours are advertised in the Sunday papers. You can see properties at your own pace and get the feel of a house without a scheduled agent's appointment. Going to open houses to look for that perfect place can be educational—and occasionally profitable.

Open houses are set up either by the agency representing the owner or by the owner himself. When you walk in the door, you'll be given a statement covering all the vital statistics of the property. Ask as many questions as you want and take notes on your statement sheet.

The agent on the premises will have you sign the guest book and will offer you a business card. If you appear at all interested, you may be asked if you'd like to make an offer. If you're working with your own agent, ask him to come and view the property as soon as possible. This way, you'll have some expert input before you make your offer.

WHEN TO LOOK FOR A HOUSE

*Y*ou can go househunting at any time of year, any day of the week, most hours of the day, but the best advice I can give is to look when no one else is coming in right on your heels. When you are the only customer a seller has to talk to, you suddenly become exceptionally attractive. If you want to make an offer, and yours is the only one, it will certainly get more than a fair hearing.

Homebuyers, like crocuses, come out in the early spring. Suddenly, real estate offices are flooded with people looking for the ideal house or apartment. Fall, when vacation is over and school is about to start, is another hot season in the property market.

Begin your househunting when everyone else is away in late summer or keeping warm in winter's cold. I've made some of my very best deals during the Christmas holidays—sellers just tend to be more giving when the holiday spirit prevails. By December, they may also be fearful that their house is doomed to sit on the market for at least another two months. While everyone else is checking presents off shopping lists and baking fruitcakes, you ought to be canvassing the neighborhoods with your agent (who may not have any other clients).

In desirable locations, house prices tend to jump a few thousand dollars as the spring season gets rolling. By purchasing at the end of the year, you get next year's home at this year's price.

TARGETING THE RIGHT HOUSE FOR YOU

*H*ow many houses or apartments should you see before you make an offer? It depends. Some experts recommend viewing fifty to a hundred properties before you even look at an offer form. But the very first place you walk into may be the best. Everyone tends to resist this notion, assuming that something better—a nicer layout, a bigger lot, a better deal—is just around the corner. That's not necessarily so. As a novice homebuyer, you are probably going to be nervous about making snap judgments, and you may walk away from that house simply *because* it's the first you've seen.

But if you've done your homework properly, and you have asked your agent the correct questions, if your aspirations for buying, renovating, and reselling at a profit match up with your gut reaction, then I say, go for it. A good agent, one who really listens when you explain what you want, is likely to take you directly to the buried treasure you've been looking for. If so, have the courage to submit an offer. You'll have at least 14 to 21 calendar days to do your inspections and check out financing before you have to make a final decision. One of the biggest heartbreaks of housebuying is realizing after several weeks of searching that the best property was the first one you saw—and then hearing that it has since been sold. Remember, if you've found the right house, chances are that somebody else has seen it and fallen in love with it too. You should act quickly and grab it before that somebody beats you to the punch.

Recognizing the piece of property that you can *transform* into the perfect home involves having an ability to see its potential, and being realistic and compromising on elements that can't be changed. It also involves lots of imagination and hard work.

Pump your agent for every bit of information he can pro-

vide about the property. You shouldn't expect him to give
you a detailed appraisal of plumbing problems, faulty electrical wiring, or existing dry rot—you'll have an engineering inspection to fill you in on those details. But you should
demand a forthright evaluation of the general condition of
the house and how it compares to other properties in physical appearance and price. It's in both of your best interests
to make a wise and informed purchase.

Most agencies' statements on a house include a dis-
claimer that says something like "The above information is
reliable but not guaranteed." This protects them to an extent, but there have been a lot of legal hassles over mis-
representation, which keep most agencies very honest.

Be sure to ask:

- How long has this house been on the market?

- Has the owner lowered the price since he
  started showing it? Do you have any idea how
  much lower he'll go?

- What can you find out about the seller's finances? Why is he selling? Is there a good possibility of seller financing? (If he's building a
  new house, he probably wants an all-cash deal.
  But if he's retiring, moving to a smaller place,
  or going to prison, he can probably wait for his
  money and would appreciate a monthly interest payment from you.)

- Will I be overspending if I put out X amount of
  dollars to improve this property in this neighborhood?

- What are a few comparable sales on the block
  in the past six months?

- What are the property taxes? Will they go up
  with the sales price?

- What type of heat does the house have—gas,
  oil, or electric—and what's the yearly cost?

- What are the charges for water and sewage? Or does the house have its own well?

- What are the arrangements for garbage disposal? Is city or private pickup? Is there a charge for this?

- Will the fact that the kitchen is upstairs and the bedrooms downstairs be a detriment to a future sale? (In most cases, yes.)

In addition to these questions, you should inquire about a few other points if you're looking at a condo or a co-op:

- Can you give me a profile of the type of person who lives here?

- How difficult is it to be accepted by the co-op's board of directors? (This is important not only for you, but for the prospective buyer of your unit.)

- Are you permitted to sublet your unit?

- Is a garage space included? How far is it from the unit? Is there guest parking?

- What kind of security system is in use?

- Can I see an engineering report on the entire building or complex?

- What's the current monthly maintenance fee? How recently has it increased? Is there a likelihood of another increase soon? When?

- Can I see a copy of the CCRs (Covenants, Conditions, and Restrictions)? I own three prize-winning Lhasa apsos and I want to know if pets are permitted in this building.

Remember that you can always back out of an offer if you decide you've made a mistake. A contract to purchase property is specifically written to include **contingencies** that let you walk away if your requirements are not satisfied. Never be afraid to make a deal just because you think you might want to break it. You are protected by a variety of clauses in your contract. This means that even if you've put in a bid on one house, you're still free to look at others and change your mind if you find a more attractive deal.

ELEMENTS OF A PERFECT HOUSE

*D*iscovering the *perfect* house is partly a product of being well informed, but it's also instinct to a great extent. You walk into a bare living room and, somehow, it seems cozy to you. You see the morning sunlight coming through the master bedroom window and you can imagine waking up there yourself. You love wandering around the spacious kitchen (even if it has a pump in the sink and a coal-burning stove), and you sense how workable it will be once you've redesigned it. That screened-in porch has more holes than a piece of Swiss cheese, but you can see yourself in there on a summer evening, sipping a margarita while you watch the dance of the lightning bugs. You like the *feel* of the house—and you can visualize yourself in it. You should trust that reaction because you have experience as a homemaker and you understand what makes a house work.

What specific elements might guide you toward making your decision?

- Layout of the rooms

- Ability to see your furniture in place

- Children's quarters separate from yours

- Views out the windows

- Size and type of plantings in the backyard or on a balcony

- Position of house on lot or location of condo in a building

- Maintenance of neighbors' homes

- Great exposures

- Marvelous light

It may be a detail as small as a leaded glass window or it could be something as big as the two-acre lot size that pleases you. Understand that there are ways to fix many of the things that don't please you. The three tiny bedrooms can be made into two spacious suites by knocking down walls; the cramped study under the eaves can be made visually larger and brighter by installing a skylight; the laundry room can be moved from the basement to the second floor for greater convenience.

But you cannot switch a house that faces north to face east, you can't make seedlings grow into stately oak trees overnight, and you can't make the neighbor paint his porch or remove the red-capped gnomes in his front yard. You can't reduce the amount of the property taxes or substantially lower utility bills. For these reasons, it's absolutely essential to make yourself a priority checklist that indicates the things you must have, the things you'd like to have, and the extra added attractions that may come with a property.

IMPERATIVES AND EXTRAS

*H*ere's a useful list that will help you compare the various properties you're seriously interested in. As you fill in the spaces, keep in mind that you are not only looking at these houses with a thought to living in one of them yourself but also checking their suitability for later sale.

Rating Property

Address	65 Terrific Terrace	39 Superb Circle	2498 Wonderful Way
List price			
Approx. sq. ft.			
Utility costs per yr.			
Property taxes			
Good location?			
Near transportation			

HOW MANY: . . . .

Bedrooms
Bathrooms
Closets

IS THERE A: . . . .

Formal dining room
Den/family room
Eat-in space in kitchen
Entrance hall/foyer
Fireplace
Central AC
Laundry room
Attic
Garage
Patio/deck
Garden
View
Security system
Income unit

CONDITION OF: . . . .

Kitchen
Baths
Heat/air conditioning
Carpeting or floors
Lighting fixtures
Windows
Interior painting
Basement
Exterior
Roof
Landscaping

This list can be endless, and you can expand it to accommodate all the particular elements of the various houses you see. For instance, under "Kitchen" you can include appliances, cabinets, counters, floors, and lighting, and under "Baths" you can include tub, shower, double sinks, and ventilation. Once you get your ratings down on paper, you'll have an amazingly comprehensive study of all the properties you're considering.

NARROWING YOUR CHOICES

*Y*ou can, of course, make a bid on a house the instant you've finished walking through it. I've done it myself, feeling impetuous and intuitive and wondering all night if I would still like the place in the morning.

If there's hot and heavy interest in the particular house, and you need at least twenty-four hours to think about it, you can always say that you're definitely going to make an offer but want to bring your contractor (husband, child, dog, psychiatrist) with you the following day to get a consensus on what work has to be done.

With a second visit, you give yourself a little breathing room, you confirm all the things you *thought* you saw last time, and you pick up on details you might have missed. Because choosing the right place, whether you're going to live in it for the rest of your life or intend to stay only one year, is very much like falling in love. It's thrilling, it's mind-boggling, sometimes it's a little irrational. But a second visit can help you take off the rose-colored glasses.

If you saw the house on a sunny day, see it again in the rain or snow. If you saw it in the morning, go back at night. If you like it in foul weather, in the dark as well as in daylight, you'll like it anytime.

BUYING PROPERTY
THROUGH PROBATE

*O*ne excellent but not too well known method of finding a house is through probate court. The houses are generally part of the estate of someone who has recently died, and the court has been appointed to handle the sale of the property for the heirs.

Local realtors are sent announcements of houses offered by the court and will show you the listings, or you can see them yourself at city hall. There are usually several days during which the house or unit is held open for public viewing. Then, on a designated day, the court accepts sealed bids. If you want your offer to be accepted, you have to bid knowledgeably. Take your agent along with you when you see the house. He can give you a ballpark figure on what it's worth. If you have plans for renovation, you should also see the house with your contractor or an engineer. You must have all your costs in order before you can come up with a price that will be advantageous for you and appealing to the heirs.

The highest offer is accepted from the submitted bids, and a court date is set for confirmation of the sale. At this time, other interested buyers who lost out have the opportunity to come to court and overbid the winning offer. It's like an auction, with all the attendant excitement and exasperation.

I remember my first experience in probate court. I'd found a wonderful property, done all the inspections, and submitted an offer. I was notified that mine was the winning bid. I was delirious. The place was fantastic, and I was getting it for a great deal less than it would have cost on the open market.

Then came the court date. The judge pounded the gavel and asked if there were any overbids. Silence.

Then an agent raised her hand and said, "Your honor, my client would like to bid on this house, but has not seen it yet." I fully expected the judge to ignore this feeble plea. Instead, he nodded and said he'd give the new bidder one hour to look at the property and return to court.

"Your honor, I object!" I cried, jumping out of my seat without realizing that I'd been watching too many courtroom dramas on TV. "It's not fair," I continued. "This house has been open every Tuesday and Thursday for the past four weeks!"

The judge glared at me, stern and unamused. "Young lady, sit down!" he ordered. "My job in this courtroom is to get the best possible price for the heirs of the estate."

I sank back in my seat. And waited for sixty endless, nerve-racking minutes.

One hour later, the interested party and his agent had not returned, and the judge was about to raise the gavel on my deal when the phone rang. The stenographer answered it, wrote something down on a piece of paper, and handed the slip to the judge. He announced that there would be no further bidding on the property. It would be sold to the original bidder.

"That's me!" I shouted.

Before a session in probate court, my stomach is always filled with as many butterflies as Yosemite National Park. After all, it's not as if you're bidding on a $30 rocking chair at a country auction. The main risk is overbidding; you must set a ceiling and stick to it. But be prepared for the inevitable temptation to go higher when the bidding gets hot.

There are also property auctions held because of an owner's failure to keep up with his mortgage payments or property taxes. These are called **foreclosures.** Foreclosure sales are often advertised in local papers and are listed in legal and real estate publications as well. Here too you can find bargains. You can obtain property for just the price of the existing loan or for the existing loan plus the total sum of all the missed payments, penalties, back taxes, and utilities. The laws vary from state to state, as do the stipulations of the lender. I feel that in dealing with foreclosure sales it's essential to be advised by an attorney.

One warning about probate and foreclosure sales: The properties are generally sold in "as is" condition and there is no financing contingency. A 10% deposit is usually required upon acceptance of your offer. If you don't have the money or a loan in place to complete the purchase, you could lose your deposit.

THIS HOUSE IS NOT YOUR LAST HOUSE

I cannot count the times I've heard people say, "This is positively the last time I will *ever* move!" And then, "I don't know how you do it, Suzanne. You change homes as often as some people change their sheets."

If they knew the profit I've made on each of my residences, they, too, would probably put up with a little inconvenience.

Now that I've logged in my twenty-third move, I have it down to a science—I guess because I do it so often. Tom, my friendly local mover, knocks on my door every six months whether I need him or not. I can organize a move in three days, and by the end of a week, I can be completely functional in my new place. It's all in the organization. You have to plan ahead before you start packing!

I look at a house as a temporary home. By the time I've finished my renovations, got the house just the way I want it, I'm ready to start another search for another property. After all, when the systems are shiny and new and the place looks spectacular, that's when your property takes its biggest profit jump.

You should stay in a house long enough to fulfill your short-term needs—and no longer. For example, you could plan your next move to coincide with a big promotion, when your toddler toddles off to nursery school, when your teenager goes to college. You could give yourself a fifty-fifth birthday present and move when you can take the maximum tax advantage—$125,000 profit tax-free.

I believe that one of the primary reasons to get started in homewrecking is so that you can eventually get the house you want but can't afford right now. By starting small and continually trading up into one house after another, you will soon wind up in the house of your dreams.

A house will always be your home no matter how long you live in it. But when you're reaping an additional income out of remodeling and selling it again, a house becomes a lot more than a roof over your head. Even as you're making the offer on this first piece of property, keep in mind that you *can* and *will* move again. You'll pack those boxes painlessly, knowing that you're only moving up from here on in.

Checkpoints

You will find the right house for your first homewrecking project if you:

- ▶ Look for the worst in the best part of town.

- ▶ Start small and think big.

- ▶ Consider selling your own house for profit or using the cash you can get out of it (your equity) to purchase a new property.

- ▶ Attend open houses.

- ▶ Househunt at *all* times of the year.

- ▶ Question your agent closely about the properties that interest you.

- ▶ Rate your final choices in terms of imperatives and extras.

- ▶ Consider buying houses through probate or foreclosure sales.

6
Making an Offer: The Formula

Y ou have driven around town for weeks, seeing two or three properties a day. You are worn out with confusion and frustration; you've seen Cape Cods and Colonials, firehouses and lofts offered as "alternative life-style housing," and the adorable "fixer-upper" that would have cost twice the selling price when you got through with the renovations. Each property has something to recommend it, but each one has drawbacks you simply can't live with. As the days pass, you despair of ever finding the perfect place.

But then, one afternoon, your agent tells you she has something new to show you. Your eyes light up as you turn into the driveway. This is the one. It's got location, it's got charm, it's got potential, and with some help and hard work from you, it will have *everything*. After you've asked all your requisite questions of the agent, after you've slept on it and thought about it and seen the house twice more, you decide to make an offer.

You'd like to clinch the deal, but you don't really want to

pay the price the seller is asking. Still, you're nervous
about getting closed out by the competition. How do you
figure out what offer to make? How much does the seller
really want? How high should you go? At what figure
should you stop bidding? How do you know exactly *what the
house is worth to you?*

Many people are intimidated by the buying process and
are particularly anxious about making an offer. They're
certain they'll be pressured to offer more than they want to
spend and will end up getting in way over their heads.

If you're on the fence, afraid to make a commitment, ask
yourself if it's the house or if it's you. You will *never* find
perfection (unless you are buying a magnificently remodeled house, in which case you'll get no bargain).

When your intuition tells you it's right, when all your
instincts point straight toward *this* front door, then do it.
Make an offer.

The initial payment accompanying the offer is refundable, and, as I've said, the buyer can pull out anytime before removing the final contingency of purchase. Buying a
house is not a roller-coaster ride. You can get off.

THE FORMULA—
WHAT SHOULD YOU OFFER?

*F*irst things first. You must get all your numbers
straight. Before you go to the negotiating table
with the seller, you should know exactly how much
cash you have on hand for your down payment, closing
costs, and remodeling. You'll have to sit down with a con
tractor and get some ballpark figures for the changes you
want to make. You don't need to know the cost of every wid-
get and screw, but you do need a general idea of what you'll
have to spend for your workmen's time and materials. If you
don't have a contractor, your real estate agent may be able
to recommend one. You'll have plenty of time before your
closing to decide whether or not you wish to use a contrac-

tor and which one to select for the job. Later on, I will show you how to choose the perfect one, the man who can make each stage of your renovation run smoothly. Right now, though, a rough approximation of costs is all that's necessary, so you can call one or two reputable contractors to give you a free estimate.

The house you've fallen in love with has been on the market for a while, maybe it wasn't appraised for the price the seller is demanding, and it's recently been reduced from $115,000 to $105,000. You're in a good position here, with a motivated seller and little competition from other buyers—no offers and counteroffers flying around the agent's office like unguided missiles. Later, after you've experienced a deal or two, you may enjoy the excitement of a competitive situation, but it's better to start with a quieter, more civilized purchase.

When you have your figures in order, you must put down your offer in writing—usually on an offer form provided by the real estate agent. This form, which states *your* terms and conditions for purchasing the property, is presented to the seller, who either accepts or counters with his own terms and conditions. A monetary binder should accompany the offer—usually a refundable "good faith" check of $500 to $1,000. If the deal goes through, this money becomes part of your down payment; if the deal falls apart, you get your money back. The binder shows that you are a serious buyer, and the terms and conditions you've stated on the form start the negotiating ball rolling between you and the seller.

You must know *before* you sign anything what you want to pay for the house. There is a very simple way to decide this. I devised a formula for making an offer the first time I bought a house, and I've used it on all my subsequent purchases, large and small. It's foolproof and exceptionally simple. You just work backward from the price you want to sell at when your renovations are completed and factor in the profit you'd like to make on the property.

Making a profit, of course, is your goal as a home-wrecker. How much you make depends on a variety of factors, but you must have some reasonable expectations before you come up with an offer.

As a freelancer in the home-renovation business, you should be paying yourself a salary. As boss of the project, you get to decide how much you should earn. When I started out, I set myself a goal of $20,000 profit per house, not really knowing whether I would be able to make it. I chose that figure after my first success, and hoped I could achieve it on every property. Some made it, some missed it, some far surpassed it. The important thing, though, is to give yourself something to aim for. You may be satisfied with less than $20,000 your first few times out, or you may think your hard work and creative genius are worth more.

Now, let's work the formula to figure out what your top offer should be on any property:

1. Ask your agent how much he thinks the house would sell for today, completely renovated. Let's say your agent reports that right now, in mint condition, the property would sell for $150,000. Subtract the selling agent's 6% commission from this figure ($9,000), to get $141,000.

2. Now subtract the profit you want to make on the property. Generally speaking, I allot three to five months to renovate a house that needs a lot of work, and then another one to three months to sell it. Let's say the net profit I want for those eight months would equal $2,000 a month, or $16,000. Subtracting $16,000 from $141,000, we get $125,000.

3. Your contractor has informed you that estimated renovation costs come in at about $14,000. This leaves you with $111,000.

4. Deduct your carrying costs for eight months. These also have to be estimated, since you don't know the exact purchase price of the

house yet, nor can you determine what your interest rate will be. But let's assume a purchase price of $100,000 with a standard 80% mortgage amortized over thirty years. At an 11% interest rate, your monthly debt service will come in at about $762. This, combined with your other carrying costs of property taxes, utilities, and insurance, will bring the total to around $1,000 a month, or $8,000 for eight months. Subtract. You're down to $103,000.

5. Finally, subtract your closing costs. These vary from state to state, but you should usually figure on paying 3% to 4% of your purchase price. Your agent can itemize these for you. Approximate closing costs on this house might be $3,000. Subtract, and you get $100,000.

   $100,000 is your top offer.

The Top Offer Formula

Today's price for a fully renovated house	$150,000
Agent's commission	−9,000
	141,000
Desired net profit	−16,000
	125,000
Renovation costs	−14,000
	111,000
Carrying costs for 8 months	−8,000
	103,000
Closing costs	−3,000
TOP OFFER	$100,000

Have you noticed that we're working with *today's* value on the resale, rather than the sale value of the fully renovated house in eight months' time? I did this to surprise you with another possible bonus: appreciation. Eight months from now, a $150,000 property may well be worth even more. This is the frosting on the real estate cake, and I've tasted frosting on nearly every property I've sold.

LEARNING TO NEGOTIATE

*W*hen you make your initial offer, you don't want to mention your top price right away. With this house, I'd begin at $95,000 and see what the seller's response was. Naturally, I'd come armed with the estimates for the $14,000 renovation costs to show exactly what would have to be done to improve the property so that it might be worth what the seller wants for it.

Admittedly, there are situations in which you will decide to give the seller his full price, even if it's a few thousand dollars higher than your estimated top offer. If the seller is offering to take back a large mortgage at a very competitive interest rate, you would probably agree to pay full price. Or if the property has just come on the market and people are lining up in the streets to make an offer, you would undoubtedly want to keep your bid high to shut out the competition. You have to weigh and balance the variables of the negotiating game and stay flexible as you go into your negotiations. You can bargain with the following chips:

- Amount of the down payment

- Financing from the seller

- Interest rate you'll pay

- Term of the mortgage

- Date of occupancy

- Competition from other bidders

One time when you can safely offer more than the top figure you got from the formula is when you plan to live in the house for two to five years before selling. In this case, appreciation will take you way above today's estimated resale price.

The art of negotiation—in real estate as well as every other field—involves some push and pull, some give and take, some compromise. In the end, everyone should be reasonably satisfied. Set yourself goals and stick to them, but remain flexible on the issues that don't really mean that much to you.

You've already learned to sell yourself in difficult situations. You've gone to family and friends and asked for their help. You've started accounts with banks, applied for credit, developed relationships with realtors, learned to ask questions about neighborhoods and houses and to probe until you get the right answers. In short, you've put yourself right in the center of the homebuying game.

In the same way, you must also keep yourself at the center of the negotiating process. Don't allow the seller to start running the show. You should let him think you're relinquishing things that are really crucial to you—that he's making out like a bandit while you are giving up the shirt off your back. In reality, though, you've decided beforehand what you can comfortably sacrifice—and where you will not bend. (Your opponent will be playing the same game, if he's smart, so keep your wits about you!) As long as you know what you want, you can feel sure of yourself and come across as strong, self-confident, and well informed.

Your goal is to make an offer you can afford that the seller can't refuse.

SELLING YOURSELF
TO THE SELLER

*I*f you're like me and enjoy the negotiating game, don't hesitate to ask your agent if you can accompany him with the offer and make your deal face to face.

Most real estate agents feel that the buyer and seller should be kept apart at all costs. I disagree. I think there's almost always room for buyer/seller dialogue. This is *your* offer—you're entitled to do the talking. If the seller is considering several other offers, it's essential that you discuss the deal with him directly. The others will merely be contracts—pieces of paper. Yours will stand out because you made the effort to give a personal presentation.

Most agents will agree to letting the buyer and seller get together as long as they can sit in on the negotiating process. When an agent is strongly against my participation, however, I bow out despite my enthusiasm for negotiating. If I'm absolutely sure that the agent is a better salesperson than I am, I hand over the reins willingly. Many agents can come up with creative solutions that I'd never think of.

I've been in situations where I was certain the deal was going to fall apart and the agent intervened and suggested some brilliantly innovative plan. On one deal of mine, the seller was absolutely adamant about getting his price. He wanted $175,000 and not a penny less. I had estimated all the renovation costs and felt that I was stretching to offer $170,000. As we began to walk away from the negotiating table, the broker suggested a wonderful compromise. The three of us—seller, buyer, and broker—would split the difference of $5,000. If the seller would come down $1,666 and I would come up $1,666, the broker would agree to take an equal amount off her commission. It was a splendid idea, and it saved the day.

It can happen, of course, that the buyer and seller simply can't get along, but that's not usually the case. My feeling is that the two parties have a great deal in common—namely, the house—and that personal rapport can navigate the deal through some very rough waters. We're all enormously sentimental about our homes and we like to know they're going to pass into loving hands.

Be excited about the property; be exceptionally flattering. Tell the seller exactly what it is about the house that grabs you and *at the same time* point out what its faults are. The kitchen is wonderful, full of sunlight and Old-World charm, but it only has one electrical outlet. The master bath is magnificent, but there's no shower and the basin is cracked. You love the 16-foot ceilings, but they do manage to keep the house at a less-than-balmy 52 degrees.

See what you're doing? You're constantly praising the

property (and the praise is heartfelt, because you really do want to buy it) while making it perfectly clear that a lot of renovation is required. The seller will be flattered that you like the house so much and impressed and perhaps intimidated by your expertise. He will also suddenly come to understand just why his house has been on the market as long as it has—and perhaps why its fair market value isn't as high as he would like. He will be coming to the ultimate and important conclusion that *you* may be right, and that only by meeting your terms will he redeem himself from allowing the property to fall into such disrepair.

I've gone to great lengths to figure out what a seller's all about, and what he really wants. In one instance, I happened to know that the owner of a house I was bidding on was a prominent member of the arts community. We'd met twice before and seemed to be coming close to a deal, but there were still a few large wrinkles to iron out.

I picked an opportune time for our final meeting—opening night at the opera. I knew the seller was going to the gala event, and I told him that I was on my way to a dinner party. I asked if we could get together for a short while before our respective appointments.

I lied. I wasn't really going anywhere at all, but I dressed as though I were dining with the president. When the seller descended the staircase in a tuxedo, I met him in the foyer wearing a black silk gown. We were well matched. The dress lent a certain elegance to the proceedings, which went splendidly. After we shook hands on the deal, his driver took him to the opera house and my chauffeur, the agent, took me home. To a meal of Chinese take-out with my son.

Being on the seller's wavelength is enormously helpful when it finally comes to dickering over terms, as is quite clear in the following sample negotiation.

Let's say Elaine has definitely decided she wants to buy Robert's house. She figures she can afford the $100,000 price, but she doesn't have much cash to put down. Also, she's self-employed, which will make it slightly more difficult for her to get a mortgage at a bank, so she wants Robert to finance the deal.

Elaine: I've decided I'd like to make you an offer of $95,000.

Robert: The price is $100,000. With a $20,000 down payment.

Elaine (*Thinking hard*): Whew! That's an awful lot of cash up front. I don't know. I *had* set that amount aside for a down payment, but you know the house needs work. It's clear from my preliminary contractor's report that at least $12,000 to $15,000 will have to go for renovations. If I get a standard 80% loan from a bank or a savings-and-loan, I won't have a cent left over for improvements.

Robert: Well, there are a few things that need fixing here.

Elaine: I have a terrific solution! If I come up with some cash for a down payment, would you consider taking back the mortgage for me?

[She's asking for seller financing, which would work out nicely for both of them, as long as Robert doesn't need all his money up front.]

Robert: You want me to take back $75,000? With only $20,000 down?

Elaine: No, actually. (*With a deep breath*) I was wondering if you'd let me put down $10,000. Then you'd finance the remaining $85,000 for forty-eight months at 10% interest.

[Elaine is asking a lot! She wants 90% owner financing at a cheap rate for four years, which is a long time in the renovation business. You will note that she referred to the time period in terms of months, because months always sound shorter than years.]

Robert (*Clutching his heart*): That's a preposterous offer! You must think I'm an idiot. I certainly would never agree to that. (*He starts to walk away, then turns around.*) I might think about taking back some of the mortgage, but only if you'll give me full price for the house.

Elaine: $100,000. (*She looks disappointed, but she's smil-*

ing to herself. This was the first point she was willing to give on.)

Robert: That's it. $100,000 with 20% down. I'll supply an interest-only first mortgage of $80,000 at 10% for one year. After that, you'll have to refinance.

[At last! Elaine has won on seller financing. She is thrilled that he proposed an interest-only loan, too. This means that she will pay only interest, and no principal, over the term of the mortgage. At the end of the deal, after she's sold Robert's house for a profit, she'll pay him the loan amount in full.)

Elaine: Well, this sounds interesting to me. But I really must insist on lowering the down payment. I've got to have that money for renovations. Let's agree that I'll put $10,000 down—how about it?

Robert: I really want $20,000. But I might agree to $10,000 if you can think of something to sweeten the deal.

Elaine: Hmm.

[She's basically home free. All she wants now is to extend the length of the loan so that she'll have ample time to renovate and sell the house before she'd have to refinance. In order to extend the term of the mortgage, she'll offer to pay him a higher interest rate.]

Elaine: I'll put down $10,000, and pay you full price. What about this? You'll agree to carry a 90% loan for twenty-four months instead of twelve, and I'll pay you 11% interest. That's higher than any of the banks around here are getting. You'll be earning an excellent rate of return on your money, and your collateral—the house—will be appreciating every day as I renovate it.

Robert (*A grin spreading across his face*): I think we've got a deal.

Elaine has carefully figured her finances before going into the negotiation. And she can see that 10% interest on $90,000 is $750 a month and 11% interest is $825. The extra $75 a month over the duration of her loan is a lot easier to swallow than the extra $10,000 down payment Robert wanted initially.

Seller financing, in this instance, was the key to the whole puzzle. Both buyer and seller were quite happy to give a little when it came down to the wire. Robert wanted a good price for his house; Elaine wanted the longest period of time she could get on her seller-financed deal, since she can't determine how slow or fast the market will be when it comes time for her to sell.

Sometimes, no matter how brilliantly you negotiate, no matter how many concessions you make or how creative your financing ideas, the seller just doesn't want your deal. I always say that it's best not to fall too deeply in love with a house. Of course you should fight hard to win in your negotiations, but don't be depressed if you lose in the end. If the house goes to someone else, my feeling is that it was kismet; it was probably not meant for you in the first place. There will *always* be another house along soon—sometimes a much better house than the one that got away.

GOING TO CONTRACT

Now that you have come to terms, they must be written down to be considered legally binding. The next step will be to have your agent, or your lawyer if you're retaining one, write up the purchase agreement. The contract should be prepared and signed by both parties as soon as possible after you make your oral agreement with the owner. In fact, if your agent was present during your magnificent negotiating performance, he should have written down all the terms you stipulated and had you both sign the document—which would be used as the basis for the formal **contract** for purchase of real estate.

The elements you've hashed out orally with the seller are then set down in writing, and one of the standard clauses stipulates that no changes from here on in can be made without buyer and seller agreement *in writing*. The contract goes on to detail:

- Parties involved

- Purchase price

- Means of payment (down payment and mortgage)

- Date of closing (this clause could change before the actual event)

- Type of deed

- Inspections (termite and engineering) to take place

- Personal property and fixtures that come with the house

- Physical condition of the property and a promise that the seller will maintain this condition until closing

- Property lines

- Transfer of ownership and transfer of possession

- Statement that the seller will pay all liens (legal claims for payment of money owed against the property)

- Adjustment of property expenses (promise that the parties will prorate taxes, water, sewage, and fuel charges, premiums on home ownership insurance policies, and so on) at closing

- Seller validation that all systems (plumbing, heating, and electric) are in good working order and that the roof is free of leaks

The contract is simply the offer made and accepted in writing. This document varies from state to state, and contingency clauses can be written in to accommodate every conceivable situation between the buyer and seller.

Remember, nothing is binding while there are contingencies on a contract—and you can include as many as you like. For example, a deal can be:

- "Subject to" the buyer obtaining satisfactory financing at the specified interest rate and terms

- "Subject to" the buyer's approving the contractor's or engineer's inspection (which may disclose more costs than your budget can stand)

- "Subject to" a termite inspection (which may uncover thousands of dollars' damage)

- "Subject to" the buyer's accountant's (husband's, children's, grandmother's) approval

- "Subject to" the buyer's selling his or her own house (many sellers will not agree to this, but you can try; some will come around if you agree to a 48-hour waiver period—that is, if the seller gets another offer, he can ask you to remove your contingency within 48 hours or lose the deal)

These contingencies offer you a way out throughout the buying process, and give you ample time to do all your necessary homework and see if the property is worth the price you're paying. They also give you time to go back for another visit to see if you're still in love.

Once you've both signed your intent-to-purchase contract, you've got a working deal. Congratulations! You're almost home. Now we're going to move on to the financial and legal matters you must consider in order to make sure the deal proceeds.

*C*heckpoints

You can make an offer that you can afford and the seller will accept if you:

- ▸ Have all your estimates in place before you make your offer.

- ▸ Sign an agency offer form and make a "good faith" deposit.

- ▸ Know the formula for your top bid.

- ▸ Learn to negotiate.

- ▸ Work with the seller directly—with your agent's input.

- ▸ Discuss all the contingencies you want in your contract with your agent or lawyer, if you're retaining one.

7
The Deal: Financial and Legal Assistance

nce you **agree** on a price and terms for your house, you must get some big systems into motion that will assure the proper completion of your deal. You should line up appointments with all your advisers at around this time—although if you found yourself in the midst of really complicated negotiations, you might wish to consult an accountant and/or a lawyer on a preliminary basis prior to signing your offer. Before you can own your house or apartment, you will need:

- *Financing.* You must obtain a loan from the seller and/or a lending institution.

- *Legal advice.* Some states require lawyer participation in a housing transaction, but even if yours does not, you may wish to retain an attorney. He will monitor the deal and help you with the negotiations, the contract, the settling of details with the seller, the closing, and the transfer of title to you.

- *Insurance advice.* You must select an insurance company to cover you and your property adequately so that you are protected from damages once you own your home.

- *Tax advice.* You should select an accountant who will be able to fit your homebuying purchase into your particular investment picture.

SELLER FINANCING

*S*eller financing, I feel, is a pure gift. *Always* ask the owner of the property you are going to buy if he will carry the loan for a short term (two to five years), or longer, if he's amenable. Most sellers are not in the business of lending money, so don't expect a fifteen- or thirty-year mortgage.

There are many advantages of seller financing:

- You have no lengthy loan application to fill out, no application fee to pay or waiting time to be approved.

- Possibly you can bargain for a lower rate of interest than you'd get at a lending institution.

- You pay no points (loan fees), which are usually 1% to 3% of the loan amount.

- You will most likely pay interest only each month. A conventional lender would want the loan amortized—meaning you would have to pay principal *as well as* monthly interest.

- Possibly you can bargain for delayed interest and pay the first three to six months at the end of your term when the loan comes due.

- You have no prepayment penalties (although they're becoming rare with big lenders too).

- You are not required to have a lender's appraisal of the house. Obviously, you and the seller have agreed on the value. (But a formal appraisal *could* protect you from overpaying for the property.)

If you are cash-poor, if you're unemployed, or if you have no sustained credit history, seller financing may be the only way to get into your first property.

Here are some of the many ways seller financing can be tailored to you:

1. THE LEASE-OPTION. THIS WAS MY WAY INTO the real estate business, and it can be yours, too. It's the arrangement whereby you, the lessee, can rent a property and are given the opportunity to buy it.

Let's say that Ann finds a place she likes that needs some work. The owner agrees to a lease-option and requests some option money up front. This money is nonrefundable if Ann doesn't purchase the property, but if she does, it will be applied toward the agreed-upon purchase price. Ann will clearly want to keep her option money as low as the seller will allow in case she decides not to buy at the end of the option period.

The lease-option is a wonderfully easy way to get into a first house, because it doesn't require a huge monetary commitment. The lessee only has to pay the monthly rent. At any time during the term of agreement, she can decide whether she's going to exercise her option. And she has a year—sometimes more—to make up her mind as to whether she really likes living there.

Ann can be pretty creative with her negotiations, too. She can ask to live in the house rent-free and agree to put all the rent money she would have paid each month toward renovations, which she will detail on paper for the owner's approval. She'll provide bills for labor and supplies and allow the owner to check her progress, of course. If the owner won't agree to 100% rent-free, she can try for 50%.

Here's another lease-option idea. If the rent is $500 a month, Ann might suggest that she pay the owner nothing during her first year when she's renovating (she can use all that money that would have gone for rent to do the remodeling) and then, if she doesn't buy the property after that time, she'll agree to pay him $1,000 a month for the next twelve months. This way, the owner can recoup his loss during the second year. But Ann, of course, will have exercised her option by this time and will have sold for a big profit without having to take a dollar of rent money from her wallet.

Still another lease-option tactic is to designate a portion of each month's rent toward the purchase price. That way, you'll get a head start on paying for the house if you decide to buy it.

The disadvantage of a lease-option arrangement when you do a lot of remodeling is that you're investing in a property you don't own. And if you don't exercise the option and buy the house, you can't take your renovations with you. However, if you are able to get the owner to agree that you will renovate *in lieu of* paying rent, then your only real loss would be time and labor.

If you're afraid to make major renovations to a property before you own it, then lease it for a year and see if property values rise around you. Remember, when the term of your option comes due, if you decide to buy, you'll be paying last year's price for this year's home.

2. SHORT-TERM HELP DURING A TIGHT MONEY market. Seller financing can be beneficial to both buyer and seller when mortgage money is tight and hard to get from a conventional lender, or when interest rates are high and there are more sellers than buyers. If you are qualified, a seller may agree to finance the purchase for a couple of years until money becomes easier to obtain.

Let's say Jim is asking $100,000 for his house. Steve and

Carole feel the value is reasonable, and won't haggle if he agrees to give them a short-term mortgage. They should offer the full $100,000 *provided* that Jim finances all or part of the sale for one to three years. Steve and Carole should also offer to pay a competitive interest rate on the loan—that is, the same or slightly above a bank or S&L. If Jim can afford to wait for his money, he'll get his full price *plus* a higher interest rate than he would on most year-long certificates of deposit.

The key here is *short-term*. You, the buyer, are in and out of the property—and the seller gets his price—within twelve to thirty-six months.

3. SWAPPING FAVORS! FULL PRICE IN EXCHANGE for full financing during renovations. Jonathan wants $100,000 for his home. The property, however, has been valued by a licensed appraiser at under $100,000. Nancy comes along on her white horse and points out—tactfully, of course—that this basically beautiful property will appraise higher once she's made some minor changes. If Jonathan will accept a minimum down payment and carry full financing (a 100% loan) while Nancy does the renovations, she'll be able to get a better mortgage later on from a conventional lender and pay Jonathan full price for the house. Keep in mind that Nancy intends to make her renovations and resell the property *before* she has to secure a new loan. She will be in and out of the deal with only a small down payment and her renovation costs.

4. THE DELAYED-INTEREST LOAN. PETE AND Christine offer Mr. Tracy down the block his full asking price of $100,000, with 90% seller financing and a $10,000 down payment when the deal closes. The catch is that they don't want to pay any interest at all for the first three months while they're renovating the house. They'll begin their interest payments on his loan 90 days after the deal closes. The payments for this three-month period are delayed and paid at the end when the loan comes due, or in this case, when Pete and Christine resell the property. Three months' delayed interest frees them in the crucial start-up months when they need all their money for renovations.

5. A SECOND MORTGAGE SUPPLIED BY THE seller. Judith wants to buy Beatrice's house for $100,000. She can come up with a $10,000 down payment, but her bank will loan her only $80,000 because the bank's policy is to finance only 80% of the purchase price. Where will she get the additional $10,000? Beatrice could offer to take back a second mortgage, secured by the property. The bank, then, would give Judith a first mortgage for $80,000, and Beatrice would give her a second for $10,000. Judith would make monthly payments to both of them.

Beatrice, in this deal, walks away with $80,000 from the bank financing *plus* a $10,000 down payment from Judith. With that kind of cash up front, it's not too painful for her to agree to carry a second short-term loan on the property. If the lender knows there's going to be a second mortgage, he will want to be sure Judith can afford to make payments on both loans. Two ways around this is for Beatrice to give Judith an interest-free note (interest would accumulate and be payable when the $10,000 was paid off) or to place a second loan on the property after the closing day.

6. THE WRAPAROUND MORTGAGE. "WRAPS," deals in which the seller holds on to his first mortgage and offers a second to a buyer who will give him a down payment, used to be very popular. These days, however, they are becoming more and more difficult to work because of the ubiquitous "due-on-sale" clause required by most big lenders. This means that the lender can demand payment in full on the existing loan if the owner sells the property. But it's worth mentioning anyway, because if you can find such a deal, it's a wonderful form of financing.

Many years ago, when Ray bought his house, he got a 7% mortgage for $60,000 from a lending institution. Tom now wants to buy Ray's house. He agrees to pay Ray $100,000 and give him a $10,000 down payment up front. Ray will take back an all-inclusive Deed of Trust for $90,000 (the bank's $60,000 plus $30,000 of Ray's equity in the house). He'll charge Tom a competitive interest rate of 10% on the entire $90,000 he's lending him.

Tom is getting a good deal—10% down, 90% seller financing, and a competitive interest rate. Ray is getting 10% on $90,000 when in fact he's only paying his lender 7% on $60,000 of that. He has wrapped two mortgages into one.

The laws about due-on-sale clauses, prepayment penalties, and mortgages change yearly. Always consult a real estate attorney to advise you on this seller financing.

7. THE LUMP-SUM-PAYMENT OR BALLOON-PAYment mortgage. I must say up front I am not in favor of this scheme—but it still may be more advantageous for you than going to a bank or S&L. Suppose Mary agrees to buy Ted's house for $100,000. She'll put 10% down with Ted carrying the balance of $90,000 for three years at a 10% interest rate.

But Ted wants to reduce the amount of principal owed to him—known in the trade as a **paydown**—so he asks her to give him a lump sum of $10,000 at the end of the first year, another $10,000 at the end of the second year, and the remaining $70,000 at the end of the third year. (The jump to $70,000 makes this a balloon payment.)

Mary should think *very carefully* before agreeing to this unless she's certain she can come up with $10,000 at the end of the first year. Even if her property is in an extremely good location in a wonderful part of town and if she is positive she can renovate and resell in twelve months and she is completely sure the market will be very active when she puts the house up for sale, I still can't recommend these terms. It would be preferable for her to pay $10,000 after the second year and $80,000 at the end of the third, knowing perfectly well that the house should be sold long before year three arrives. But it's still a very risky proposition.

I agreed to a lump-sum deal once, and that was the last time! I made an agreement to buy a big building in San Francisco and was able to assume the seller's first mortgage and got her to carry back a $500,000 second mortgage with a paydown of $100,000 a year for five years. I was making payments on the first mortgage to a bank and on the second mortgage to her. I was certain I could complete my renovations and conversion of the apartments to condominiums before the end of the second year. But it took much longer than I had anticipated, and I had to borrow $100,000 every year to satisfy my loan commitment to the seller.

8. BUYING PROPERTY AND PAYING THE SELLER in installments. Instead of coming up with the total sale price of $100,000 at closing, Maureen can make installment payments to Joe—say, $5,000 the first year, $10,000 the second, and so on. Maureen doesn't need a large down payment the first year, and she can spread out her payment as her wages or other monetary resources increase over the years.

BANK FINANCING

*C*urrently, all conventional lenders—banks and S&Ls—will offer mortgages to you, if you're a qualified applicant, for around 75% to 95% of the appraised value of the house you wish to purchase. That means that the lender wants you to come up with anywhere from a 5% to a 25% down payment. (The most typical arrangement is 20% down, 80% mortgage.) Sometimes you will get more advantageous terms if you put a larger amount of money down and the property is to be owner-occupied than you will if you want 100% financing or it's to be used as rental property.

If you intend to buy and sell property as often as once or twice a year, you should develop a working relationship with a commercial bank as well as one with an S&L. Once you have a track record of buying and selling at a profit, the bank may be very accommodating about lending—you can even borrow money for renovations and carrying costs.

Whereas a seller may be rather loose about checking out your credentials, a bank or S&L will be very tight indeed. You will have to present a bank with:

- A financial statement
- Your tax return for the past one to three years
- A statement about the size of your down payment and where you're obtaining it (is it your money or are you borrowing it?)
- A description of the property (including location, size, and estimated operating costs)
- A description of your renovation and an estimate of costs (sometimes you can get a loan that will include renovation costs)

Before you even think about calling a major lender, you should familiarize yourself with what I call "mortgagese," the particular vocabulary of mortgages. Here are a few of the catchwords:

Amortization: The length of time over which the repayment of the loan is calculated. Monthly payments are prorated over a number of years—most commonly, ten, fifteen, or thirty.

Assumable Loan: If you qualify for the existing loan on a property you are purchasing, the lender may permit its assumption. According to the terms of the loan, he could adjust the interest rate to present conditions.

Bridge Loan or Swing Loan: A short-term loan offered to bridge the time between closing one home and selling another.

Due-on-sale Clause: The stipulation that the balance of the loan still owing when you sell your house will be paid in full to the lender.

Escrow: A deposit of agreements, money, or papers between buyer and seller, held by a third, uninvolved party until all the conditions of the contract are met. Very often, a title company acts as the escrow agent.

Lien: Any outstanding debt against the property. A

plumber can place a lien for an unpaid plumbing bill; the city can place a lien for unpaid property taxes.

Mortgage or Deed of Trust: A document by which property is pledged to secure the payment of a debt. Promisory notes are secured by mortgages or Deeds of Trust.

Note: A signed, written document acknowledging a debt and promising payment.

Points: A percentage of the loan amount charged by the bank for writing the loan. Two points on an $80,000 mortgage is $1,600.

Prepayment Penalty: A fee (usually six months' interest) that you must pay the bank if you pay off your loan early. I feel this is one of the nastiest, most unfair practices in the lending business.

Refinancing: Terminating your loan and writing a new one because economic or personal conditions have changed. If you got your loan when interest rates were around 16% or 17% and they're now down to 10%, and if you intend to stay in your house for several more years, it's to your advantage to refinance.

Title: The guarantee that the property belongs to you, free and clear. Title companies are hired to research the ownership of your property and to make certain that all liens and encumbrances against the property are settled. To ensure a clear title, the company sells the buyer title insurance, which is included in the settlement costs paid at closing.

Now that you can speak the language, it's time to do some very thorough comparative shopping. Don't fill out any applications until you've canvassed *at least* four to six different lenders and examined all their various loan programs. Believe it or not, you can bargain for terms. When money is easy to get, lenders are in hot competition for your business. It may take you a little longer, but by asking these questions of each bank's loan officer, you'll be certain of getting the best deal you can:

- What types of loans are available?

- For what length of term are they being offered?

- What are the current interest rates for each? Is this a fixed or adjustable (fluctuating) rate?

- When are these rates set—at commitment or at closing?

- What's the minimum down payment?

- Is there a limit on the amount of the loan?

- How many points are charged, and when are they paid—at commitment or at closing?

- Is there a prepayment penalty?

- Is the loan assumable (built-in financing for a qualified new buyer)?

- What are the various fees?

- How long does it take to get a decision on a mortgage?

Mortgage-loan specifics vary from state to state and from month to month, but the following are some of the most conventional and long-standing mortgages available.

1. FIXED-RATE (CONVENTIONAL) LONG-TERM loan. In a fixed-rate loan, the interest rate never changes over the life of the loan, which may be anywhere from ten to fifteen to thirty years. If you get a 10½% fifteen-year mortgage, you are locked in. The amount you pay in principal will increase each month; the amount you pay in interest will decrease over this time, but you will pay the bank the same amount each month for fifteen years. Major lenders generally require a 10% to 20% down payment and charge a loan origination fee, about 1 to 3 points (that is, 1% to 3% of the amount of the loan), as well as an appraisal fee

(which runs around $200 to $300, depending on the state). Fixed-rate loans are usually not assumable and are likely to have prepayment penalties.

2. ADJUSTABLE-RATE MORTGAGE. ARMs ARE based on fluctuating national economic factors—the prime rate, U.S. Treasury bills, or the Consumer Price Index (CPI). If you select an ARM mortgage, you are assuming that your own finances will mirror the economy. You may get a one-year adjustable that starts at 10%, for example, that will increase or decrease 1% to 2% a year. After the initial term is up (usually at the end of the first year), the interest rate adjusts upward or downward, reflecting the national index. It's important to find out if there is a cap on this type of mortgage—typically, it can't go higher than 2% per year on the periodic adjustment or higher than 5% over the life of the loan. The borrower will also be expected to supply a 10% to 20% down payment and will pay 1 to 3 points, as well as the loan fee. ARMs usually have a lower initial interest rate than fixed-rate loans, which makes them easier to qualify for. Furthermore, ARMs are usually assumable.

3. BALLOON-PAYMENT LOAN. THIS IS *NOT* THE mortgage of choice for most people, but it's perfect for the homewrecker who knows she'll sell within two years. A balloon mortgage is predicated on a long-term payout schedule (meaning that the monthly increments are about the same as they would be on a fixed-term loan), but with a difference. At some point in the near future (most banks will only write a five-year balloon), the entire amount of the loan must be paid to the bank. Either that, or you must refinance. Some banks require a 25% down payment for a balloon mortgage. Again, you must pay your loan fee, points, appraisal, and legal fees, if any.

There are, actually, dozens of different variations of the above loans, one of which will be right for you. And you can still get an FHA (Federal Housing Administration) loan or, if you're a veteran, a VA loan. Loan programs change yearly depending on existing rates and money available. Who would ever have thought that mortgage rates would go below two digits as they did in 1986? I stood in line like thousands of other Americans and refinanced my home at a substantially lower interest rate.

You must have a signed contract for the purchase of a particular property when you apply for a loan from a bank. While processing your forms, the bank will send an appraiser to the premises to be certain that the property appraises for at least the amount of your loan. (If you default on payments, the bank wants to make sure it can sell the house for the amount you owe.)

Some lenders can give you an answer on your loan in a few weeks. This is important—you want that mortgage contingency lifted quickly. If it takes your bank over a month to process an application, as it sometimes does, you could lose your deal.

When your loan is approved, you'll receive a commitment letter. A copy should go to your lawyer, if you are retaining one, and to your real estate agent. If your loan isn't approved, you have every right to call your loan officer and ask why. If there are good reasons for your being turned down—such as a bad debt or insufficient credit history—you ought to get to work and fix the problem before applying to another lender for another loan.

HOW A LAWYER
CAN ADVISE YOU

*I*n certain states, you must retain an attorney in order to close a real estate deal; in many states, you don't need one. I personally feel that a licensed real estate agent can capably handle the negotiations, contracts, and settlement of nearly any standard real estate transaction. And the title company—if your state requires one—will guarantee free and clear title to your property. So do you really need a lawyer?

When deals get complicated or when the slightest question arises on any legal issue, then yes, by all means consult a competent real estate attorney. Or you may simply feel more comfortable having legal counsel when you buy a house.

Real estate lawyers work on property transactions full-time, every day, so retaining one for his experience and creative input may be worth the fee. (A lawyer's hourly charge varies widely, from small town to big city.) And if you're in the midst of a big, expensive deal, a trade or exchange, an estate or foreclosure sale, or any situation where there are rental units involved, you certainly want a lawyer. If you get bogged down in complex negotiations, a creative lawyer may come up with suggestions and solutions that might never have occurred to you. And before you do something rash, like agreeing to let the seller take your down payment out of the escrow account to buy another property, your lawyer can advise you of your rights.

Lawyers can help a real estate transaction move smoothly—or they can complicate it so badly the whole thing may fall through. I remember one house deal I had where time was of the essence and it was vital that the seller's attorney and my attorney iron out specifics so that the contract could be signed. But the two men could never get together. When one of them was in the office, the other was in probate court. When *he* was in the office, the other was arguing a case before the planning commission.

After a week, the seller, the agent, and I finally took matters into our own hands and we cleared up our differences in two days.

How do you select an attorney if you've never retained one before? Always get referrals from your real estate agent or friends. You want to find someone who knows his stuff but is not so popular that you can never get him on the phone. Try to make a get-acquainted phone call or visit (for which you're generally not charged) *before* you get yourself in the midst of a deal. And make certain you've got yourself an attorney who is an expert in residential real estate transactions.

Let's assume that you need some professional legal advice on this, your first deal. After you've signed the agency's binder or offer to purchase and the agency has drawn up a formal contract for buyer and seller (subject to financing, inspections, and lawyers' approval), you should get your attorney to review the document before you sign it. If you're having terrible problems figuring out what to bid, how much to put down, and the various kinds of contingencies to include, you may want to call your lawyer before you submit an offer.

The attorney will make sure that all essential clauses have been included and that anything detrimental to you—his client—is struck out, and will see that the contingencies are properly phrased. It will be your lawyer who'll advise you of when they can be removed—you can't lift your mortgage contingency until you get a commitment from the bank; you can't lift your inspection contingencies until you get a formal report from the inspectors. And then only a removal in writing can be used to lift them.

Your real estate agent can perform most of these services for you, but if you are retaining a lawyer, he will:

- Order the title company to do a title search and check into the intricacies of ownership of the property—whether the seller owns it free and clear; whether there are liens against it.

- Hold down-payment monies in escrow, generally in an interest-bearing account. (A title company or a bank can also do this.)

- Set the time and place of closing in conjunction with the seller.

- Make certain that any code violations on the building are removed and any damages repaired before closing.

- Deal with any tenants who may be living on the property, serve them with a notice to vacate if you wish and are permitted to do so by the particular occupancy law.

- Make sure that the outstanding property

taxes, insurance, and utilities are adjusted at closing.

- Make certain that you, the client, are protected in all circumstances. For example, if the closing date stipulated in the contract passes, he'll get an extension from the seller. If the seller pulls out of the deal, he'll see to it that you are reimbursed for fees already incurred.

- Possibly, renegotiate the sales price during the escrow period. Suppose your contractor comes in with a renovation budget that far exceeds your initial expectations or the termite inspection shows $3,000 worth of damage. A lawyer can explain this to the seller and try to convince him that it's necessary to take some money off the top.

The only time I really feel a lawyer's services are essential is when I need a creative contract written. Sometimes the linchpin of a deal is not how much money the seller wants and the buyer will pay but the way the deal is constructed.

HOW AN INSURANCE AGENT
CAN ADVISE YOU

*Y*ou never want to drive a car without insurance, because it's potentially dangerous for the driver and everyone on the road; and for similar reasons, you don't want to own a house without insurance.

It is possible, of course, to continue coverage with the seller's insurance company. He informs them that he is canceling his policy and wishes to recommend the buyer.

But suppose you've bought the house for a great deal more than your seller paid for it. Suppose the seller hasn't kept up with tax values in his neighborhood. Clearly, his house has appreciated in the years he's owned it. The house is worth a lot more today than it used to be—which would mean it's vastly *underinsured.*

If you're taking a mortgage from a bank or lending institution, it will insist that you insure your house for the amount of the mortgage—at least. You can mail the insurer a copy of your mortgage-commitment letter, or if you had your property professionally appraised, the appraiser can send the insurer a letter.

I believe in covering a house for the full replacement cost—the insurer can estimate this for you—plus the contents. More is better, because the cost of building materials and labor rises each year.

How do you value your personal property? Many policies have a blanket coverage for personal property equal to half the value of the house. If you own lots of computer equipment, some valuable antiques or paintings, and all your jewelry comes from Cartier's, you may need special coverage.

Then there's liability. Most companies automatically write a $100,000 liability clause which covers you if, for example, anyone slips and falls on the sidewalk outside your house. But for a few dollars more, you can get $300,000 worth of coverage. And when you think about all the people who will be coming and going on your property when you begin remodeling, you may wish to consider special workman's compensation in addition to the coverage the contractor will have.

Homeowner's insurance should be tailored to cover the particular house and the particular owner.

Call the seller's insurance company at least three weeks before closing and get an estimate. Prepare a list of your personal effects and all the particulars about coverage that may occur to you. If you aren't satisfied with this company's estimate, you can ask your real estate agent, your lender, your lawyer, or a friend to recommend another company, and get a second appraisal. Whichever company you decide to go with must know the date of closing so that all appropriate papers can be prepared and your policy drawn up. It must be paid for on the day you take possession of the house.

If you're buying a condo or a co-op, the homeowner's association already has an insurance policy in place. Part of your monthly maintenance includes your portion of the insurance—the cost of which is split among all the owners. The insurance includes the floors and walls of your unit and the exterior. The wallpaper and carpeting, plus all the furnishings in your apartment, are your responsibility.

Insurance policies in multiple-unit dwellings should keep up with increasing values, in the same way that those covering single-family detached houses do. Be sure to check and see that the existing coverage on your building is sufficient for you and the other homeowners.

HOW AN ACCOUNTANT
CAN ADVISE YOU

I might consider buying a house without a real estate agent; I would certainly consider buying a house without a lawyer. However, I would *never*, under any circumstances, enter into a real estate transaction without the advice of my accountant. She is an extraordinary person who thrives on the awesome activities of managing, saving, and making me money on what I've already earned.

In these days of creative financing, rapidly changing tax laws, retirement and pension plans, variable interest rates, and tax forms running the length of *War and Peace,* an accountant is not a luxury but a vital necessity. Homewrecking can be a high-profit business, but you need all the expert help you can get to make sure that, whenever possible, the profits stay where they belong—in your pocket.

When you're househunting, overseeing construction on a part-time or full-time basis, selecting materials, raising roofs and maybe a family on the side, it's simply impossible to keep up with the latest requirements from the IRS. And it's not worth it. Just when I think I've finally understood a particularly arcane facet of tax law, my accountant informs me that it's obsolete!

A really smart tax accountant can help you with your real estate purchase in innumerable ways. He or she can:

- Get the deductions you deserve on your taxes.

- Come up with clever means of financing.

- Tell you when to close the deal (timing is always crucial).

- Tell you exactly how much down payment you can afford.

- Tell you how much of a monthly mortgage payment you can afford.

- Explain all the tax benefits that accrue from owning real estate.

- Tell you how to figure your profits from a sale.

- Help you invest for your future.

How do you select an accountant? Again, referrals are the best means of finding someone creative and responsive. Friends who invest in real estate and are happy with their CPA (Certified Public Accountant) will probably be your best source. You do *not* want an accountant who's a scared rabbit. You want someone who's creative and reliable, with plenty of financial imagination.

Get a few names, interview a few people (they generally won't charge for the interview). Bring along tax returns for the past three years, and be completely open about your financial situation. How much liquidity do you want? How much tax-free income? Be sure to explain your real estate investment plans in detail. Remember that the information you share with an accountant can be very personal. You'll be telling him or her more about the intimate details of your life than you may care to divulge to your parents, children, or spouse. For this reason, you should pick a professional you really like and can talk to easily and comfortably.

When I bought and sold my first apartment, and then bought my second right afterward, I was totally ignorant about what these deals meant—other than making me a nice profit. But real estate investment is complicated, because the government sets certain rules and regulations that impinge on every move you make. You can get into a good deal of financial hot water if you don't know what you're doing.

Let's look at some of the areas where an accountant can help you:

1. TAX DEDUCTIONS. I'VE ALREADY TOLD YOU about the nice benefits you get deducting the interest payments on your mortgage and your property taxes as well. The Tax Reform Act of 1986 has changed none of that.

Then there's depreciation (cost recovery) on your investment property. If you own a house with a rental apartment or manage a piece of rental property, you can claim a depreciation expense. Depreciation means that the improvements (what is on top of your land) wear out as they get older. Interesting how the government lets you depreciate a building that appreciates in value each year!

What about the deductions you get just from closing your house deal? An accountant will explain that the points you pay to a bank for your mortgage are deductible, as are the majority of the costs itemized on your closing statement.

2. ROLLING THE PROFITS. YOUR ACCOUNTANT won't tell you what to buy or where to buy, but he will tell you how and *when* to buy. He wants to make sure you negotiate a deal that will have the lowest tax impact on you. So your timing is crucial. Let's look at a specific deal.

Jan bought her house for $50,000 four years ago. Her renovation costs totaled $10,000. This year, she puts her house on the market and is delighted to accept an offer of $80,000 for it. Now she's going to buy a new house that costs $100,000. Looks like Jan has to pay taxes on a $20,000 profit from the sale of her first house—right?

Wrong. For two reasons. First of all, the IRS allows you to roll that profit from the first house into the second tax-deferred—as long as:

- You buy another property within two years. (This time period changes occasionally. Ask your accountant what the current ruling is.)

- Your second property is equal or greater in value.

- The property you are buying is your primary residence.

These rules make it very clear that the government rewards the diligent home remodeler. You will be rolling your profits, buying increasingly more valuable pieces of property, and paying no current taxes on the profits you make.

This is my theory behind starting with a small residence and continually moving up into the nicest house in town.

3. FIGURING YOUR TAX LIABILITY ON A HOUSE sale. But just suppose Jan bought a property that was *cheaper* than the one she sold for $80,000. Let's assume she buys a condo for $75,000. Jan only has to pay taxes on the difference between the adjusted sale price (after broker's commision and expenses of sales) and new purchase price.

4. DELAYING OR SPEEDING UP RESALE. AN AC- countant might tell you to delay or speed a closing date, depending on your particular circumstances. Or if you were into homewrecking in a big way and happened to be buying and selling more than one piece of real estate at a time, your accountant might advise you to incorporate. When you get into the habit of buying and selling property that's not your primary residence, the government may consider you a "dealer" and tax you heavily for that privilege. But if you're a corporation, you get many breaks that individuals don't get. Ask your accountant to explain the benefits.

The real estate business often seems like a game—but

you cannot pass GO unless you know all the rules. Your accountant understands how the game is played. It's unlikely he'll consider risking his license, his reputation, and his business to bend them for you. It always hurts to make out a check to the IRS, but that check will be minimal if you have a good adviser telling you when to buy and sell.

There is only one more adviser you must consult before the property can be yours. This is your contractor or your engineer—who will conduct a structural inspection of the premises. You want your property to be given a clean bill of health, and an engineer can tell you all about its aches and pains. In the next chapter, we invite the doctor over—to make a house call.

Checkpoints

You can successfully close a deal if you:

- ▸ Explore financing options at several major lenders.

- ▸ Negotiate creative seller financing for part or all of your mortgage.

- ▸ Make sure you have adequate insurance coverage on your property which will take effect on your closing date.

- ▸ Decide to retain an attorney for difficult negotiations.

- ▸ Listen closely to the advice of your accountant. He or she will counsel you about the various tax benefits you'll receive from buying and selling property at the right time.

8

The Inspection: Finding the Skeletons in the Closet

*Y*ou are about to become an expert home-wrecker—but you don't want to buy a home that's a total wreck. *As soon as you have an accepted offer, you must get the house inspected. This is the time to find out whether the property you're planning to buy is structurally sound.*

Now ask yourself: What do you really know about this house? I mean, *honestly.* You may know a man intimately for months—even years—and still not realize what it's like being married to him until you actually take the plunge. Well, it's almost the same with a house, except, thank goodness, you can get an expert to warn you about major problems before you tie the knot.

The detractions that strike your eye when you first walk

in the door—the chipped paint on the woodwork, the peeling wallpaper, the torn shades on the windows—can all easily be replaced or fixed with time, money, and a little physical exertion on your part. But what about the antique dinosaur of a boiler? What about the leaking roof? What about the fireplace that's been cemented over?

One of your contingencies to purchase will be a favorable report on your house inspection. After you and the seller have agreed on terms and gone to contract, you can—and should—order an inspection. This service will cost you anywhere from nothing at all (a contractor can perform the service, so he may not charge you if you've already agreed that he'll do your renovations) to $100 or more. The price varies enormously from small towns to big cities. I usually order a separate roofing inspection by a professional roofer as well. Making sure you don't have termites or uncovering the damage they did twenty years ago requires a separate termite inspection—well worth the cost of the report. If you find out you've got them, you may not be able to afford them.

WHY HIRE A PROFESSIONAL INSPECTOR?

I can usually size up the general condition of a property by myself—and you can too, even if you've never bought a house before. Just by being alert, you'll know if the basement is damp and smells of mildew. You can see that the carpeting has a few stains, but nothing that you can't get out with a commercial shampooing. You may not be wild about the olive green refrigerator or the red flocked wallpaper in the entry, but those can—and will—be replaced. At least you can see that there are no settlement cracks in the concrete floor. The ceilings and floors in the rest of the house seem plumb, square, and level.

But I have to say that most of the time I don't really understand the severity of the house's illness—is it only sniffles or is it terminal? And I want to be absolutely sure what certain things mean *before* I buy. How serious is that cracked plaster under the peeling wallpaper? Is it due to a slow-leaking pipe in the upstairs bathroom—easy for any plumber to fix—or is there a hole in the roof? That might mean getting a brand-new one, to the tune of several thousand dollars.

Regardless of how many times I've bought and sold, I still don't trust myself to pick up on every skeleton in every closet, every potential pitfall of structure or equipment. That's why an engineering report and a termite inspection are so essential. You'll find out exactly what comes with the purchase price—good and bad. A trained inspector will give you the grand tour, telling you how to work the furnace, when to replace the filters, how to drain the hot-water heater, how to work the well pump if you have one, whether you should insulate the attic.

Another benefit of having a professional inspection is that it gives you financial leverage. You can always renegotiate the price downward if there's any major disaster you think the seller should pay for.

You'll have to decide whether you want to use a home-inspection service or a contractor to perform this function for you. Since you're going to be developing a close relationship with a contractor a little later on, when you begin renovating, you might consider having the same person do this preliminary report. The only cautionary note I'd sound here is that somebody who knows you want work done may *make* work appear like magic, so he can do it for you. He may exaggerate the danger of cracks in the plaster so that they turn into veritable craters. Beware of contractors with inflated ideas—get a second opinion if you're leery of the first.

WHAT THE
INSPECTOR INSPECTS

*T*he following list will give you a general guideline of what the pros look at when they examine a house. They are checking to see that all systems are functional, and that there are no safety hazards. You can use this list yourself when you're coming down to the wire on your negotiations and impress the dickens out of a seller. If he sees you looking at his roof with binoculars and checking for termite tracks with a flashlight in his cellar, just like a contractor doing his report, he will know he's not dealing with an amateur.

Exterior of the House
  drainage
  grading
  utilities (gas, water, sewer hookup)
  siding (brick, masonry, shingle, clapboard)
  roof
  leaders and gutters
  paint job
  garage or outbuildings
  windows
  doors
  porch or patio
  deck or balcony
  driveway
  sidewalks

Structure
  walls
  floors and floor joists
  masonry
  girders and columns
  heating system
  hot-water system
  electricity
  cellar drainage
  plumbing; water pressure
  ventilation
  insulation
  central air system
  security system

Interior
  walls
  floors
  ceilings
  windows (Are they hung properly? Do they have storms and screens?)
  electrical outlets (How many per room?)
  heating (Do all radiators work? Do they need bleeding?)
  fireplaces and chimneys
  closets
  storage
  doors (Do they stick? Do they buck square?)
  bathroom (fixtures, tiling, caulking, ventilation, leaky shower pans)
  kitchen (appliances, cabinetry, countertops, lighting, exhaust fan)

EXAMINING A CO-OP
OR CONDO

*W*hen you're thinking about buying an apartment in a multiple-unit dwelling, your inspector's report is slightly more involved. You want to make sure that the unit you're considering is in good order, of course, but you can't overlook the rest of the building, either.

Suppose you've made an offer on an apartment in an older building that's just gone condo. The inspector informs you that the plumbing is not copper, the plaster is cracked on the bedroom ceiling, the appliances date back to the year one. Nothing to get excited about.

But then he takes you down to the boiler room, and the superintendent gives you a tour. You both notice that the service company's most recent sticker on the side of the boiler is dated last month, and the sticker beside it is dated thirty days earlier. The inspector will want to know why this boiler is getting so much attention. Is something chronically wrong with it? You should make it a point to ask a number of residents of the building about the heat, and about any recent problems they've noticed.

If the building has only one hot-water heater and several units, will there be enough hot water for all the occupants?

How's the electricity in the building? Is there a 220-volt line? Will the electrician be able to increase the amperage in your unit to handle the new dryer, microwave, and dishwasher? Will the width of the old drainage pipes handle garbage from your new disposal? Many older buildings won't accommodate your needs.

With a co-op or condo, you have to take other people into consideration. Will your renovation affect someone else's apartment? Are there particular multiunit-dwelling building codes you must consider before completing your plans?

Remember that you are paying not only for the unit but for the building's upkeep as well. If the boiler goes—or the roof, or the elevator—the monthly maintenance will undoubtedly be kicked up (sometimes way up!) to pay for replacements and repairs.

LESSONS FROM
THE INSPECTOR

*B*uilding inspectors rarely jump up and down about anything. The ones I've encountered over the years have perfected the art of deadpan delivery and emotionless praise. "You've got brass piping throughout the house, lady—they don't make 'em like that anymore" when translated means "These pipes are worth their weight in gold."

How can you find out the really good points about the house or apartment you want to buy? The inspector will probably keep his mouth shut unless he sees something totally atrocious. All he's technically supposed to do is complete his printed report, in which "Satisfactory" is the highest grade. But if you're an informed buyer and ask pertinent questions, you can wangle some priceless gems of knowledge out of your time with this expert.

- What kind of pipes and bathroom fixtures are best? Does this house have them? Is there copper piping, or is it all galvanized? Should I up-grade the galvanized pipes to copper? What might it cost me to take out the old bathtub and put in a new one?

- How long will the water heater last? Should I wait until it goes, or would it be safer and less expensive to replace it immediately?

- Does it matter that the support beams are old? (In many cases, old is better. For example, the cellar beams and joists in an old house may be made of oak—as opposed to pine in a new house. Pine has a great deal more cellulose than oak, and cellulose is the favorite food of termites.)

- Can I patch the roof, or is a new one necessary? There are two layers of felt and tar on there already—should I go over it a third time or remove it all for a better job?

- Is it energy-efficient to insulate wherever pos-sible? As long as I'm opening up walls to do some new electrical and plumbing work, should I install a layer of fiberglass insulation?

- Is it better to have fuses or circuit breakers? (If the inspector tells you the wiring was done in 1910 and today it's done very differently, you should be aware that it may be costly to rewire. If he tells you that the attic fan was customary in those days, ask him if it's still good for any-thing. He'll tell you that it provides wonderful ventilation—an attic fan can help cool off an entire three-story house!)

When you receive your written report, go over it care-fully and write down any questions you have. If you don't know what certain terms mean—what's this about the "spalling and mortar joints that need repointing" in the cellar?—don't be embarrassed to call the inspector and ask.

What Should Be Fixed and About How Much Will It Cost?

I once bought a turn-of-the-century mansion with a boiler that had been converted from coal to gas. The thing took up most of the basement and roared like fury when fired up. The building inspector told me that this eighty-year-old monster was "reaching the end of its useful service career." (That's an engineer's euphemism for "on its last legs.")

Well, I had nightmares about this furnace breaking down. Every time I went down to the basement, I could hear the monster growling at me. But I didn't really want to put $3,500 into a new one. I wondered if there were any halfway measures I could take.

So I had a gentleman from the gas company come in and do a simple test. To my surprise and delight, I discovered that the old clunker was up to standard (72%) efficiency and still running smoothly after all these years. I could spend $125 for parts and labor and replace one valve on the furnace, which would bring the heating system up to 80% efficiency. Four years later, the family I sold that house to is still using the old furnace. Who says that new is better?

TAKE NOTHING
FOR GRANTED—
CHECK EVERYTHING

*W*e hire the experts to tell us about the property we're buying because they know more than we do, but they can't always uncover everything. Your engineering report deals only with those portions of the house that can be seen by the inspector when he comes for his visit. He's not going to tear up the carpeting to see whether termites have eaten the floorboards; he's not going to crack open a wall and check the wiring. He will help you to make your decision, but in the end, you're the one who has to decide whether you're going to pay your money and take your chances.

Ask yourself the following questions, and don't overlook any of these points:

- Did you see the house in the rain? Was there standing water in the basement? Did water collect in impromptu swimming pools in the backyard?

- If you saw the house during a dry summer, did you look for signs of water damage that might have occurred months ago? Look for stained walls and ceilings.

- Did you inspect the house in summer when the boiler wasn't running? Can you get a written representation from the seller or his lawyer stating that the boiler, burner, and hot-water heater are in good working order?

- If the house has a central air-conditioning system and it's winter, can you turn it on? You may not be able to if the heat is running, so get a written representation that it works. If air conditioners in every window are part of your deal, it's up to you to turn them all on even if it's the coldest day of the year.

▪ Find out about the city services. Is there adequate water pressure in your part of town, or will you have to install a pump to regulate it? Is your water meter accurately recording your usage? Will the gas man come the instant you smell a leak? How's the garbage collection?

▪ If you're not hooked up to city sewer services and the house has its own cesspool or septic tank, how has it been maintained?

Renegotiating for Repairs

*Y*our inspector has uncovered a few flies in the ointment. You confront the seller with the fact that he has misrepresented (just slightly) the wonderful shape his house is in. You are still interested in purchasing his property, but you think it is only fair that certain things be fixed before you take ownership. And you shouldn't have to pay for them.

Let's say you initially offered him a purchase price of $100,000. Your inspector has pointed out that the wood on the greenhouse is rotted from termite damage, a pipe in the downstairs bathroom is rusting and needs replacement, the tub in the master bath should be recaulked and watersealed, and the back burner on the stove doesn't work.

Your inspector can give you a rough estimate of what each item will cost, and if you want to be really accurate, you can get another professional (a plumber for the plumbing problem, for example) to give you a second opinion. But chances are you won't be able to renegotiate up to the full price, anyway. And you may not wish to have the seller repair everything if you intend to replace some of the items immediately.

Approximate Replacement Costs

Foundation, greenhouse (concrete sill to replace rotted wood; labor)	$800–1,000
Plumbing, pipe	50
Tub, caulking (you can do this yourself)	10–30
Stove burner (maybe it's just dirty and needs to be reamed out with a toothpick)	0–100
TOTAL: no more than	$1,000

Try to get the seller to leave that amount of money in escrow. If he won't pay the whole thing, maybe he'll split the difference with you. Or if he won't budge at all on money for repairs, what about asking him to pay a portion of your closing costs? If he simply refuses to discuss accommodating you on money at all, consider bargaining with some of the other terms of your agreement—perhaps moving out of the house a week before closing, for instance, so that you'll have more time to plan your renovation. You might also consider asking him to throw a few other items into the deal—the extra refrigerator or freezer in the basement that he planned to take with him, the power lawnmower in the tool shed, or the kitchen stools that fit so perfectly under the butcher block counter.

Be sure to put your new offer in writing. Just because you have a contract doesn't mean it can't be changed, but you must be certain that your renegotiation is just as businesslike as your original deal was. Remind your seller that you've had an expert's eagle eye on the property—you aren't just suggesting these modifications for a price reduction. If he balks at the modifications you want to make in the original deal, ask what he would suggest. It's the rare seller who won't move on anything at all.

THE BOTTOM LINE— TIME TO CANCEL THE DEAL

If you discover a blight on your property, you have every reason to terminate your contract with the seller. The contingencies you've built into the deal protect you from loss, and you'll have your deposit back in no time, so you can start looking for another property. The only expense you've incurred is paying your inspector—and he's saved you from pouring your money into a bottomless pit.

*W*hat's so bad you may decide to walk away?

1. Tons of termites! Your engineer or inspector will undoubtedly suggest a separate termite inspection, even if there's no visible damage to the property.

   If there's evidence of heavy infestation, either around the house or in the cellar, well, you've got some trouble, my friend. Termite damage, or wood boring as it's known in the field, is identified by tubular mudlike tunnels in a vertical pattern up the wood from the floor or along the beams. It may not look like much to you, but any inspector will tell you how extensive it can become. And you don't just get one termite chewing away, you get families, colonies of them invading your property. Repairing this kind of damage can be very costly.

   If your inspector tells you he's found termites, ask how he recommends treating the problem, get a firm estimate for the treatment from an exterminator, and find out how long he'll guarantee the work. If the seller won't pay all or part of the costs, or if the inspector can't estimate the extent of the damage, you may want to pass on this property.

2. You need a new roof. The seller refuses to pay for it. And it will run you thousands of dollars. You may want to resume your house-hunting.

3. Extensive water damage. The roof has been leaking so long that water has caused dry rot in the beams of the house. Replacing structural beams can be a major expense.

4. The house needs a new cesspool. If you're not hooked up to the city water and sewer system and the cesspool has to be replaced, you've got a huge expense on your hands.

5. The building is structurally unsound. This might be the case in brand-new buildings or condos where hasty workmanship and poor-quality materials were used.

6. The house is situated on a cliff, and nature is eating your backyard away. Investing in this property would mean putting your money into a depreciating asset.

But if your inspector tells you that you have no really serious problems, and you're in love with the house despite its few quirks and detractions, and you're reasonably sure that you can fix whatever is wrong and not run your renovation costs over the limit, then you're in business.

The next step is to get yourself ready to work. And work. You're about to turn this ugly duckling into a dazzling swan.

Checkpoints

You can get the most out of your housing inspection if you:

- Accompany the inspector and ask questions about each system and element of the property.

- Ask the inspector to point out the positives as well as the negatives of the house or apartment.

- Find out where all your emergency shut-offs are.

- Ask to see an engineering report of the entire building, if the property is a co-op or condo.

- Be sure to ask the seller about elements you weren't able to see on the inspection.

- Use evident problems as bargaining chips in your deal.

9
Planning Your Renovation Campaign

ime is money. In the renovation business, time is heavy money. The moment you complete a real estate purchase and the property officially becomes yours, your expenses start mounting up—loan payments, insurance premiums, utility bills, and property taxes. You're paying hotel prices on empty rooms. Each day you don't work on your property is a day of money wasted.

But if you work hard and fast during your escrow period, and are so prepared by the time you close on the property that you can get your renovations done a few weeks ahead of schedule, you may have earned yourself a holiday in the Bahamas.

On closing day, as soon as the final papers are processed, you want to be ready to start work. Ideally, the seller will hand you the keys to your new front door and hear a faint but significant "boom" as his car pulls out of the driveway. The first wall has fallen and you haven't lost a nickel's worth of time.

TIMING YOUR PURCHASE

*T*o avoid extra weeks of carrying costs, *it's essential that you do all your plans before you close the deal.* Your timing should go like this:

1. You've made an offer and it's been accepted by the seller.
2. You've taken ten to fifteen days to carry out inspections and secure an oral, preferably written commitment on financing.
3. You've received the report on the structural aspects of the property (it needs work, but you knew that!).
4. You and the seller have mutually agreed to split the costs to cover the termite treatment.
5. All the contingencies have been removed and you've decided to buy.
6. You sign the contract and increase your deposit from the initial binder ($500–$1,000) to around 5% or at the most 10% of the selling price. (Commit to as little as possible; no reason to tie up a lot of cash at this point if you don't have to.)

The house is not yours, legally, but you're fully committed, and so is the seller. *You should be working from this point on.* Now is the time to make all your preparations, design the new layout room by room, organize a new kitchen, draw up floor plans, finalize estimates, obtain permits, and shop for decorating ideas. You're not actually going to buy anything until after your closing, but you should be lining up all your future purchases.

This is also the time to select your contractor or put together your crew if you're supervising the job yourself. You have already received an estimate from one contractor before you made an offer, but you should now get several more and choose the person you want to do the work.

Generally, a closing takes place thirty to sixty days after the signature of contract, although it can be extended for several months if you and the seller mutually agree. If you are currently renting, the only question of timing is how soon you can get a mortgage and how quickly the seller can find somewhere else to live. The situation gets more complicated when you are selling one home and buying another.

There are many factors that can hold up a deal. Your lender may take more time than expected to process your mortgage, or your seller's deal for his next property could fall through, which might mean he would want to stay in his house longer. It's also possible that your buyer will change his mind at the last moment, and you will be left owning the house you thought you'd sold.

Try to sell your own house before you buy another. You can generally control what you are buying; you can rarely control being bought. If you time your new househunting to start a few weeks after you put your own house on the market, you'll at least have a few showings under your belt to give you an idea of how fast your property might move. This way you can arrange your schedule for getting out of the old house and securing financing for the new one at your own convenience. Selling first means that you will know exactly how much you've got to put toward your new home and its renovation.

Of course, if you reverse the process and stumble on the house of your dreams before you've marketed the one you live in, you should request a distant closing date to give you time to sell your house and avoid carrying two properties simultaneously.

What do you do if you must purchase your next property before you've closed on the one you're selling? You can take a swing or bridge loan. This short-term loan is available from most lending institutions for three to six months, offering you a bridge between the amount of money you have on hand and the amount you need to close your deal. The loan is often secured against both the house you currently own and the one you're buying.

If the owner of the property you're purchasing or the buyer of the property you're selling changes the deal at the last moment, somebody—or everybody—will have to make some compromises. If you can't complete the sale and get into the property you're buying as scheduled, the owner may have to share costs with you for the storage of your furniture and a week of hotel bills—especially if you've just flown into town expecting to take occupancy. And the laws vary from state to state as to whether you can keep all or part of the deposit on the property you're selling if your buyer backs out.

It is possible—if everyone cooperates and money is quickly available to the buyer—to close on a house within days or a week after an offer is made. If your buyer wants to conclude his deal in December for tax reasons, but you have nowhere to go, you can close on the property and then rent it back from the buyer.

A short escrow means that a deal is sewn up quickly with few hassles. But I feel a long escrow period is better for a renovator, since the property market—and your new house—will appreciate monthly while costing you nothing. You've also got more time to get all your ducks in a row so that work can start as soon as the closing is over.

THE ESCROW PERIOD IS FOR PLANNING

*T*his is the time to get organized. You need to have a very good grasp of all the elements that will be involved in your renovation. What should you do before you close on the property?

- Decide on a contractor, and hire an architect if you feel you need one.

- Put together your crew if you're supervising the job yourself.

- Arrange to meet with an interior designer if you wish, for some direction on your decorating ideas.

- Give everyone the proposed starting date.

- Design your new layout room by room with a complete set of floor plans. Your contractor or architect can draw these for you.

- Organize the design of your kitchen and baths if you're redoing them.

- Look at all available appliances on the market; take down model numbers of the ones you think you want.

- Apply for any needed building permits from the city or have your contractor do it. Don't pick them up or pay for them until you actually own the property.

- Shop for decorating ideas on wallpaper, carpeting, tile, faucets, hardware—the finishing touches that will cap off the major work.

- Finalize estimates and apply for a home-improvement loan if you need one. You will need to present the lender with a detailed budget for the work to be done. Your bank may not lend you 100% of what you need, and you may run slightly over budget on your first renovation job, so it's a good idea to figure in a cushion of your own. You probably won't be sitting on it by the time you're finished!

Do you want two new bathrooms? How close are they to existing water lines and drains? If they're miles away, those are expensive plumbing miles to travel. Do you want to add a dishwasher, disposal, trash compactor, microwave oven, and washer-dryer? The electrician can tell you whether you have sufficient amperage or will need to add more. What if you remove a wall to enlarge a room? You have to be certain it's not a bearing wall supporting floors above. This is the time to ask questions of your professionals, formulate ideas, and add or eliminate remodeling choices depending on your budget.

You will need access to your new home in order to measure for accurate plans and discuss alterations on the property with your contractor. However, you don't own it yet, which means you will be dependent on the seller to let you in. This is usually no problem if you schedule well in advance with the owner and arrange several appointments for the same day. Sometimes a seller may insist that his listing agent come along to make sure that no damage is done and that his rights as current owner are respected.

Always accompany the contractor, architect, plumber, or electrician on these visits. I think it's important to go into the property every chance you get. Each time you see it, you get a better perspective on how you want to reorganize it. About the third or fourth time I request entry, I bring a large bouquet of fresh flowers as a thank-you to the owners for their patience.

FLOOR PLANS: THE KEY TO GETTING ORGANIZED

*A*s soon as you've signed the contract to buy, you should have a **floor plan** drawn up by your contractor or architect. This is the most valuable visual aid on any renovation project. There is nothing as helpful as seeing your new purchase all laid out on paper. A floor plan shows:

- The size of all rooms and closets on every floor

- The location of hallways, stairways, and fireplaces

- Which walls will stay, which will go, and which must be built

- The size and location of windows and skylights

- Location of the doors to each room and which way they swing

- Location of bathrooms and all fixtures in them

- Arrangement of the kitchen with all cabinets and appliances

- Electrical plans, including new outlets, switches, and fixtures

- Where new plumbing, or heating and ventilation ducts are to be installed

There, with a floor plan of the house you can shuffle, reorganize, plan, visualize, and dream about moving around thousands of square feet by making changes in inches.

I look at those plans, and go back to them again morning, noon, and night. I pencil in bursts of creative thought to see if my ideas work in the layout. If I'm going to live in the property, I plan out where every piece of my furniture will go so I can be sure there's an electrical outlet or a phone jack where I'll need it.

Developing well-thought-out floor plans will obviate the need to make major changes once renovation has begun. Be sure to tack up a plan on each floor of your house, outlining what's to be done. The tradesmen will then have a reliable reference point and will know what's going in, what's going out, and how to continue if you're not around.

Never, under any circumstances, rip out one piece of wood or hammer in one nail before you have *finished floor plans* for your property. It doesn't matter whether you're planning to renovate your house board by board, piece by piece, over the next five years or whether you intend to finish in a couple of months and resell. The key to any successful renovation job is *getting organized and paying close attention to detail.*

Do You Really Need a Contractor?

*F*or your very first homewrecking job, I strongly suggest that you seek professional assistance, if for no other reason than to see how the game of home renovation is played by the experts. You've got to learn the language—pick up the right terms and vocabulary. Ideally, you should have an overview of a house, a sense of what makes it function, the division of space, the way to achieve good traffic patterns, and an understanding of all the ingredients and how they work. It's difficult to get that kind of perspective if you're a novice. A good, experienced contractor can lead you through the maze of home-renovation procedures and make certain that the work you want accomplished is done—and done properly.

What, exactly, is a general contractor? He is similar to an orchestra conductor, in that he coordinates and arranges the talents of many different people so that their work overlaps in perfect harmony. He is a master builder who is able to alter an existing property to produce functional and comfortable space. He is a smart shopper who deals with the suppliers in his community and knows the best products—from lumber to light fixtures. He is a boss, commanding respect of the various tradesmen he employs on a job. If he's good, he is an exceptionally organized professional who can get the most work done in the shortest period of time.

That's all very nice, you say, but what about those horror stories about the contractor who created $5,000 worth of work for himself and abandoned the project midstream with two bathtubs in the living room? What about the guy who measured the kitchen cabinets incorrectly and had them all special-ordered and delivered only to find they didn't fit? What about that man your Aunt Ruthie took to small-claims court for ruining her hardwood floors—and nobody can even find him to collect? Isn't it better to subcontract the job yourself, maintain complete control, and save the extra fee you pay to have a contractor do it?

Absolutely not. Subbing out is a huge responsibility. You need endless time and patience, and you must be as organized as a GM assembly plant. The only two times I would recommend that you even consider it is when you're redoing your own home over a long period of time with very limited funds and the project is a true labor of love, and when there is only minor work to be done—painting, wallpapering, carpeting, maybe installing new toilets—and you can't find a contractor who's interested.

Subbing out the work yourself entails:

- Redesigning your property with the help of an architect if you're not able to do plans yourself

- Finding and then hiring the plumber, electrician, carpenter, taper, plasterer, tiler, roofer, painter, and any other workmen needed for odd jobs

- Scheduling the arrival and departure of subcontractors so that the right work is done at the right time (you can't install the kitchen cabinets until the plumbing is in, or the sink and faucets until the counters are set)

- Ordering materials in advance, checking to be certain that they will arrive on schedule and that they are first-quality—i.e., straight lumber that has few knotholes

- Paying for all materials as they are delivered

- Knowing how to remedy disasters if they occur

- Dealing with the city planning commission when necessary

- Ordering permits for new construction

- Scheduling inspectors to approve the work going on

- Hounding recalcitrant workers to show up on time and stay until the work day is officially over

- Being on-site nearly all the time to make decisions and reevaluations

You may save a little money by subbing out a job yourself, but you can also lose valuable time. A professional contractor can move a job along more quickly because he's done it so many times before. Your contractor sees to it that one job finishes and the next begins immediately.

The smart renovator is one who knows how to use the services of professionals to help her make up her own mind. When renovation runs like a well-oiled machine because you've planned ahead and made your selection of appliances, moldings, faucets, carpeting, and light fixtures, you'll save inestimable amounts of time and money.

FINDING A GOOD CONTRACTOR

*I*t took me several jobs to find a great contractor. On my first renovation, the contractor I hired brought in two plumbers who worked for three days and drank for four. I had another crew who were installing a shower pan and drilled right through my floor into the unit below, sending pounds of debris and plaster dust into my neighbor's closet. In yet another property, I received custom-made cabinets painted white when I had ordered them stained in light oak.

You need a reputable, experienced contracting firm, one that knows its business, can work fast, and *guarantees* the work. You want a contractor who'll return with a smile if anything goes wrong. In short, you want the best.

How do you find this paragon? Here is one instance where the Yellow Pages will not do. I would suggest that you limit your search to licensed contractors, who have put up a performance bond of several thousand dollars in the city in which they practice. This way you know you can trace your man in case you're forced to seek retribution. You need personal references, and lots of them, when you're looking for a contractor. Ask your friends, your neighbors, your local building inspector, your real estate agent (who has undoubtedly seen many houses being renovated), or an acquaintance who has just completed successful home remodeling.

When your prospective contractor gives you a reference to check, ask pertinent questions of his client:

- What work was done on your house?

- Did your contractor follow your ideas and add to them?

- Were there any emergencies, and did he perform well under pressure?

- What were his workmen like?

- Did they clean up each day?

- How was the overall quality of construction and finish work?

- Did he and his subcontractors guarantee their work, and if so for how long?

- Did he complete the job on schedule and on budget?

- Would you hire him again?

When you have consistently high recommendations for a contractor, you must go and see his work. Be certain that the work you're viewing bears some resemblance to what you want done in your own house. It would be useless to inspect three beautifully constructed decks when you want to have a new bathroom installed. You may not know a two-by-four from a piece of plywood, but you can undoubtedly tell a shoddy finished product when you see it. Ask yourself:

- Are mitered corners done properly?

- Are Formica seams matched inconspicuously?

- Is there toe space at the bottom of kitchen and bathroom base cabinets?

- Are there enough electrical plugs in the kitchen?

- Are the moldings and baseboards matched properly?

- Do doors and windows operate well?

Once you have narrowed your sights to two or three possible contractors, start collecting final bids. (If you are getting a home-improvement loan from a lending institution, you will be required to submit at least two competitive bids.) Ask the contractor to meet you on-site and walk him through the property. Most do not charge for estimates, but you should ask in advance.

An experienced contractor who does estimates knows how to come up with pretty accurate figures for the work to be done. He will listen to your ideas and suggest some of his own. If he's a real pro and has put together lots of houses, he'll be able to reorganize your rooms with his eyes shut.

He'll spend an afternoon measuring up a property and appear in the next day or two with plans of each floor. Then the two of you can discuss which wall can come down, how to rearrange the kitchen, and where the new downstairs bathroom will go. Ideally, you'll work so closely that you'll begin to second-guess each other.

Never pinch pennies when you select your contractor. The one who gives you the least expensive bid may not necessarily be the best choice. I gradually discovered as I learned the homewrecking business that the contractors who come in with the highest estimate rarely run over budget, while some of those who come in at lower prices do.

It was only when I picked the contractor with one of the highest estimates and one of the best reputations in town that my true love for renovation began. Yes, his bids were high, but I sincerely feel that he gave me the quality I demanded and an hour and a half's worth of labor for every hour's pay.

A large contracting firm is generally preferable on a big job, because such firms:

- Buy in large quantities and, in turn, receive priority service from suppliers.

- Warehouse materials themselves for immediate use.

- Have their own in-house woodworking shops for any custom cabinetry.

- Usually have large, time-saving power tools delivered to the site.

- Can employ enough extra labor to help out on a job if needed.

- Generally maintain excellent relationships with city planning offices and can obtain work permits right away.

If your first job is a small one, hiring a large firm may be unnecessary. A better solution may be to choose a young, independent, up-and-coming contractor who'll work day and night building your house and his reputation. If you find a real gem—especially if you're thinking of making home renovation a lifelong career—you may want to consider marrying him.

Whether you select the biggest or the smallest firm in town, the quality you insist on will pay off. *In the long run, first class costs less.*

If the contractor you'd like to work with comes in over your budget, talk with him about various ways to trim costs. The two of you should use the escrow period for fine-tuning. Budgets do not have to be graven in stone at this stage, but they should be pressed in wet cement and dry by the time you start work. Do you want to install a skylight in the kitchen, or will a less expensive set of recessed lights be acceptable? Do you want to go the whole hog and create an extra bedroom, bath, and playroom in the attic space? Or is that completely out of the question financially?

Hiring a contractor can *save* you money. He'll be able to get your appliances, hardware, and light fixtures whole-sale. He will usually tack on a percentage—cost plus 10%—for doing the ordering, but that's still likely to be the cheapest price in town. Remember, too, that everything he purchases and installs for you will be his responsibility. If anything goes wrong with the installation of these prod-ucts, he should take care of it.

Quality shows—and quality sells. When you get ready to go to market, and you're showing an unfurnished prop-erty, you will never be able to hide poor craftsmanship. Without furnishings, paintings, or palm trees to act as coverups, your house or apartment will be completely ex-posed. But if you have taken the time and effort to hire the person who will make sure each addition is done perfectly, you will overwhelm your buyer. The property, in effect, will sell itself.

The Contractor's Contract

*Y*ou should have a written contract with your con-tractor spelling out the terms of your agreement. You may want to check out your man with the local Better Business Bureau before you sign anything. If he has any registered complainants, regardless of the good refer-ences he's given you, you should find out just what went wrong. If he won't tell you, you don't want to hire him.

Here are the essentials of a standard construction con-tract:

- Contractor's name, address, and license num-ber

- Your name and the address of the property to be renovated

- Full description of jobs to be done and who will do them

- Complete set of approved plans and a list of all specifications (these are always attached to the contract)

- The names and model numbers of all fixtures and appliances if they're included in the estimate (all warranties on appliances supplied by the contractor are to be given to the owner of the property)

- Full description of the manner in which on-site changes will be handled and paid for

- Starting and completion dates of the project (some homeowners insert a penalty clause if the job runs beyond the estimated time)

- Proof of insurance for workman's compensation, liability, and property damage

- A statement that he—not you—is responsible for all payments to the subcontractors and suppliers

- Assurance that he will be responsible for securing all building, electrical, and plumbing permits

- The total price of the job

- A payment schedule (I usually stipulate 10% or 20% increments as the work progresses, paying out only as it's completed, and reserving a final 10% until everything is done to my satisfaction)

- Schedule of events showing the timing of demolition and rough and finish work

- A guarantee on all work from the general contractor and his subordinates specified with a
  time limit (usually one year)

- Provision for termination of contract if work is
  not proceeding satisfactorily

DISMISSING A CONTRACTOR

This is a terrible thought to consider before you've
even started, but it is possible that things simply
won't move ahead the way you'd like them to. You
certainly don't want to proceed if the contractor is going in
the wrong direction. How bad is bad? How do you know
when it's time to cut out?

This is a very subjective decision. I would say that if
you've had too many arguments with your contractor during the first half of the work, if you feel you're way behind
the schedule he's set, if you are gravely dissatisfied with
some element of the whole job, then you should consider
terminating your contract for cause. This means, legally,
that you have a legitimate reason to dismiss him.

Because you've set up a payment schedule, you only owe
him for the work he has performed. Unfortunately, you are
out of pocket for the bad work you *didn't* want him to perform. Be sure to get a signed release from the contractor
when you cancel the contract. This will protect you from
any future legal action for nonpayment that he might
bring. In turn, he may ask you to sign a document releasing
him from responsibility on work that was never completed.

If you owe him $1,500 or less, he may take you to small-
claims court, where a judge or arbitrator will decide on the
validity of his case—or yours. If the amount is higher, your
lawyers will discuss your various grievances and probably
arrive at a settlement agreement out of court. Don't expect
to come out a winner when you have to change contractors.
Since most contractors don't like fixing up the bad work of
their colleagues, they may charge accordingly.

Are you responsible for paying subcontractors if your

(Laurie Black & Roslyn Banish ARX)

*W*hite ceramic tile, which I arduously laid myself, adds brightness to an entry garden room.

(Laurie Black & Roslyn Banish ARX)

A giant movable skylight and clawfoot tub make this one of my favorite renovated bedrooms.

*S*everal pieces of molding were added at ceiling height to give this room more character. Leftover moldings were used to create a mantle over a new marble fireplace.

$\mathscr{A}$ small narrow kitchen bene-fited from a 30-foot extension to the main house, creating a wonderful kitchen–family room.

(Laurie Black & Roslyn Banish ARX)

$\mathscr{H}$igh narrow lighting, sur-
face-mounted medicine cabinets, and
dark tile on an inexpensive vanity
cabinet were replaced with a full
cedar bath, carefully finished inside
the shower with five coats of
polyurethane.

The walls of three rooms were removed to make one large country living room with dining area. The original fireplace (opposite page) was unaltered, the dark panelling was whitewashed, and a double door entry was added to the adjoining bedroom.

(Laurie Black & Roslyn Banish ARX)

A small dark kitchen was totally gutted and redesigned, adding a large window, knotty pine cabinets, new appliances, and random plank oak flooring.

$\mathscr{R}$emoving three walls and using open shelving extended this country kitchen to the living space around it.

$\mathscr{A}$n original bath was enlarged by three feet for a walk-in wood shower with a ventilated skylight and eye-level window.

$\mathcal{N}$ine feet were added to the master bedroom, creating a new wall for a fireplace, large windows, and built-in bookcases. The bed wound up in the middle of the room.

(Laurie Black & Roslyn Banish ARX)

$\mathscr{M}$ajor renovation in an old mansion resulted in an open kitchen with good light, dark stained oak cabinets, and the popular center island with butcher-block top.

*E*nlarging a small window and adding a French door provide extra light and direct access to the backyard.

$\mathcal{B}$y cutting a hole and installing a piece of glass in a solid-wood door, we created a great view to the outside. A *faux-marbre* painted finish on the woodwork adds a whimsical touch.

(Reprinted from Decorating and Remodeling/Laurie Black & Roslyn Banish ARX)

$\mathcal{T}$wo rooms were opened up to create a master suite with bedroom, bath, and four closets on one end (shown below) and large sitting room opposite it.

$\mathcal{U}$nless you need the privacy, why cover windows that have great architectural detail?

$\mathcal{B}$all casters were added to the bottom of four shutter panels, providing a movable window covering with controlled light.

(Reprinted from Decorating and Remodeling/Laurie Black & Roslyn Banish ARX)

deal with your general contractor falls apart halfway through? This depends on whether you agreed to such a provision in your contract. You should ask the workman requesting payment if you can see the paperwork that exists between him and the contractor, as well as his paid receipts for materials. If the contractor has not paid him for work rendered, then yes, these bills are your responsibility. If you like the subcontractor and he will agree to finish the job for his original bid, then you should pay him when he's completed it to your satisfaction.

AVOIDING LIENS

A lien is a debt against your property, most commonly placed there by a disgruntled workman who's been unable to collect payment for work rendered. If you refuse to pay your contractor because you feel that he did a bad job, he may put a lien on your property.

When problems with workmen grow into legal headaches, it can be unsettling and uncomfortable—particularly for the homeowner. And the reason is that any lien against a property shows up on the title search and prevents the owner from refinancing, selling, or borrowing extra money on his home.

To remove a lien, you either pay up, negotiate a settlement with the lien-holder, or institute expensive and time-consuming court proceedings. Another solution is to wait it out. Depending on the state, a lien can only remain on the property for one to two years, after which time it is automatically dropped if the lien-holder doesn't go to court to collect on his debt.

HIRING AN ARCHITECT

W hen do you need an architect? When you're stuck for ideas. When you or your contractor can't draw up the plans for a major renovation job that requires extensive structural changes. When you want a professional trained in the art of design and reconstruction to supervise the job for you.

You definitely need an architect for major alterations or additions to the exterior of a structure. In this case, the plans for the proposed additions must be approved by the community's planning commission. Certified working drawings, with the architect's seal, must be submitted for approval, and perhaps an engineer's report. You should, of course, hire an architect for a huge job like converting an eighteen-room boardinghouse into condos or turning an old warehouse or firehouse into a family home.

If you've decided to enter the world of homewrecking but wish to stay at arm's length, an architect can direct the project for you. I can't endorse this approach myself because I like to be there with my own T-square, tool chest, and overalls, but it's ideal for some people.

I used an architect for only two of my seventy-one projects, but both sets of plans I commissioned were invaluable. One was for an eight-car garage with a landscaped deck above it that I was adding onto an apartment building I owned. The other entailed a 30-foot extension of my present home onto an empty adjacent lot. Together, the architect and I created an extra garage, bedroom, and bath on the ground level, a 25-foot extension plus balcony onto the kitchen, which then became a cooking/entertainment center, and a 30-foot deck on top which extends the view from my living room right over San Francisco Bay.

There are occasionally terrible knock-down, drag-out fights between architects and contractors over the method of construction and the way a design is executed. An architect's creations are intended to be built exactly as stated on his plans—a 40-degree angle, not one that's 45, a ceiling that's 9 feet, not 8¾.

Architects are purists; most contractors are not. I stay pure in design most of the time, but when my contractor and I can find a less expensive route to the finish line, I compromise. I'll settle for that 45-degree angle—as long as it produces the desired result.

There are a variety of ways you can benefit from the talents of an architect, and a variety of arrangements you can make with him. You can pay very little for a consultation (generally, $50 to $100 per hour), or hand over a substantial chunk of your budget to have him draw all the plans, recreate the interior and exterior, get bids on the job, select a contractor, and supervise all the work. This service usually runs 10% to 20% over the cost of construction or else is determined in advance as a set fee. The architect's price should be discussed long before you finalize your renovation budget so that you can factor it in.

HIRING A DECORATOR

When do you need a decorator? Like an architect, a professional decorator is a wonderful source of ideas. If you don't feel you have the confidence to choose the elements that will make your property a knockout, then hire a decorator. And if you *know* you're not artistically inclined, if you can't tell peach from orange, then by all means consult an expert. Regardless of the painstaking work you do on the underlying structure of a property —the plumbing, electricity, and carpentry—what makes the first and most lasting impression is the decorating.

There is a solution to getting top decorating advice for a fraction of the usual cost. How? By doing the legwork yourself. You should pick up:

- Color charts from paint stores

- Tile samples

- Formica chips

- Carpet swatches

- Wallpaper samples

- Wood and stain samples

- Brochures on lighting fixtures, taps, hardware, knobs, basins, tubs, toilets, appliances

Get pamphlets on everything—including the kitchen sink. Gather together all the samples you like best, take them to the new house, and set up a miniature showroom for your consultation with the decorator. She will inspect the property, go through your display, and make recommendations. She may also have access to wallpapers and flooring you can't buy yourself, and will be able to place an order for you.

For an hourly consultation fee, you can get a real sense of what colors would work and which products might not. This is really worth it on your first few homewrecking jobs, when you'll be selling an unfurnished property and don't need the full-time services of an interior designer.

How do you find a good decorator? Through friends who've just had homes redone, referrals from other professionals, or the nearest ASID (American Society of Interior Designers) office. You might also try a decorator showcase house—a yearly event in many areas where lots of designers have their work on display.

CLOSING ON
THE PROPERTY

*S*ee how much you can get done before you've actually closed your deal? It may seem anticlimactic to stop all the preparation and finish up the paperwork, but finish you must.

Closings—or settlements, or completions, as they are sometimes called—can be short or long, tricky or blissfully easy. Closings can be quiet events—just you and an escrow officer in the title company's office. In some cases, they can even be carried out by telephone and express mail. Other closings are Cecil B. deMille productions, with a cast of thousands (the buyer and seller, two lawyers, two real estate agents, an officer of the title company or a third neutral party who's handling the transaction, and perhaps a few friends or relatives for support).

If all the documents are in order, it really should take no more than fifteen minutes to read and sign the closing papers. A few more hours may elapse before the deal actually goes on record at city hall. But unexpected events do pop up—like a promised repair that didn't take place or a delay in receiving the insurance policy—and there are closings that extend over days rather than minutes.

You should receive a copy of the closing statement well in advance of the completion day so that you can have an opportunity to read and understand all the closing costs for which you are responsible. If you have any questions or problems, try to settle them on the phone or in person with your lawyer, escrow officer, or real estate agent *before* you go to sign the final papers. It is also wise, in order to avoid last-minute hitches, to arrange a final "walk-through." This inspection of the property is to ensure that everything is just the way it was when you signed your contract.

Now what about those closing costs? Here's an idea of what to expect:

- Title insurance (based on amount of loan)

- Title search

- One-year insurance policy

- Survey (optional in some states)

- Recording fees

- Mortgage application fee, if not paid at commitment

- Appraisal fee

- Mortgage origination fee and points (percentage paid to lender for making loan)

- Inspections of the property (these are usually paid outside of closing)

- Real estate property taxes, adjusted between buyer and seller

- Attorney's fee, if you are retaining one (he may bill you separately)

- Miscellaneous charges: credit report, notary fee, transfer tax, if any

When the closing papers are signed, money has exchanged hands, and you have gone on record with the city, you can open the champagne. The property is yours now to do with as you like, even before the deed arrives in the mail. Lift your glass on high, enjoy the celebration, and then get into your workclothes. It's finally time to start homewrecking.

Checkpoints

You can use the time during your escrow period to best advantage if you:

▶ Budget, plan, and do preliminary legwork on all of your renovations.

▶ Try to sell your own property before you buy another.

▶ Think twice before you decide to do the remodeling yourself.

▶ Select your contractor—and architect or decorator, if you plan to use one—through references and visual inspection of their work.

▶ Read and understand all the closing documents thoroughly before the day you obtain title.

10
Becoming an Expert Renovator

You closed the deal at noon and went on record an hour later. You celebrated over lunch and then phoned your contractor to confirm that work would begin at 8:00 A.M. tomorrow.

It's at this time, after the agent gives you all four sets of keys, that you can go over to the property and open the front door. *Your* front door. That's what I always do. That afternoon, all by myself, I get acquainted with my new acquisition. It's quiet, it's empty. It looks so different. I walk through each room, inspecting every inch of my purchase. This is the first time I can stand, touch, and investigate the property without the agent, inspector, appraiser, contractor, or the owner and his dog hanging around.

I raise the shades and marvel at the wonderful light that permeates the whole house. I can never wait to get all the blinds, sheers, shades, and draperies off every window and let the sunlight in.

The bedroom carpeting bears deep indentations where heavy furniture has stood for umpteen years. The closets look twice as big now that they're empty—I'll remember that when it's time to resell. The chipped paint on the woodwork really shows up without the furnishings in the room. The old wallpaper has completely faded around the pictures that once hung there, so that the walls still seem to host a ghostly gallery of artwork. The stairs have a slight creak, a personality—I like that.

The old brass dining-room chandelier which I negotiated in the purchase price is all alone in the empty room. It looks fabulous. If I never added another piece of furniture, the room would still be splendid.

The kitchen is going to be ripped out, so the dirt doesn't bother me. The refrigerator is a classic—something like the one I grew up with in the fifties in Binghamton, New York. I open the door and find, predictably, the half-empty jars of pickle relish, olives, and maraschino cherries.

The view to the garden is spectacular, even through the busted screen door. Tomorrow we open up the entire kitchen, visually linking the inside with the outdoors.

An era has passed. The former owners raised three children in this house and have moved into a retirement community in the Sunbelt. They never bothered doing much to their property, which has fallen into considerable disrepair. But I don't mind. I love it.

It's 5:00 P.M. I pull the blinds and check all the locks, and before I leave through the front door, I turn around for one last glance.

"Get ready for a change," I shout into the front hall. "By August, you're going to feel like you've spent four months at Elizabeth Arden!"

Joining the Team

*T*he remodeling show's about to begin. You are the boss of this production, which means it's your responsibility to make decisions, large and small, during the entire renovation process. The work crew needs you as much as you need them, and the excellence of the job they perform depends in great part on the communication and rapport you develop over the weeks and months ahead.

If you've hired a contractor, an architect, or a designer to help manage your renovation, you will have to collaborate closely with him. If you're subbing out the work yourself, the management of the entire team is on your shoulders.

In a world where every profession, from jet piloting to mud wrestling, has been infiltrated by women, the construction site still remains a bastion of masculinity. While there do exist female painters, plasterers, carpenters, and an electrician or two, these women are in a distinct minority. Over 90% of the people working on a job site are men— men who are about to become your closest colleagues. And, you might hope, your closest friends.

The success of your renovation project stands or falls on your commitment to be present every day, from the first crumbling wall to the last polished doorknob. Success depends on your willingness to be available—making decisions, offering support, being an active player on the team, pointing the way throughout the entire remodeling project.

Many first-time renovators worry about being around too much. They're certain that they will hinder the progress of work rather than hurry it along. And, too, they feel that their contractor, a consummate professional in the home remodeling business, won't want any interference. They figure he's being well paid to do a job, and he probably doesn't want any amateurs horning in on his territory.

On the contrary. A good contractor welcomes the opinion and interaction of the owner/renovator. Instead of plowing ahead and making costly mistakes, the contractor can rely on the renovator who actively participates. As leader of

your team, remember not to interfere with the workmen—
but keep tabs on their work.

You don't need to adopt a macho attitude to be accepted
by this male fraternity. You don't have to prove you're one of
the boys. It's obvious, you're not.

Be calm, reasonable, and professional. That's what it
takes to be accepted, respected, and admired by your em-
ployees and colleagues. Don't make an issue of your sex.
Invade the industry with delicate force.

When I go to work, I always dress impeccably from the
neck up, makeup and hair perfect, earrings in place. I take
the same care with my appearance as I would for any other
job. From the neck down, I dress for the construction site in
work shirt, work shoes, and jeans or overalls. Dress sensi-
bly when you go to the property—it will be the dirtiest,
dustiest house on the block.

THE STAGES
OF RENOVATION

*E*ach day brings a new job and a new challenge on any
work site. Once the walls are demolished and the
rubble cleared, new vistas open up, and with them
new design possibilities. A good contractor may suddenly
come up with a cost-cutting alternative to a job. The two of
you may decide to eliminate another wall, enlarge an opening, cut a window, or raise the ceiling height. Or you might
discover that a wall you're removing to bring more light
into a room has been hiding two water lines to the next
floor. Rerouting them would be extremely expensive. But if
you leave them where they are and cut an opening beside
them, you are solving the problem without creating new
ones.

Window Placement

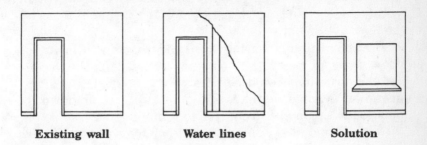

Existing wall   **Water lines**   **Solution**

If you are on-site to make a decision about what should be done, the work can proceed smoothly. And these are decisions you won't be able to make if you're just dropping by once in a while.

How much you participate in the physical work will depend on you. There's no need to make yourself miserable doing manual labor if the main reason you've decided to become a homewrecker is to get away from the heavy housework you do at home. There are dozens of ways to keep busy without looking like a lost soul who doesn't know a hammer from a hairpin. But if you enjoy physical labor and want to plunge in, don't be shy about it—there's plenty of work to do.

There are four stages to any major renovation:

- Demolition

- Rough work

- Finish work

- Decorating

STAGE 1
OF RENOVATION

*D*emolition is tearing down and removing all parts of the property that will not be used in the reconstruction. You'll be amazed at how fast this stage goes—on average, it takes a day or two to tear down as opposed to the months required to rebuild.

This is one of my favorite parts of renovating. It's the first opportunity you have to see the possibilities of improvement and to confirm that the plans you've made on paper can actually be executed in three dimensions.

Demolition

Unless you're very familiar with the way a house should be dismantled, have the strength to swing a sledgehammer, and look good in a hard hat, let your contractor supervise the rip-out. There is still plenty for you to do:

- If you're subbing out the job, order a dumpster, a large debris box, to be parked outside your house. (If you've hired a contractor, he'll do this.)

- Buy a lot of heavyweight plastic bags for the debris and garbage that will accumulate daily. You might also purchase a few sturdy garbage cans with lids.

- Throw everything you don't want into the dumpster—the partly used paint cans in the basement, broken furniture, three years of accumulated newspapers.

- Cover everything you don't intend to replace or refinish to avoid damage. This would include wood and tile floors, mirrors, chandeliers, a clawfoot bathtub.

- If old timbers are being removed, collect the small- and medium-sized pieces of wood and stack them in the cellar or garage for firewood.

- Buy a 6-foot ladder, tools, and a tool chest. Mark the tools with red nail polish so you can quickly identify them if they make their way onto someone else's workbelt. Measure your hand, spread out from thumb to little finger (around 8 inches), so if you misplace your tape measure, you'll be able to estimate approximate lengths.

- Take down all window coverings, send any draperies you're going to use to the cleaners, and keep the others for rags or protective coverings until the end of the job. Drapery linings make great drop cloths.

- Remove all the hardware—curtain rods, switch plates, doorknobs, backplates, hooks, and handles. If you plan to put them back, place them in a plastic bag with all the screws and label them to indicate which room they belong in. You'll have time to clean and polish them later.

- Be sure your carpenter saves any old moldings and baseboards he rips out to reuse where needed when the finish work begins.

- If you're not keeping the carpet, tear it up and remove it. Keep the old padding down if you want to protect the wood floors.

STAGE 2
OF RENOVATION

Rough work includes the reconstruction or repair of the "guts" of your property. It involves all the stuff that's behind the walls, under the floors and on the roof, such as:

- Studs, supports, and beams
- The foundation
- Plumbing lines
- Electrical wiring
- Duct work and fireplace flues
- Insulation
- Termite work
- Prewiring for burglar-alarm systems, phones, cable TV

Should this hidden work require as much time, attention, and expense as the finish work? There is only one answer to this question, and it is a resounding yes.

You must now decide whether to repair existing systems and structures—the plumbing, the electrical wiring, the insulation, the foundation, the roof—or to replace them. Your initial inspection report, of course, indicated where the problems lay, but this is the time to confirm how much you should do to the systems that are "behind closed doors."

Not a day goes by in our twentieth-century lives when we don't turn on the faucets, open the refrigerator door, cook a meal, or switch on the lights. We take the amenities of our homes for granted as long as they're functioning, but the minute a fuse blows, a pipe bursts, a roof leaks, the heating breaks down, or a toilet overflows, we are suddenly and painfully aware of the systems underlying our comfortable abodes. And we want them to be perfect.

Never skimp on the items that don't show. For peace of mind—yours and your buyer's—and for the sake of your business reputation, you must ensure that the hidden work is perfectly done. Visuals may attract the buyer, but what really counts is the quality of the structural work. *If your house could be magically turned inside out, you would want to be as proud of what's inside the walls as what's on them.*

Vital Systems

Plumbing is the most important system of a well-functioning home, and because I'm always adding new bathrooms and redesigning kitchens, I have found it to be one of the most expensive parts of renovation. Plumbing material and labor are costly!

Following are a few important plumbing pointers I have picked up over the last fifteen years:

- Always hire a licensed plumber who works with a city permit. This will guarantee you that the materials and his labor will be inspected by the city.

- When adding baths to a house or apartment, try to locate them above or below one another, or back to back on the same floor. This way they can share the same water lines.

- Every city or county has its own plumbing code which describes what can be done and what can be installed in residential property, including the size and kinds of pipes. Copper pipes—the most expensive—are generally required, since they don't deteriorate as do galvanized iron pipes. Plastic piping doesn't either—it's practically indestructible—but many contractors don't like it, and some codes don't permit its use.

- Old-fashioned galvanized pipe doesn't necessarily have to be replaced if it functions well and there's adequate water pressure. Sometimes the plumber and I decide to redo only the hot-water side, because hot water destroys metal faster than cold.

- Patching new copper to galvanized pipes can create problems because there's a chemical reaction between the two metals if they're not joined properly.

- If you're on one of the top floors of a condo or co-op, be sure to check the available water pressure before you make a drastic plumbing alteration like removing the tub and adding your marble walk-in dream shower. You may only be able to get a trickle up this high.

- Find out where the individual shutoff valves, called stopcocks, are to the sinks, tubs, and toilets in case of an emergency. You should also know the location of the main shutoff valve to the entire water supply. It's usually where the main water source enters the house.

- If you want to heat or cook with gas and you don't have a gas line, you can have one installed. If the line runs through your street, chances are you have a meter connection at your house. Your plumber can take it from there and connect you to the system. Be sure you know where the shutoff valve is in case you have to cut off the gas supply.

When the cost of plumbing throws you into near panic, remember that buyers do care and will pay for quality pipes. In fact, in this day and age, buyers won't tolerate less than perfect water works in a fully renovated property for which they're paying top dollar. "New copper plumbing" in the ads can be as tempting as a spectacular view or a hot tub.

One of these days, I swear, I'm going to put a glass wall or floor over newly installed plumbing. This idea strikes me forcibly whenever I look at new-laid copper pipes and realize that I'm about to cover a sculptural masterpiece with sheetrock or floorboards. It's like draping a sheet over a Ming vase! What a crime to keep such beauty—and such *expense*—hidden away.

Electrical work runs a close second in importance to

plumbing. Safety, of course, is your primary consideration. If existing wiring is old, frayed, or overloaded, you've got to change it to eliminate a fire hazard. Your second concern is whether there's enough power—**amperage**—in an older property for all the various gadgets you will install, from TVs to toaster ovens.

Plan in advance for the juice you'll require. Install a sufficient number of outlets in every room—put in more than you think you'll ever need.

A utility company supplies power to your property, then meters and bills you for kilowatts used. The power is fed through your home on many different circuits. There are fail-safe devices (fuses or circuit breakers) that shut down when you've overloaded a particular circuit. When you blow a fuse, you have to change it. With circuit breakers— the preferred method—you only need to flip the switch to get back in business.

Here are some of the electrical pointers I've picked up over the years:

- Always hire a licensed electrician who is familiar with the city's building code and the standards of safety for residential property.

- Find out where the source of electricity is so that you can change fuses or flip circuit breakers when the power goes off.

- Walk through the property, floor plans in hand, and confirm where you want light switches and new plugs. Don't forget lights in closets, the basement, and garage, plugs in the bathrooms and laundry room, and outlets at counter level *every 5 to 6 feet* in the kitchen.

- Plan where you intend to place your TV, stereo, and computer so that you can put an electrical outlet within 3 to 5 feet of them.

- Consider putting your computer on a separate circuit to keep interference at a minimum and prevent the loss of unstored data.

- Don't forget outdoor lighting and a waterproof plug for an electric barbecue starter.

- Use three-way switches to control a light from two different places—up and down stairs, or at each end of a long hall, for example.

- Now, during the rough work, is the time to hide wires for cable TV, telephones, stereo, alarm systems, an intercom, and the entry buzzer to the front door.

Heating a house well means providing maximum comfort for all family members. I remember getting dressed over a heat register on cold schoolday mornings, and even now, when I'm in London, I still warm my clothes over a radiator on chilly mornings. The inefficiency of old systems makes me long for perfectly regulated temperatures and reminds me how important good heating is to the success of a well-renovated house.

If the existing system is in working order or just needs minor repair or updating, stick with it. If forced-air heat with ducting throughout the house is not functioning well, or if pipes and radiators are not bringing up an adequate amount of heat, it's possible that the furnace just needs a good cleaning or a repair job. It may simply be a question of new valves on the radiators, or a new burner on the boiler.

Replacing the furnace itself is still less costly than designing and installing a whole new system. But if you've tried the small solutions and they really don't work, a new system may be the only way to go. Be sure to select several competent, licensed heating specialists to give you estimates and to describe your various choices: forced air, (hot water) steam, oil burning, electric and, perhaps, solar.

You should also compare the relative costs of fuel, since monthly utility bills are always a big consideration for you as well as your buyer. If you're living in a climate that requires both heat and air conditioning, consolidate the two systems by using the same ductwork for cool and hot air.

Be sure to select a system that can be serviced locally.

Whether you're adding new parts to an old furnace or installing a brand-new system, get a written guarantee from the service company.

Insulation completes the heating and cooling job. If you've committed a good amount of money to make sure that your property will be warm in winter and cool in summer, don't lose all that "temperatured" air through crevices in the window frames and cracks around the doors. Seal, caulk, or weather-strip all problem areas. I think I could go in the *Guinness Book of Records* for sticking the most miles of weather stripping around windows in America.

The largest areas to insulate in a house are the space under the roof (where heat rises and escapes), inside exterior walls, and under the building. If you're tearing out ceilings so that you can incorporate attic space as another level in your property, you must insulate properly to keep winter's heat and summer's cooled air in.

Fiberglass padding, I find, is the best and easiest kind of insulation to use, but blown-in insulation is great for difficult-to-reach areas.

A condo or co-op in a high-rise building doesn't have the same heat and cold retention problems as a house, except perhaps for drafty windows. These can and should be carefully caulked and weather-stripped.

Good insulation means lower utility bills. That, alone, is argument enough for installing it.

The foundation is the base on which your property sits. Any problems it may have, such as termites, dampness, or dry rot, must obviously be put right before you resell your property.

The inspector's report or termite inspection will have revealed any areas of damage from wood-boring insects. Your carpenter may take care of a great deal of this problem as he rips out walls and replaces old, chewed timber with new wood. He'll eliminate deteriorating wood sills and weathered wood framing around windows and doors.

But if you know that your house has previously had an infestation, have a licensed termite company check it out and chemically treat any infected areas if necessary. After the work is done, the company will award you with a one- or two-year guarantee and a certificate of completion, your pest-control diploma. This is a nice item to have in your back pocket when you go to sell the house.

A thorough treatment, however, does not always mean the house is completely free of termites. It is possible that the technician will miss a nest—and this is precisely why your guarantee is so important. If there's a new infestation during the next termite season—usually in the early spring—the company must retreat the house at no extra charge and repair any damage that's occurred in the meantime.

The roof must be as tight as a waterproof watch. Settling for less is like wearing an Yves Saint Laurent outfit into a thunderstorm without an umbrella. You risk ruining everything you've worked so hard to put together.

Your housing inspector or roofing contractor will have pointed out any problems in the existing roof and given you a pretty good idea of its life expectancy. If the roof is not too old (less than ten years) and in fairly good shape, repairs may be all that's necessary. Minor problems usually involve the flashing, the material that covers and seals valleys in the roof and junctions with walls, chimneys, and ventilation pipes.

If the roof is old but doesn't leak, you can leave it alone. Just be mentally and financially prepared to replace it after one or two bad winters.

But there's nothing like a new roof! To me, a 10- to 20-year new roof guarantee is as splendid as that termite certificate of completion. When you've got both, you have a clean bill of health from top to bottom.

Rough Work

This is clearly no time for amateurs. Though your physical participation in the rough work may be minimal, there are still many things you can do on-site:

- Select one room or area in the property to be your office. This will become your center of operations for talking to workmen, doing your ordering, and getting your samples and catalogues together so that you can make final decorating selections. Set up two sawhorses and a piece of plywood for a desk, have a telephone installed, and pull up a stool.

- Remove old wallpaper. Pick a room where no one else is working and use a steamer or liquid wallpaper remover, a soapy solution that you paint or spray on, let soak in, and then scrape off. It's available in every hardware store.

- If you've previously removed wall-to-wall carpeting, now's the time to take up the tacking strips. Get a small crowbar or a long screwdriver and hammer and start yanking—carefully. These strips scratch!

- Fill in small holes in the walls with spackling compound and sand them smooth. This will shave hours—and money—off your painter's estimate.

- Strip layers of paint from woodwork, fireplaces, banisters, and balustrades, if you can stand it. This is a hard job—one I always pay the pros to do.

Now it's time to do the job you can't pay anyone else to do for you, and that's go shopping. Serious shopping.

You must select all the appliances, bathroom fixtures, faucets, tile, floor coverings, light fixtures, and hardware.

You will now be buying all the items you need from show-rooms and paint and hardware stores.

Take your time; lie down in a few bathtubs, stand over a few sinks, sit on a few sample toilets. Figure out whether brass or porcelain knobs will look better on your kitchen cabinets. And consider putting that huge brass chandelier you found for 75% off retail price in the master bedroom.

A few pointers on your final shopping spree:

- Let your contractor buy all your bathroom and kitchen fixtures, sinks, faucets, and appliances for you. That way, he's responsible if anything goes wrong.

- If you special-order light fixtures, let the sales-man know you need delivery by a certain date. Be sure to pick out second choices, just in case.

- Get charge accounts at your local paint and hardware stores.

- Ask for discounts everywhere you go. You'll be surprised how often you get them.

- *Never* buy secondhand appliances.

STAGE 3
OF RENOVATION

*F*inish work is the longest part of any renovation project, and it involves the materials and elements that cover the guts of your property, from sheet-rock, plaster, floors, and moldings to cabinets, fixtures, and appliances.

This is the part of the job where the carpenter, the first workman to arrive and the last to leave a site, is center stage. He directs the installation of all the new items and repairs whatever can be salvaged of the old.

After the rough work is done, the finish work begins. This is the most important part of remodeling, because it involves all the things we handle, see, and use every day.

Finish Work

Because the finish work takes the longest, there may be days when you think you're making little progress. The metamorphosis is slow, but your active participation will move things along.

What to do during the finish work:

- Sandpaper everything in sight. Old wood trim invariably needs some smoothing, especially where paint has chipped off. New wood moldings require sanding at joints and mitered corners.

- Fill in holes and undercoat newly installed wood. I always hire a painter to do the majority of this work, but accomplishing part of it yourself could save the pro time and you some money.

- Wipe down existing doorways or window frames with liquid sandpaper, which eliminates the need to sand old woodwork before repainting. This marvelous product dulls the finish so that the new enamel goes on better.

- Help with the painting if you like. Just take time when you roll or brush to make it a professional job.

- Polish all the old brass hinges and return them to their proper places.

- Wallpaper. This is one of my favorite jobs. It's therapeutic as well as being visually rewarding at the end of the day.

- Line all your cabinet drawers and shelves with

leftover wallpaper, or buy a prepasted roll to do the job.

- Clean up! This is a job anyone can do. Just bring your own broom and you'll be welcome anywhere.

Communicating with Your Crew

On-site work is not all hard labor. You should allocate a good deal of time to watching the transformation in progress, seeing how materials are used, and observing the installation of everything from plumbing lines to kitchen cabinets.

By being on-site, you'll learn twice as much twice as fast as you would from studying all the construction and decorating manuals ever printed.

As you walk through the sawdust and shavings, becoming well versed in the arts of floorboarding, tiling, sanding, and supporting, make it a point to offer support yourself. Your crew will appreciate it if you compliment good work. Very often we think to criticize and forget to praise. But there's nothing like a pat on the back to keep morale high and good work flowing.

Communicating with your crew is essential. It is the *only* way to make sure what you want done is done right the first time—the second time gets very expensive.

Similarly, it is very important to express your real opinions as soon as a particular problem arises, but criticism should be meted out gently, like salt on well-prepared food. Good work flows from good feelings. Demanding quality in a professional manner will earn you the lasting respect of your workmen. And a positive attitude will earn you their friendship and loyalty. The whole team—including you— will look forward to coming to work each morning. There's nothing more rewarding than being part of an enthusiastic group who love their work and do it well.

Your dedication to your job will affect everyone's per-

formance. I often wonder what the construction crew think about my working alongside them, unafraid to handle hard tasks. I believe that when they see me hauling debris, stripping wallpaper, sanding walls, and eating lunch beside them on a dirty floor, they think, here's a woman who is committed to her profession and who cares about her work. Because I *do* care, they do too.

STAGE 4
OF RENOVATION

*D*ecorating your property is the fourth and final phase of home remodeling. Whether you're moving in or preparing this masterpiece for immediate resale, your next set of decisions will be crucial. I'm not talking about furniture, but rather, those finishing touches that make even an unoccupied property sparkle. The colors you choose and the faucets, hardware, towel bars, floor coverings, and lighting fixtures all make up the decorative accents that complete a fine remodeling job.

When it comes to decorating, ask yourself, what can I create that is so special it will make a buyer want to buy? How can I package my property so irresistibly that no one can refuse it?

Developing Great Taste

There are two decorating principles to keep in mind as you design your homewrecking project:

- Make it tasteful.
- Make it simple.

An important point to remember is: *Don't do too much.* Go slowly, selecting attractive but simple accessories at first. Once they're in place, you may discover you don't need another thing to make the room perfect. Never worry about not doing enough. If you've kept it simple, your new buyer will have the option to dress it up with his or her own style. Not so, if you go overboard and it has to be undone.

Never overdo. Leave the crowd begging for more.

Now, you will say, everyone's taste is different. If I intend to live in this property for a while myself and then sell it for a profit, how can I be certain that my taste, simply executed, will please both me *and* a prospective buyer?

What is "good taste," anyway? How do you know if you have it? And if you don't, how can you acquire it?

You may not feel confident in your decorating skills, but you can probably recognize what you like when you see it. Look everywhere for ideas—visit showrooms, hardware stores, department stores, do-it-yourself shops, friends' homes, restaurants, offices; read design books and magazines.

If you discover something you really like, *copy it.* There's no copyright on colors, room arrangements, kitchen designs, or bathroom layouts, so take advantage of the decorating that's been tried and tested at someone else's expense and duplicate the results in your own home. Gleaning at least one good idea a week from someone else's creativity and good taste should be a part of your homewrecking education.

An easy decorating principle anyone can master is: *Only one of each.* One color of carpeting per floor, one wall color in each room, uniform moldings for all the trim, one kind of hardware (I prefer brass), a monochromatic scheme in the kitchen, one color for all bathroom appliances, and one helluva lot of light.

Finally, *avoid fads.* Forget about the latest hanging lava lamp, long shag carpeting, or sparkles in textured ceilings. Fads generally have a small following, so think of the big picture. Classic elements and ingredients that attract a large audience will create a tasteful, simple, beautiful home.

Simple Elegance

Like the shoes, bags, belts, scarves, and jewelry we add to dress up our wardrobes, the color, hardware, carpeting, and chandeliers you choose for your property are essential. They can be all right or all wrong, so they must be selected with care. You may need some help from a friend or a professional designer if you're unsure of what to select. Your property is an enormous investment, tailor-made by you, so think couturier.

Never skimp on these design elements. Not that you can't find bargains, but beware of fixtures that are cheap and look it. It's the difference between brass and brassy.

I believe in color and the way it can be effectively used to create a mood. Think about warm, natural colors—earth tones like beiges, browns, grays, cream, and almond; warm pastels, like peach and pale yellow. If you're selling your property unfurnished, you must use pleasing, unaggressive colors that will give order and continuity as a prospective buyer walks from room to room. I've had great success, especially in a home with a lot of wonderful woodwork and ceiling-height moldings, using a warm beige with white enamel woodwork. It's calming, inviting, and comfortable. It goes with anyone's furnishings—yours or your buyer's.

There will be massive planes of undecorated wall space, floor space, and ceilings in an empty property. You want these to *blend together* rather than jump out at you. Don't experiment with wild colors, dark shades, or iridescents.

Bold colors such as forest green, burgundy, chocolate brown, navy blue, or a dark yellow—which I love—should only be used in a fully decorated room and then as a *background* for furnishings, plants, and paintings. With the proper lighting and room arrangements, the effect of such colors can be exciting and dramatic. And, although I've never done it, an all-white kitchen is smashing. It's a virgin canvas to which a new homeowner can add any color she likes. If you're really stumped, plain white walls, beautifully polished hardwood floors, and brass accents create a clean, elegant impression that few buyers can resist.

Add one element at a time, then step back and see if you can stop there. A bathroom doesn't need a gold-veined cultured marble vanity, rococo patterned taps, a harvest gold tub and toilet, foil wallpaper, and plastic beads hanging in the window to match a hand-painted sink you inherited with the property. That extraordinary sink could well be the focal point of the room with no other pattern around it. Just all-white fixtures and one color on the walls that's repeated in the basin. *Then* you'd have a stunner of a room.

In the final analysis, your colors and decorative touches should show off all the beautiful finish work, not interfere with it. You've spent six months renovating this house, so don't hurry the last details. Don't ever stop thinking top quality and first class. Make the prospective buyer know he's in Tiffany's, not Woolworth's.

Checkpoints

You can become an expert renovator if you:

- Are on-site every day.

- Join the work team, offering your opinions and supporting your crew with praise and intelligent decision-making.

- Make yourself lists of tasks to accomplish during the four stages of renovation and tackle them one at a time.

- Participate the way you want to—either helping with manual labor or working behind the scenes in your on-site office.

- Never skimp on the things that don't show.

- Create a masterpiece no buyer can resist by adding one element at a time, keeping it simple, and, if you like, copying the good taste of others.

11
Three Areas That Sell a House: The KCBs

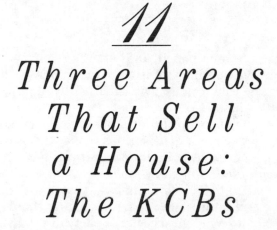eople are attracted to one property rather than another for many mysterious and personal reasons. It's impossible to second-guess a buyer. But in my fifteen years of homewrecking, I've learned that there are three specific areas that sell a house: the KCBs—kitchens, closets, and bathrooms.

When you are renovating, keep the following truth in mind: *The toughest nut you have to crack is the woman homebuyer, and she is primarily interested in kitchens, closets, and bathrooms.*

Regardless of who does the cooking or who takes out the garbage or who makes the most money in a marriage, it's nearly always the woman who makes the actual decision when it comes time to buy a house. And it's invariably the man who decides how and where to finance it. Even if there's a single male purchasing your property, nine times out of ten he'll bring a woman friend along for her opinion.

Singles, couples, and families today rarely need or want a four- or five-bedroom property. It's much wiser, therefore, to turn any extra bedrooms into baths and closets. Ideally, you should have one bath per bedroom, unlimited storage space, and a kitchen that takes the cake.

KITCHENS

*S*harpen your pencil and your ingenuity—kitchens deserve special attention. This is one room in the house that comes furnished, fully equipped, and permanently installed.

Here's your opportunity for a spectacular presentation. Design your kitchen for the serious cook—there are plenty of them out there. *Never exclude an extra if there's space for it, and go for quality in every inch.*

The kitchen is a room that serves many functions. Workplace and family headquarters during the day, social center at night. What good cocktail party ever stayed in the living room? That's why you want to make the kitchen a welcoming place—warm, well laid out, easy to work in, and casually elegant.

Kitchen prices vary enormously, depending on the size of the space and what you intend to do with it. You can redo a kitchen for a few thousand or for tens of thousands.

Color

One of the first things to recognize when designing a kitchen is that there's a lot going on visually. The lighting must be wonderful and the walls pleasant to look at, and the cabinets and countertops should blend with the appliances and sit on a proper floor. If all these elements aren't properly coordinated, the eye will jump from one spot to another searching for a place to land.

The best way to get started designing a kitchen is to select one element first. If you have one idea to start with (it may just be the desire to use almond-colored appliances), consider yourself lucky. You have direction. From here on in, you can choose all the other items to blend or match. It's the homewrecker who's found thirty-two wonderful things she wants to try who's going to have a hard time making that first decision.

Think of a kitchen as a whole unit—don't focus too much on its parts, because there are just too many parts. There are appliances, surfaces, angles, textures, and patterns. Color is your common denominator, the thread you can weave through everything you choose for the room. Begin with a monochromatic color scheme.

It's always easy to add color to a kitchen—in fact, it's almost impossible not to. Just try to find a nice-looking beige dish towel. It's like searching for the Holy Grail. They're all covered with bright red peppers, pink watermelons, or smiling dachshunds.

It is, however, difficult to subtract color, particularly when you've built it in. For this reason, keep the big things—cabinets, floors, appliances, and countertops—neutral and completely color-coordinated. Don't use anything too bold, overwhelming, or heavy. This is crucial when you're renovating for resale.

Start out simple in your design and color scheme. A kitchen will grow busier as you add more elements.

Lighting

It is my firm belief that kitchens want natural light just as plants and people do, and any architect who designs a kitchen without a window deserves to have his plans torn apart. A kitchen without a window to the world is hard to work in and hard to love. Unfortunately, many condos and co-ops are cursed with windowless interior kitchens. These are difficult to sell to someone who actually cooks.

If your house or apartment kitchen is graced with big windows and/or skylights, *develop the workspace around the source of natural light.* When the window faces onto the backyard, a sweeping stretch of lawn, or a great cityscape, install the work areas so the cook will have a view while preparing a feast. If you are short on window space and plan to put in a skylight, be certain to position counters or a butcher-block island to take advantage of the light. Skylights should be clear, not just translucent, so that the blue skies or clouds that pass overhead can add another dimension to the room—instant weather forecasting.

How can you develop natural light in a kitchen?

1. CUT A WINDOW FOR AN EXTRA EXPOSURE OR enlarge the ones you've got. Costs depend, obviously, on whether you're boring through a brick wall, concrete, or studs and shingles. The city must approve the addition of most new windows, and you must also have written permission from your neighbor if the proposed window is on the common property line.

2. INSTALL A SKYLIGHT. YOU CAN DO THIS IF you've got a one-story house or an extension with just a roof over it, or if you're on the top floor of a condo or co-op. In a multi-unit building, you must have the other homeowners' approval since you're cutting into a common roof area.

3. USE GLASS IN YOUR BACK DOOR IF THE kitchen leads outside. You can replace a solid exterior door with large glass panes or a lovely French door, or if you have the space, you can install sliding or folding glass doors.

4. OPEN UP THE KITCHEN TO AN ADJACENT room that does have a window. In certain cases, this may be the only solution to a windowless kitchen. With an open kitchen plan, you informalize the property, but at the same time, you gain a marvelous family or entertainment space.

5. ADD A GREENHOUSE WINDOW OR ROOM. These usually prefabricated units can fit right into the existing window frame and extend out from the wall. Or, if you have space outdoors, you can add or build an entire greenhouse extension on one end of the kitchen.

6. Eliminate any heavy window coverings.
Consider using shutters, shades, or miniblinds which can
be fully opened during the day and closed at night for privacy. Or use nothing at all.

In addition to natural light, every kitchen needs well-
planned artificial light. The stove, sink, counters, and dining area must be well lit.

How can you develop artificial light in a kitchen?

1. Install recessed spots (high-hats) over
all task areas. These are an excellent solution, especially
when you're reconstructing walls and ceilings in a kitchen,
prewiring and positioning the fixtures wherever you need
them. Recessed spots, set flush with the ceiling, give you
clean-cut lines as well as good illumination.

2. Use track lights mounted in a strip on
the ceiling. Individual lamps can be moved anywhere along
the strip and positioned in any direction for specific high-
lighting.

3. Install a dropped ceiling of light. An
entire ceiling of plastic panels can cover fluorescent-tube
lights, turning a dark, windowless kitchen into a Broadway
stage set. I personally like to leave fluorescent tubing at the
office. It's hard on the eyes, it can buzz and flicker, and it's
not flattering to the complexion.

4. Put a chandelier in the kitchen. In
older homes, which usually have a single fixture in the
middle of the ceiling, I often hang an enormous chandelier
with eight to ten bulbs for excellent general lighting. I aug-
ment the illumination with lights under cabinets if necessary.

By installing dimmer switches—rheostats—in any
kitchen, you can control the intensity of your lighting. You
can have bright lights for chopping and cooking, soft, mel-
low ones for dining.

Appliances

Appliances can make or break a kitchen. If your appliances don't work, your kitchen doesn't work. Most people abuse their appliances unmercifully, which means that only first-class products that can take such abuse will do.

Appliances are expensive investments, whether you get top or bottom of the line, so don't waste good money on a cheap unit. Ask your local appliance dealer which models are popular and sell best and which have a high rate of complaint. Read *Consumer Reports* to find out which are recommended. And make sure that everything you buy is backed up by a manufacturer's guarantee.

As for color, don't make any bold statements. In other words, white. Almond comes in second. There is no third. I personally don't like olive green, harvest gold, copper brown, or red appliances. They add too large a dose of color, and they're expensive to change if the next homebuyer wants something different. (There is a way to change the color, using a baked enamel finish, as you would spray an automobile but it's very expensive—which means you might as well replace the unit as paint it.) The only exceptions I'd make are wood-paneled fronts that match cabinets, and stainless steel or a custom color done to blend with the rest of the room.

It's crucial that all the large elements of a kitchen be well laid out, because their location controls the traffic flow. This is where we apply **the triangle theory.** The three most-used items—the sink, the refrigerator, and the stove—should form an equilateral triangle. They are the focal points of any kitchen. If that triangle gets too acute, too obtuse, or too isosceles (making it a long haul from sink to stove), then you need to rework the layout.

Kitchen Layouts

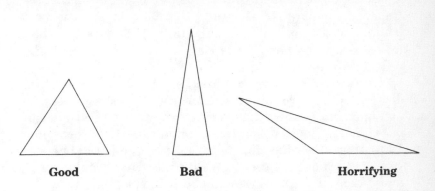

Good   Bad   Horrifying

Here are some pointers about the individual appliances:

1. REFRIGERATORS. IF YOU HAVE A GOOD-SIZED kitchen that supports a three- or four-bedroom home, you should plan space for a large refrigerator-freezer (24 cubic feet). A 12- or 14-cubic-foot refrigerator is adequate for two people; add 3 cubic feet per person after that. A 4-cubic-foot freezer is adequate for two; add 1 cubic foot per person after that.

Most refrigerators, except for those manufactured by Sub-Zero, stand out from 24-inch-deep counters, whether they are designed with the freezer above, below, side by side, or under the counter. Be sure the door swings in the right direction, and have your plumber install a water line if there's an automatic icemaker or water dispenser.

2. STOVES, OVENS, AND COOKTOPS. YOUR choices are endless, depending on the available space. If the cook's quarters are small, a single drop-in or freestanding range with one oven below and burners at counter level will take up less space than wall-hung ovens and a separate cooktop. Residential ranges come in gas and electric, and include one or two ovens with a choice of self-cleaning, continuous cleaning, microwave, convection, and warming ovens.

If you have the room and the money in your budget, add

a **microwave.** These ovens are growing in popularity and will help you sell your kitchen.

Once you've defined your needs and available space, it's time for comparative shopping so that you get the best equipment for your money. Pick units that cook well and look great, too. They should be color-coordinated with the refrigerator and dishwasher.

Cooktops, used in conjunction with wall ovens, are dropped into the counter much the way a sink is. I like this arrangement because the ovens are at eye level and you can use the area under the burners for storage. Cooktops come 12 to 42 inches wide, depending on the number of burners you want. There are cooktops with interchangeable equipment, including rotisseries and built-in charcoal grills.

If your kitchen is good-sized and it's drama you're after, consider a large commercial gas range. They're expensive and impressive but they require big ventilating fans, as well as twice the amount of insulation of a normal cooktop or range. Keep in mind that they're not for everyone—especially the mild-mannered cook. You may or may not recoup the price you've paid for this beauty when you sell your house.

As far as heating source goes, most cooks prefer gas. I like to cook and broil with it and bake in electric ovens. Gas gives a lot more control for cooking, but electricity is tidier to maintain.

Unless you are blessed with a kitchen full of windows that open, you will probably have to install a hood. A **ducted hood** vents grease and smoke and odors to the outside. A **ductless hood** filters the air and returns it to the kitchen. The ventilation fans or blowers in a hood are noisy, but they are a necessary evil. Just be sure to blend the design of your hood into the kitchen. Making it a focal point, I feel, is a mistake.

3. Sinks. A sink sees a lot of activity in a kitchen. Every meal begins and ends here. There are over a hundred configurations to choose from, with one, two, or three bowls in enameled cast iron, enameled steel, or stainless steel.

I'm sold on an enameled cast-iron double sink with a self-rimming edge. It comes in wonderful accent colors, eliminates the need for metal trim, and looks beautiful year after year. If you try really hard, you can chip it, but it takes a heavy hit to crack this baby. Enameled steel chips much more easily.

Stainless steel is the most popular choice for kitchen sinks, but it's prone to dents and scratches. And, of course, if you're fussy, as I am, you waste a lot of time wiping up the water spots every time the faucet is turned on.

Space will determine whether you have a double or single sink. I recommend that you get the widest one you can fit in your workspace—tiny ones are useless. If you really want a second sink and don't have room for two side by side, consider installing another bowl somewhere else in the kitchen for the convenience of washing vegetables or having a wet bar.

There are as many kitchen **faucets** as there are sinks. Time and again, I put in a plain single-lever fixture for easy cleaning, easy use, and simple lines. Old brass faucets look wonderful the day they're installed, but when the plumber sends his bill for special fittings and labor to install recycled fixtures and your polishing arm wears out, you'll wish you'd gone the modern chrome route.

4. Disposals. A disposal is a great help in any kitchen—a lovable critter that eats all the eggshells and carrot scrapings you put in the sink. Of course, children and guests sometimes feed incredible things to a disposal, so be sure to buy a real chewer. Older apartment buildings—whose drains can't handle the waste—may not permit their use.

5. Dishwashers. I recommend that you buy the low end of the top line. The "on" button is all you're really interested in. Forget the pot scrubber, dish warmer, and carpet-cleaner attachments—you'll never use them.

6. Washer-dryers. Although I prefer to have my washer-dryer near the bedrooms where most of the dirty laundry originates, it's not always possible to grab space that might otherwise become a closet or bathroom. My second choice is to put the washer-dryer in the kitchen. There are several under-the-counter front-loading units available, which give you a wonderful folding space or countertop for kitchen use. There are also stackable units which can be built into a corner.

If you have the space, create a utility room. As well as keeping the washer-dryer here, you can store brooms, mops, dustpans, a vacuum cleaner, and cleaning supplies. If you can, build in a fold-down ironing board—a pure time saver.

7. TRASH COMPACTORS. IF THERE'S SPACE, ADD one. Just remember that you may need a course in bodybuilding before you are able to carry out that bricklike bag, full of a week's compacted bottles and debris.

Cabinets

New base and upper cabinets are usually the most expensive addition to a new kitchen. If they're custom-built, your contractor will have to know just what you want early in the game, as they take a good deal of time to build.

Custom-made cabinets are my first choice for a renovated kitchen. I prefer wood custom cabinets, which generally cost less than Formica to construct. I stain them in a wood tone or paint them to match my color scheme. Your contractor can give you the price differences between the many available woods: oak, maple, birch, ash, or paint-grade woods.

You can go another route and select special-order cabinets, either manufactured in the United States or imported from abroad. These come in various sizes and shapes and will make your kitchen look as customized as a tailor-made suit. The cabinets are displayed in showrooms in most major cities. You may also pick up some clever ideas there for storage and layouts.

Special-order cabinets can be as expensive as carpenter-built ones. Try to get a guaranteed delivery date if they're shipped from Europe. If some cabinets arrive damaged, they could hold up the installation of your entire kitchen. Let the cabinet manufacturer do the measuring and ordering, so that if something doesn't fit, it's because of his figuring, not your miscalculations. And always have a professional do the installation.

Stock cabinets, a third possibility, are the least expensive. These mass-produced, modular units work well and can look great dressed up with some handsome hardware as long as your kitchen can accommodate their selection of sizes. Order "fillers," pieces of wood that fill in small gaps, and have an experienced carpenter install them so they're tight and level.

You might also consider using the cabinets that came with the property. Okay, they're old and tired. But if a coat of white paint and some shiny brass knobs will improve them, or if you can remove their terrible doors and use the shelving, you may save yourself a lot of money. If you're fortunate enough to have inherited an old kitchen with glass-front cabinet doors, keep them. Paint and a new set of hardware may be all you need.

Experience has taught me that when you're painting kitchen cabinets, there are three colors from which to choose: white, off-white, and ivory. Maybe you can stretch it to light beige, champagne, and almond, but don't get any darker than that. The lighter the better—unless you are a designer yourself or you've hired a professional who knows exactly what she's doing with bold colors.

If those old cabinets are simply awful, irreparably dirty, or ugly, and if they interfere with the new design of your kitchen, my advice is that you spend the money and replace them. Stripping paint off old cabinets just isn't worth the agonizing hours spent digging into every nook and cranny. Often my biggest dilemma is getting a kitchen that's not good enough to keep or bad enough to scrap. I wind up following the advice I give many others: When in doubt, rip it out.

Avoid ornate, expensive cabinet doors. Fancy hinges and expensive front panels can make a kitchen look busy. Dress up your cabinets with simple, elegant hardware such as good-sized brass knobs. Thirty knobs, even at $3 a shot, give you kitchen elegance for under $100.

If you are planning an open kitchen/family room, never hang overhead cabinets where they will obstruct the view between the two areas. I prefer to build cabinets to the ceiling for added storage, but when cabinets don't go all the way up, you or your buyer can arrange plants and baskets on top for decoration.

An alternative to closed cabinets is **open shelving.** New or old, I love it. Because they eliminate the high cost of manufacturing and installing cabinet doors, open shelves cut expenses considerably. And they can look most attractive if you arrange your china, crystal, mugs, cookbooks, and *objets d'art* effectively.

Try gluing custom-fit mirrors to the back wall of each open shelf. This inexpensive trick dresses up and enlarges the room, doubles your sparkling champagne glasses, and allows you to see what's going on behind you when you're facing the shelves.

Granted, not everyone likes open shelving. I've had buyers call the carpenter and request that he come back and install the doors that Suzanne forgot. If you're worried about clutter, combine shelving with cabinets that do have doors. This way you can keep the canned goods, foodstuffs, and less attractive equipment out of sight.

Storage

I discovered the secret of a perfect kitchen one evening when, right before a dinner party, I spilled a canister of sugar on the floor while reaching into the depths of a corner closet for the electric mixer. I then proceeded to upset the avocado I'd been rooting for several months as I plugged in the mixer to whip the meringue. I had no sooner righted the avocado than my cookbook slipped into a sink full of soapy water. The mixer followed thereafter—short-circuiting the entire kitchen. Spontaneously, I yelled,

"Space! Storage space. Counter space. Space!" This, my zealous renovator, is the good cook's mantra.

Utilize every available space for cabinets, every available inch for counters. Eliminate clutter. Hide it, bury it, eat it—but get rid of it.

List your basic kitchen equipment and be sure to create storage where it's needed. In a perfect kitchen, there must be a place for everything and everything in its place.

- Roll-out drawers near the stove for pots and pans
- Cupboards for dishes and drawers for silverware near the dining area and not far from the dishwasher
- A cupboard near the sink for drinking glasses
- A big, deep drawer beside or underneath the cooktop for utensils
- Revolving shelves in corner recesses for easy access; sliding shelves to prevent jars and cans from getting lost at the back of a cabinet
- Adjustable shelves for different-sized items
- A drawer for dish towels and potholders
- Cabinets and shelves to store small appliances
- A garbage can or trash compactor near the sink
- Narrow base cabinets for stand-up trays and cookie sheets
- Wine-storage cabinets
- A place for the telephone, message pad, and phone books
- Walk-in pantry
- And where does the 25-pound bag of dog food go?

Keep in mind that kitchen storage space can go beyond the conventional cabinetry and even open shelving. A large country armoire, for instance, can be adapted by adding shelves. Depending on the style of your kitchen, an antique breakfront or a wire baker's rack may be a good storage solution, and the perfect decorating accent.

You should have separate storage for **small appliances.** If you kept all these wonderful items on your countertops, you'd never have any room to cook! The blender, toaster oven, electric can opener, sandwich grill, coffee maker, food processor, ice cream and yogurt maker, juicer, mixer, wok, crockpot, pasta machine, and espresso machine should all be housed in cabinets and make their appearance only when needed.

All major kitchen manufacturers and experienced carpenters can tell you how to hide these appliances while keeping them at your fingertips. There are many clever storage tricks. One thing I always do is put electrical outlets in the cabinets. This way a toaster oven, for example, can operate from inside an upper cabinet. A food processor on a pull-out shelf will be handy, yet hidden.

By providing a place to store small appliances, you get cleaner lines in a kitchen, uncluttered counters, and a more functional cook.

If you still need more storage after including all of the above, there are two more possibilities:

If the room is large enough, I strongly recommend installing a versatile **center island.** You can buy one ready-made or have it custom-built. It can be constructed completely for storage with cabinets and drawers and a butcher-block top for cutting and chopping, or it can house a cooktop or a sink and dishwasher unit *plus* storage and eating space. Your plumbing and electricity comes from underneath, from lines set into the floor.

If you're having a center island constructed, and there's sufficient space, extend the top 10 to 12 inches to accommodate 30-inch-high stools, providing dining space for informal meals. There should always be at least 30 inches, preferably 34 to 36 inches of free space all around the island in order to move, work, and lower dishwasher and oven doors.

Hanging pot racks and wall hooks can free up drawers for storage. Racks are generally made of wrought iron or stainless steel and come in different styles with as many hooks as you need. It's best to install hanging racks out of the flow of traffic and over the stove or center island for easy access. Attractive pots and pans, colanders, or baskets hanging from ceiling racks or wall hooks give a charming, informal country look to a kitchen.

Countertops

Your base cabinets don't come with countertops, which must be selected separately. The work surface should be durable, attractive, and easy to clean. Think about backsplashes as well; they can extend 4 to 6 inches up from the counter or reach all the way to the upper cabinets—about 18 inches (my preference). You can mix and match countertop material with a different backsplash—for example, a Formica or butcher-block top with tile on the wall—but I prefer to use the same material. I like countertops to be 37 inches from the finished floor, a little higher than the standard 36 inches used by most builders. The higher counter is easier on the cook's back because she doesn't have to bend over while chopping, stirring, or washing up.

Tile is my current favorite for countertops, because it looks elegant and natural. Glazed tiles are impervious to heat and stains, although there's a high breakage factor—a falling wineglass doesn't stand a chance. Occasionally, tiles themselves can crack, so always order more than you need.

I use a medium-sized tile, 4 × 4 inches or 6 × 6 inches, all of one color, but I love to place a hand-painted decorative tile at intervals in the backsplash. Tiles can create a lot of pattern on the countertop, so use a grout that matches or is only slightly darker than the tile itself. It's best to seal the grout to make the counter easier to clean and protect it from dirt and food buildup. When reselling a property, tile is a real crowd pleaser.

Plastic laminate (Formica) is a popular and versatile material for counters, backsplashes, and cabinets. It cleans easily but does show scratches, and a burn can mean having to replace an entire surface. Like dark clothes, dark Formica shows everything—water spots, glass rings, crumbs, and fingerprints. Wood-grained Formica patterns, in my view, are poor imitations of the real thing. I'd rather have a light solid-color Formica than one that pretends to be butcher block or marble. Who wants to wear a bad knockoff of a real Chanel?

Formica is a good choice of countertop material for a small kitchen. Because it is installed in a continuous, unbroken plane, it makes a small area look larger.

Wood butcher block creates a beautiful, natural look, and is convenient for impulsive cooks who like to chop at a moment's notice. This material is impractical to use in quantity, though, because it needs tender, loving care. Wood, even when sealed or oiled, stains and burns more easily than other surfaces. Removing stains means sanding it down and sealing it again. And again. Unless it's coated with plastic, butcher block is also porous, which means that it can absorb food and liquids. If it's installed around the sink, water is bound to penetrate.

Professionally installed butcher-block countertops throughout a kitchen are expensive. Consider settling for a built-in chopping board or just using it on a center island.

Corian is an attractive solid material, manufactured by Du Pont, that looks like white or slightly variegated marble. Corian is slick, clean, and impervious to most stains. Light sanding will remove stubborn burn spots or ring marks. It can be cut to any size, and a one-piece combination sink and countertop unit creates simple, sleek lines for a contemporary look. This rather costly material can be used most successfully in the kitchen, but actually, I like it in the bathroom even better. Avonite, a similar synthetic, solid material designed to look like granite, marble, or onyx, is another possibility.

Slate, granite, and marble are all pretty to look at and pretty expensive. The diehard pastry chef may consider a built-in marble slab because its cool surface keeps the dough from sticking, but for a whole kitchen? Some friends of mine just spent $8,000 on granite counters. That's rather extravagant if you're considering an imminent resale.

Flooring

Think of the amount of time you spend on your feet in the kitchen! The right floor can make your day; the wrong one can spoil it. Your choices for flooring range widely in terms of expense, comfort, and attractiveness.

Wood is my first choice for kitchen flooring, after much experimentation. If you've got a hardwood floor already, keep it! Sand it, stain it, and seal it with several coats of polyurethane. It's easy to maintain, needs no waxing, washes with a wet mop, and is a delight to the eye. You can bleach it or stain it light for a warm, countrified look, or go with a dark stain for a more formal effect.

If you don't have hardwood floors, you can lay them. This is expensive, but one way to cut costs is to use reject oak planking, which will run you about one quarter the price of hand-selected narrow strip oak flooring. The planking comes in random widths with knotholes and wormholes—rejected by most builders and therefore cheap. This type of flooring has personality and works especially well in a country-style kitchen.

Tile looks as wonderful on floors as it does on counters and backsplashes. It's expensive and not particularly gentle to your feet, but like wood, it lands a buyer every time. Ceramic tile floors speak of natural elegance and quality. I use 8 × 8 inch or larger tiles for floors—the smaller ones look too busy. I prefer solid, muted colors—plain terracotta, quarry, or white are wonderful when sealed—and I like a matte finish rather than a highly glazed surface. If you do decide on ceramic tile, soften the blow to your feet and back by putting area rugs (on top of rubber pads to prevent slipping) in key places, particularly in front of the stove and sink. And keep some extra tiles on hand in case of breakage.

Vinyl tiles that are very good representations of ceramic tile are now available everywhere. Kentile makes one that looks a lot like terra-cotta. These tiles are relatively inexpensive, easy to clean, and easy to install if your floor is absolutely smooth.

Linoleum has gotten better in recent years and comes in patterns that, if not actually attractive, closely resemble wood, brick, or stone. But I can barely spell linoleum, let alone use it. Admittedly, it's waterproof, so spills bead up. It's also cheaper than wood or tile, and easy to clean. But so are polyester leisure suits.

Carpet is kind to your feet and back and absorbs noise, and spills can be easily sopped up with soap and water. It's great in an open kitchen–family room where the flooring can tie two areas together. People protest that carpet looks tacky, collects food, and is generally to be avoided in the kitchen. But I'm not talking indoor-outdoor carpeting (Ozite) that looks suspiciously like furry linoleum, or that so-called kitchen carpet that comes in a bilious turquoise-scarlet-mustard hurricane pattern. I'm talking good carpet, a tightly woven short shag, a tweedy Berber, or commercial-weight ribbed nylon in dark brown, beige, or gray. Convinced? I didn't think so. I've about given up the fight for carpet in the kitchen.

Walls

You may have very little wall space to worry about if your kitchen is completely outfitted with base and upper cabinets. In that case, the color on your walls should be a continuation of the colors you've already introduced in your appliances, countertops, and flooring. But if there's enough space to make a statement, choose an attractive color or wallpaper that blends well with everything you've done so far.

If you've put in an all-white kitchen and you're dying to spin the color wheel, a strong hue on the walls could be dramatic. Instead of a semigloss or a matte-finish paint, you may want to try a high-gloss enamel for a shiny, patent-leather look. This paint is especially good in small areas because it reflects light. High-gloss paint, however, should be applied only on a well-finished, smooth wall, because it accentuates the slightest bump or nailhead. A matte finish, on the other hand, can hide imperfections. Always use enamel paint on kitchen walls and woodwork. It repels water and it's washable—a necessity in every kitchen.

Wallpaper is a mood-creator, and will make a dull room happy, calming, or frenetic, depending on the pattern. Large, bold prints that come on like gangbusters may have you crawling the walls you've just papered. If you're going to use a paper, stick to small patterns like pinstripes, prints, checks, or plaids. Don't make your final selection of a paper in the store or showroom—take home some samples and pin them to your wall. Live with them for a day or two, and see what they look like in both daylight and artificial light.

Eat-in Spaces

I go to extremes to provide an eat-in space in the kitchen. I will often sacrifice a formal dining room by tearing down the dividing wall in favor of a large, open kitchen where everyone can sit around and enjoy himself before, during, and after mealtime. It's always a prize creation—the most loved, most used, and most versatile room in any home.

But if the formal dining room is to be kept intact, then some form of eat-in space should be created in the kitchen for casual meals, quick snacks, coffee breaks, or solitary dinners with the newspaper or TV.

If the kitchen is big enough, a breakfast nook set into a large recess, preferably near a window, is ideal. I'll design a permanently installed booth if space is tight, or use a table and chairs if there's room.

Eat-in space in a small kitchen deserves serious thought. Consider a fold-up or roll-out table from under the counter, or just a large pull-out chopping board which can double as work space and then slide back out of sight when not in use.

If you have enough storage in the room, eliminate a cabinet to give yourself knee space under a counter. You'll need 18 to 24 inches in width per person to accommodate a stool or chair.

Informal eating at a center island is my favorite solution. There are so many variations, depending on the available space and the design of this special piece of kitchen furniture:

- You can extend the top on one side 10 to 12 inches to create knee space and accommodate several 30-inch stools.

- You can add a shelf at 28-inch dining height for standard chairs.

- You can build a circular extension at one end to serve as a table.

- You can buy a freestanding, ready-made island table at a department store or shop specializing in butcher-block furniture and kitchen equipment. Such tables come in a variety of sizes with open storage below, and you can use the top alternatively for chopping and cutting or informal dining.

Pullman Kitchens

Usually one short wall chock full of cabinets, shelves, and appliances, a Pullman kitchen requires organization from side to side, top to bottom. The key is building up and out, using every available inch.

Here are some tips if you're squeezed for space:

Center-Island Seating

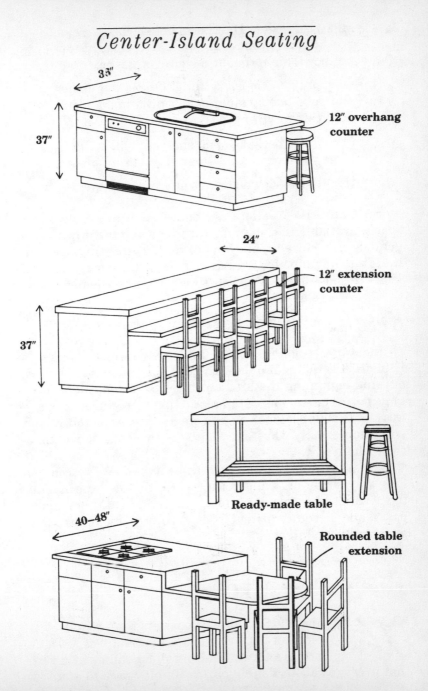

35″

37″

12″ overhang counter

24″

12″ extension counter

37″

Ready-made table

40–48″

Rounded table extension

- Hang things up. Hang pots on overhead racks, put up hooks that could hold an awkward copper bowl, an apron, or a string of garlic.

- Own only one of everything. One set of dishes and pots, one strainer, one soufflé mold. Don't duplicate anything.

- Mirror the backs of open shelves. This will enlarge the look of a Pullman kitchen.

- Install drop-down shelves on sturdy hinges.

So many city dwellers are squeezed into the smallest spaces available that manufacturers have come up with ingenious new storage solutions to help utilize tiny areas to their maximum potential. Kitchen decorating manuals and visits to showrooms are a must for a Pullman owner.

Kitchen Research

In every bookstore, you'll find an enormous array of home renovation manuals with good suggestions for laying out and equipping the kitchen. Interior design magazines are another great source of ideas; clip out pictures of every kitchen that appeals to you and start a file. Your contractor will know exactly what you want when you can show him a color photo of it.

Let your imagination go in the kitchen. We've come a long way since meat and potatoes. We're now experimenting with ethnic cuisines and dining on sushi, homemade pasta, and mesquite-grilled foods. As our palates expand, so too should our kitchens.

CLOSETS

*H*appiness is having more closets than rooms. Most of us are either moderate or serious packrats, and we tend to collect things at a rate that averages about double our available space to store it.

Therefore, the more closets and storage space we have to hide our clutter, the more attractive our living space can be.

Rooms not needed for personal or family use should be surrendered to storage. This means that if the house you buy has four or five bedrooms, and today's average family produces 1.7 children, you would do well to turn one bedroom into a glorious storage space. Not a place to stash lawn chairs, rubber rafts, flagpoles, luggage, skis, or football trophies, but rather a whole dressing room of built-in closets, complete with storage cubicles, hanging space, shelves, cupboards, and a hundred hooks. A room of pure luxury!

Of course, most people, particularly co-op and condo apartment dwellers, don't have the option of stealing rooms from the basic layout of their property. But it's possible to take dead space—in a corner, under a staircase, in an alcove, even air space in a high-ceilinged room—and turn it into some form of storage.

The point is, whether you're working with a one-room studio apartment or a three-story house, you want to create as much closet space as you can. The more built-in storage your property offers, the more useful it will be for you, and the more impressive it will be to potential buyers.

Good Storage

Every room needs a storage closet. Architects and developers should recognize the fact that we're all basically searching for the one-to-three-bedroom twenty-two-closet house!

When you are looking at the floor plans of your property, remember to consider the following storage necessities:

- The entry hall needs a place for coats.

- The living room or family room needs bookshelves and TV, VCR, and stereo storage, as well as cabinets for records, cassettes, compact discs, and videotapes.

- The dining room needs space for silver, crystal, china, and table linens.

- The kitchen or hall needs a utility closet for the vacuum, brooms, and mops.

- Bathrooms need medicine chests for toiletries and drugs.

- Kids' rooms need plenty of storage space for toys and books.

- A home needs a linen closet for sheets, blankets, pillows, and towels.

- Garages or basements need storage space for tools, ladders, paint, garden equipment, and bicycles.

With the proper storage, you won't spend endless hours searching for that continually lost item.

Clothes Closets

When planning your bedrooms, particularly the master bedroom, forget about the furniture for the time being. You don't need to know where a bed will go until you have your well-organized, spacious closets in place. The very first thing to figure out is how you're going to remodel the closets—stretching and stealing space from the rest of the room.

If you've planned your closets properly, you won't even need the beastly bureau. A large bedroom dresser is, without a doubt, the ugliest piece of furniture made. It dominates a room because of its size, and it takes up your best and longest wall. Although it's designed for storage, it creates a lot of unusable space on either side of it. I haven't put a dresser in a bedroom for fifteen years—instead, I've built wall-to-wall and walk-in closets that house all the clothes that usually sit in dresser drawers. This is a boon to me while I'm living in a property, and it's a fantastic selling point to a potential buyer.

Here are a variety of innovative closet designs:

1. A SEPARATE DRESSING ROOM. MY FAVORITE solution for clothes closets is to take a whole extra room, if it can be spared, and turn it into a dressing area. Since a luxury master suite is high on the priority list of new home-buyers, the best room to steal for this purpose would be adjacent to the master bedroom. The room would include:

- Two separate areas for his-and-hers space

- Built-in shelves

- Poles at different levels for hanging clothes

- Drawers for underwear

- Hooks for ties, scarves, belts, and beads

- Cubicles for sweaters, purses, hats, and shoes

- Full-length mirrors

- A makeup table if space is short in the master bath

2. WALL-TO-WALL CLOSETS. IF YOU ARE UNABLE to allocate an entire room as a dressing area, your next alternative is to take a bedroom wall with no windows or doorways and construct wall-to-wall closets. You need 2 feet inside the closet—that's the necessary width for a clothes hanger—and at least 6 feet in height, but you can go straight to the ceiling for unlimited storage. This makes your room 2 feet smaller, but if you put mirrored doors on your closet, you'll visually double the space in the room instead of cutting it down.

I like to install standard hollow-core doors that open outward on heavy hinges, mounted flush to the sides with full-length mirrors. I have a hole cut in the mirror for a large brass handle or knob. Use clear mirror—never smoked or veined—for extra light and a true reflection.

Mirrored Wardrobe Doors

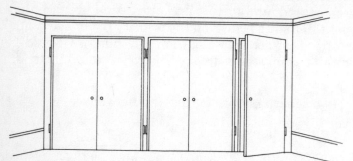

Mirror mounted on flush doors

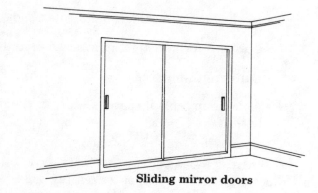

Sliding mirror doors

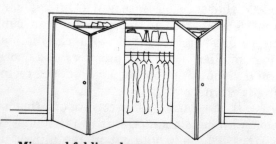

Mirrored folding doors

A ready-made alternative which works quite well is mirrored folding doors set on tracks. Sliding glass doors are cheaper still, but look it.

3. REDESIGNING THE INTERIOR OF EXISTING closets. If you own a tiny co-op apartment and have no room to expand, or if there's no room in your budget to rebuild, you can probably do a lot with the closet space you have. Just don't make the mistake of putting in one clothes pole and a shelf above it. If the closet is wide, put a divider down the center, install one high rod for dresses 80 inches from the floor and several rods for skirts, shirts, and pants 40 inches from the floor. Build more than one shelf above the poles and a row of compartments down the center.

Closets

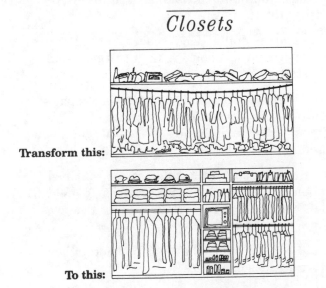

Transform this:

To this:

4. COMBINING TWO CLOSETS INTO ONE. TWO SMALL his-and-hers closets side by side in a master bedroom can be combined to make a luxury space. Cut through the division between them and make one walk-in closet with open shelves or extra hanging poles in the center.

Storage Tips

You can find all kinds of good storage ideas in decorating books and manuals, some of which are included in the recommended reading list at the back of this book. There are also plenty of closet stores around the country to help you plan your space. Here are a few tips to get you started:

- If you have a window alcove, build in window seats with flip-top lids.

- The space under a stairway has unlimited storage possibilities. You can house linens, coats, sporting equipment, Christmas decorations, or a washer/dryer.

- If there are sloping dead spaces behind the walls on your top floor, break into them and build storage centers.

- Create high-up storage as "deep freeze" space for things that you need only occasionally, like luggage, snow skis, and off-season clothes packed in mothballs.

- Buy or build a custom headboard for your bed with plenty of shelves and drawers to hold books, reading lights, a clock, radio, tissues, pillows, and the telephone.

- Use old pine or cedar chests as bedside tables to store off-season clothes.

- Build a sleeping loft over one side of a child's room and put a desk or storage for toys and clothes beneath it.

- Use vinyl-covered wire baskets and shelves in your closets. They provide good ventilation and maximum visibility.

- Buy inexpensive flat wicker baskets to separate clutter in the closets. They can be used for underwear, scarves, toiletries, or toys. An attractive wicker hamper in the closet, hall, or bathroom can hide laundry.

- Store shoes off the closet floor. Put them on shelves or racks, in pouches or cubicles to keep them organized and dust-free.

- Buy a big antique armoire and have shelves installed in it. Or put hanging poles in an old linen press. These are both much better looking than a dresser in your bedroom.

- A sewing closet is ideal for the seamstress. The machine can be permanently set up, and doors can quickly close off the shreds and threads.

- Store the television in an armoire, étagère, bookshelf, or cabinet unit so that it can be hidden when not in use.

Organized closets create an organized life. If you can get your possessions in order, you will look better, feel better, and *be* better.

BATHROOMS

*I*n the mid-1800s the White House got its first bathtub and Buckingham Palace got hot running water. Half a century later, British architect Sir Edwin Lutyens suggested that every bedroom in every house should have its own bath. He was thought to be exceedingly eccentric.

In fact, the concept has become popular only within the last twenty years. In the late 1950s, developers were *still* building three- and four-bedroom houses with one and a half baths.

A bathroom is like a toothbrush—you want your very own, you want it to be available when you need it, and you don't want anyone else messing it up. For this reason, and in the interests of resale value, try to achieve the following equation in your properties: 1 bedroom = 1 bathroom.

I know this is not always possible. One place you can successfully consolidate is with children, but remember that little kids eventually become teenagers, and then their bathroom time doubles.

A good contractor or architect can help you redesign your layout so that you can exchange that extra bedroom for closets *and* an extra bath. If you have a big pantry beside your kitchen, he can show you how to steal a portion of it and put in a half-bath for guests.

Working closely with your contractor and plumber, you may be able to install new waterworks in a variety of locations. It's not as difficult as it sounds to plumb rooms that don't already have plumbing. You go through the walls or floor and extend the existing hot- and cold-water lines from the nearest bathroom. The idea is to do this in the most economical and efficient way possible.

Ask a lot of questions about the location of plumbing fixtures. Is it expensive to move the toilet 6 feet? Should bathrooms be located back to back to utilize the same water lines? Does every bathroom have to be ventilated? Is a cast-iron tub really the best?

The answers to all of the above are "yes." Your plumber, an expert in the world of copper pipes and sewer lines, can educate you thoroughly, and together you can design your baths and select all the fixtures that will fit your budget.

Lighting

A bathroom without natural light is like a greenhouse without windows. If the existing bath has no window, and there's no chance of adding one, stealing one as you expand into another room, or installing a skylight, then you should make the damn thing what it wants to be: a closet. And put the bathroom somewhere else.

Of course, in many urban, high-density areas where you're sandwiched between other condos and co-ops and cutting a window can bring you nose to nose with a brick wall, the concept of an open, airy bathroom may be just a pipe dream. In that case, you'll need to install a good ventilation and lighting system.

How can you develop natural light in a bathroom?

- *If your bathroom has an outside wall, knock a hole in it.* Get permission from your local planning commission and your immediate neighbor, and create the biggest window possible.

- *If there is an existing window, for heaven's sake don't cover it up!* Never block natural light in the interest of privacy. It makes absolutely no sense to keep the blinds drawn all day just so no one will see in. Although I dislike translucent glass, it will give you daylight without prying eyes.

- *Install a rectangular or half-moon window above the tub or shower.* It should be high enough to retain privacy but open enough to give light.

- *Install a skylight in an upstairs bath.* There's nothing better! You can have the great outdoors right inside with you.

- *Add a skylight that swings open as a window* in an attic with a slanted roof. This provides ventilation and light, and you may not need the planning commission's permission to install it.

- *Use miniblinds, vertical blinds, or shutters.* You can get maximum light or complete privacy when you want it.

Most bathrooms require two kinds of lighting—overall illumination to get you to the tub, toilet, or Tylenol, and task lighting to highlight the area for making up or shaving. Small baths usually have one strong lighting source over or around the mirror, but larger bathrooms may require two or more locations.

How can you best use artificial light in a bathroom?

- *Install recessed lights* (high-hat canisters recessed into the ceiling) for general or task lighting. They enable you to keep clean lines in a small, crowded room and are ideal for the things you do in a bath that require excellent visibility. A good choice if you want a light in your shower stall or over the tub for a long soak with a good book.

- *Use vanity bulbs or professional makeup lights* in or around the mirror over the sink. Their bright light allows for serious attention to detail.

- *Put in overhead or wall-mounted spotlights,* which can be individually directed to various spots for task lighting.

- *Place fluorescent tubes* in a soffit—an overhang—above the sink for strong diffused lighting.

- *Add a chandelier.* It gives lots of light and can really dress up a bathroom.

- *Install a heating lamp.* These wonderful little coils in the ceiling make a gigantic difference in the temperature of the room on a chilly day.

Fixtures

The bathroom is a specific-purpose room—you rarely go into it if you're not planning to use the sink, tub, or toilet. It's the smallest room in the house, and the larger you can make it feel, the more successful it will be.

Fixtures dominate the bathroom's design and layout. There is only one color choice to consider for them, and that's white. Period. White fixtures are less expensive than colored ones, they're easier to obtain from a plumbing supply house, and they offer you and your future buyer the chance to add any accent color you wish on the walls, countertops, rugs, towels, and accessories. Why tie someone you don't even know to your love of avocado?

Good fixtures are costly, so keep the old ones if they're white and in acceptable condition. A chip in a cast-iron tub or sink's enamel finish can often be successfully repaired by cleaning, painting, and then heating the powdered-glass paint for a permanent enamel finish. There are professional "fixture fixers" who do this—your contractor can find one for you, or look under "Bathtubs & Sinks, Repairing & Refinishing" in the Yellow Pages.

A large old pedestal sink is like a piece of sculpture in a remodeled bath. I kept a pull-chain toilet in my present home with a wooden cistern at ceiling height and a flush few modern toilets can match. And my old clawfoot tub is a foot deeper than any of today's standard baths. Old can be beautiful, but don't pay good money for old fixtures you've found in a salvage yard unless they're perfect. You can also find impressive collections of reproductions through renovators' catalogues or in specialty bathroom stores.

If you're buying new bathroom fixtures, here's what to look for:

1. BATHTUBS. TUBS ARE AVAILABLE IN CAST iron, enameled steel, and fiberglass. You'll find them in special-order 4½-foot lengths as well as 5-, 5½-, and 6-footers. Enameled steel is less expensive than cast iron, but it chips more easily and sounds tinny when you stand or sit in it. Fiberglass tub units are lightweight and won't chip, but scratch and stain easily. They sound like hollow drums when you stand in them and look cheaper than metal tubs, which they are.

Enameled cast-iron tubs are my favorite. They weigh a ton and cost a lot more than steel, but they look, feel, and act like the Cadillac of bathtubs. Jacuzzi tubs are for those with a healthy budget, as are Kohler's clawfoot reproductions and big sunken whirlpools.

I'm not in favor of glass enclosures on tubs because I like to show off my cast-iron beauty. And did you ever try bathing a child with sliding doors and metal trim in the way? Uncomfortable for both of you. Keeping your bathtub exposed when not in use also visually enlarges the room and shows off the walls you've just paid dearly to decorate.

2. SHOWERS. A SHOWER SHOULD BE PART OF every tub, unless you have space in the bathroom for a separate shower stall. The width should be no smaller than the distance from elbow to elbow measured with arms raised at your side. The shower head should be at least 5½ to 6 feet off the floor, but not so high that you get your hair washed whether you want it or not.

Ideally, you should have a tub in the master bath, but if you have no room for one in the other bathrooms, just put in a shower stall. Use quality materials on all sides—tile, marble, or Corian—with a nonslip surface on the floor. One-piece fiberglass stalls that include everything—top, sides, and the pan you stand on—are popular, but I'd only install one on a very limited budget. If the bathroom is on the top floor, be sure the size stall you order can be maneuvered up the stairs and through the doorways.

A redwood or cedar shower gives a warm, rich, rustic look. I suggest a matching brown tile for the shower floor. The trick of a wood shower is in the installation: The wood must be sanded and polyurethaned over and over again so that the surface is splinter-free and watertight. It is easily maintained by wiping off any soap buildup with a liquid cleaner—never an abrasive scouring powder. Talk about resale value! Few buyers can refuse this specialty item.

3. SINKS. THERE ARE AS MANY DIFFERENT types of bathroom basins to choose from as there are different colors for toothbrushes. There are sinks of vitreous china, enameled cast iron, enameled pressed steel, cultured marble, hand-painted porcelain, and even hand-hammered brass. They're mounted under the counter, on top of the counter, with rims and without, attached to walls, and on freestanding pedestals.

For my own use, I prefer a self-rimming sink (no metal

trim) or a good, deep basin mounted under the counter. If I want to wash out some lingerie, I can slosh water around the sink without causing a flood.

And if your house plans aren't set up to help lower the divorce rate in America with his-and-hers separate baths, at least put two sinks in the bathroom that he and she share.

4. FAUCETS. SPEND THE MONEY FOR GOOD-looking faucets. You or your buyer will handle them several times a day. The choice is difficult, because manufacturers give us too many options. You can select old ones or new ones, or copies of old ones. There are marvelous reproductions of the Victorian era and sleek, modern, one-handle models. They come in chrome, brass, and gold—polished or brushed—and in enameled colors, ceramic, porcelain, and clear plastic.

You should go into a showroom and handle all the faucets before making a final selection. My favorites are lacquered, polished brass with white ceramic handles and one spout, not two, so you can mix the hot with the cold.

5. TOILETS. YOU HAVE A CHOICE BETWEEN TRA-ditional two-piece models and the more expensive low, contemporary one-piece toilet, in standard or elongated sizes. A toilet seat, like sales tax, is not included in the price. Select a quality seat—you guessed it, in white.

VANITIES AND COUNTERTOPS

*U*nless you're using a freestanding pedestal sink, plan on buying or building the largest vanity that will fit your space. It will provide a much-needed storage cabinet, possibly a dressing table, and a spacious countertop for toiletries.

Countertops are available in a variety of materials:

- *Tile* countertops are attractive, but don't get

carried away with pattern. Bold designs can make a small space seem busy.

- *Real marble* is fabulous, elegant, and expensive. It can't be scoured, and it may crack or chip.

- *Plastic laminate (Formica),* which is available in unlimited colors, can be cut to almost any size. Priced right.

- *Cultured marble* usually comes with a basin already molded into it. These counters are easy to clean, easy to install, inexpensive, and available in a variety of sizes. In most cases, they are not luxurious enough for the master bath.

- *Corian,* a wonderful synthetic marble, can come molded with a basin, or in sheets that can be cut to accommodate a deep sink. It's moderately expensive but looks elegant. This is my favorite.

- *Wood* is a possibility, but no matter how many coats of polyurethane sealer are applied for waterproofing, water manages to seep through and eventually discolor it.

To create some Old-World charm, I've often taken an antique dresser or breakfront and cut a hole in the top for a self-rimming sink and a hole in the back for the plumbing. I do this in a powder room or bath where infrequent usage will preserve the wood.

Flooring

The bathroom floor gets heavy traffic. It's a small area, so put down the best. You may select:

- *Marble.* A small number of large square slabs will yield an elegant look. Price it and see!

- *Ceramic tile*. The most traditional bathroom flooring, tile is easy to clean and looks neat. Use a dull, glazed finish so nobody slips.

- *Carpeting*. This is my first choice, because I'm generally barefoot in the bathroom. I use a top-quality nylon wall-to-wall carpet, but I don't tack it down, so that it can be removed for cleaning or pulled back quickly in case of a leak.

- *Wood*. Finished with several coats of polyurethane for an impervious surface, wood bathroom flooring is another favorite of mine.

- *Vinyl tiles and linoleum*. Two of the least expensive floor coverings. Easy to install, maintain, afford, and get bored with!

Walls

A bathroom and bedroom should be color-coordinated if they are attached. You can cleverly mix and match different hues of the same or complementary colors.

Before I decide on the wall treatment for a bathroom, I ask myself where and how much mirror I can install. More mirror is better in a bath, because it's necessary for primping and also because it visually enlarges a small room. You may do some tiling on the walls—especially around the tub.

Painting the walls is the easiest and least expensive wall treatment. Use enamel paint on everything; it will hold up under extreme moisture and steam.

One of the most dramatic wall treatments I've done was on a job with a very low budget. I couldn't afford new fixtures in a bathroom that had a green sink, tub, and toilet, surrounded with black, green, and purple tiles. I hired an artist who specialized in Rousseau-like jungle scenes and asked her to paint all the available wall space. With lions peeking from behind lush green foliage, wild purple flowers, and cats on the doorframe, she created a tropical fantasy that totally overpowered the ugly tiles. One long day's work: $150. An affordable solution to a problem bath.

If you use wallpaper, keep it light and warm in color to compliment skin tones. Select a strong, washable vinyl paper and cover all the walls. Because steam rises, don't paper the ceiling or it will eventually join you in the tub.

Bathroom Additions That Sell a House

Every buyer loves a luxury bathroom. When you're remodeling, be sure to add some or all of the following:

- Large medicine chests—two if you have two sinks (you can recess them into a wall between the studs)

- A built-in hamper if you have the room

- A built-in dressing table—a great extra, providing a space to sit down and convenient drawers for all your makeup, brushes, and hair paraphernalia

- Storage for toilet paper, cotton balls, and tissues

- Shelves for towels, soaps, perfumes, powders, and rarely used items like hot-water bottles, vaporizers, and heating pads

- Simple, elegant towel bars, toilet paper holders, and hooks on the door (my preference is brass)

- Enough electrical outlets for dryers, makeup mirrors, shavers, hot-rollers, and curling irons

- A book or magazine rack near the toilet

- A telephone—a marvelous convenience

The bathroom—the master bath in particular—should be an extension of the bedroom, which means that it ought to offer the same feeling of luxury and quality all the way. Keep the doors open and the toilet seat down.

Bathroom Additions That Don't Sell

Saunas, hot tubs, and bidets are nonessential items for your renovation budget and only of passing interest in terms of resale value. Buyers can always add these later on—they'll never make or break a deal.

You can spend a little or a lot on home renovation, but the secret is to budget most of your money for the KCBs. With a kitchen worthy of a master chef, a set of closets to store all your treasures, and luxury bathrooms that speak of comfort and elegance, the home you redesign will be absolutely irresistible to your future buyer.

Checkpoints

You can make the KCBs something special if you always remember to:

- ▸ Keep the color scheme simple and coordinated.

- ▸ Make the most of natural and artificial lighting.

- ▸ Add sufficient storage.

- ▸ Buy quality fixtures and appliances.

- ▸ Include interesting extras.

12

The House Beautiful—Inside and Out

lthough the KCBs are the three rooms that sell a house, they are not the rooms a prospective buyer sees first. In fact, they can often be buried in the middle of the tour. First come the exterior and entranceway, then the living and dining rooms—and *then* the kitchen. After that come the bedrooms—and then the closets and baths. For this reason, it's wise to make these introductory areas—exteriors, entries, formal rooms, and bedrooms—the tantalizing hors d'oeuvres before a luscious feast.

EXTERIORS

*T*hey say that beauty is only skin deep. Appearances can deceive. Don't judge a book by its cover. Rubbish! Don't believe any of those old clichés. Anyone who invests in real estate has to recognize the importance of exteriors—and of first impressions.

Like you, all prospective buyers preview properties, comparing and contrasting one particular house to the rest of the block, the rest of the neighborhood, and the rest of the market. Beauty may be skin deep, but a pretty facade is what persuades a buyer to look further. Unlike you, most buyers are not seeking a place with potential, but a place with pizzazz.

Translated into bricks and mortar, this means some interesting architectural details, a great front door, and an attractive exterior and entrance. You certainly don't want to present a sagging porch, a set of broken steps, or a peeling paint job to a prospective buyer. You want to give your house "curb appeal."

There are a variety of simple alterations that will greatly improve the first impression of the exterior of any property. To figure out what can be done to give the outside of a plain house some character, I sit out front and study the building, mentally adding, subtracting, and changing elements. I take photos and study these, and draw up a few sketches or pay an architect for an hour of his time to give me some good ideas. I explore other streets and neighborhoods to find properties that look great, then I figure out just what it is that gives them their appeal. The simplest details—a set of shutters, good landscaping, a new color, a lovely porch light—may be all that's needed.

If you're a condo or co-op owner, you won't be able to alter the front of your multiunit dwelling so easily. But as a member of the homeowners' association, or a member of the co-op board, you can recommend and campaign for a needed face-lift to the exterior or lobby of your building.

When you own a house, you are fairly free to do what you want, as long as you're not in a developed area where there's architectural control. You will also have to work within the strictures of your city's zoning ordinances. If you live in an area where all the houses are painted the same color, you should respect this uniformity for the benefit of the other homeowners. Following are some improvements you can make to a house without taking up a substantial part of your renovation budget.

A New Paint Job

A rich new color is an easy way to add distinction to a nondescript house. It pains me every time I see someone spend a fortune on first-class interior renovations, only to complete the job with a bland exterior—say, an off-white that blends perfectly into the tired white next door. An outstanding house that attracts the eye may be just what the neighborhood needs.

You don't want your property to stick out like a sore thumb, but you shouldn't play it too safe, either. There are certain strong combinations of color that work wonderfully well on houses. I've tried each of the exterior color combinations listed here with great success.

Exterior Colors

House	Trim	Sashes/Door
forest green	cream white	burgundy
camel beige	white	navy
gray	white	navy or burgundy
blue-gray	white	black
rust	cream white	chocolate brown
chocolate brown	cream white	burgundy or rust
dusty rose	cream white	cocoa brown

It's unnecessary to use more than three colors on a house. Use your first color for the bulk of the building. Use your second—and usually lightest—color for the woodwork, the gable overhang, window frames, shutters, and roof trim. Use a dark color for accents like window sashes and doors.

Natural, unpainted materials on the exterior of the house—weathered brick, wood shingles, or stone—should not be painted unless they look ugly. They were intended to be used in their natural state, and you can point out to prospective buyers that it's a *big* savings in exterior maintenance if you don't have to paint every five to seven years. If you think a natural brick building is too bland, paint the trim a dark green, burgundy, beige, gray, or black.

If your property has a concrete or masonry facade that's been painted many times and it's beginning to crack off, you may be forced to **sandblast.** If your painter advises this drastic measure, alert your neighbors and resign yourself to lots of noise and grit. It's best to have sandblasting done during the interior demolition work, because no matter how you seal the windows and doors, sand will find its insidious way through the crevices.

When you're dealing with a historic building, say a brownstone from the mid-1800s or an old brick structure that's been painted over many times, you may want to opt for a gentler form of sandblasting, known as **feathering.** This procedure uses a finer sand, but takes more time, and therefore, more money.

Sandblasting is too harsh a treatment for wood, which is porous. Instead, layers of paint are **burned off** with torches. The torches don't burn the wood because the process is done so quickly that it just singes the paint, which rolls off with the help of a scraper. The exterior is then sealed and painted over.

Perhaps the exterior only needs a cleaning. If water jets won't do it, **chemical cleaning** is a successful treatment, particularly on brick.

Exterior Additions

Rarely do you have to take the outside of your property apart by the seams and redesign it. Just adding some interest and character could do the trick. For example:

- Window boxes. The simplest and most inex-

pensive solution to a plain exterior when kept
overflowing with plants and flowers

- Wooden shutters. Still another economical addition—and an opportunity to add a second
color

- A big handsome exterior light—small ones get
lost against a large facade

- A new front door or decorative molding added
to a plain one

- Attractive hardware for the front door

- An awning over the door or windows

- Glass "sidelights," narrow windows on one or
both sides of the front door, will let light into
the foyer. Always use clear glass, or perhaps
clear glass etched with sand

- A white picket fence or a wrought-iron gate—
whichever fits the style of the property

- A brick walk from the street to the house to
replace broken concrete paving

- A new set of steps—perhaps safer as well as
better-looking

- An arched entryway—more interesting than a
square doorway

- A paneled roll-up garage door, operated with
an automatic opener—a true luxury for any
homeowner

- Thermopane glass windows with nice wooden
frames to provide good insulation

- A potted plant or container of flowers beside
the front door, but out of the way so it won't
trip a visitor

- Large numbers in shiny brass, or hand-painted numbers above the door

Unless you are selling a property in the Sunbelt, don't go to the expense of putting in a swimming pool or tennis court. These exterior additions will raise the price of your property, but may limit your market.

Landscaping

Plant the hell out of your front yard. There's nothing as welcoming as a lot of flowers, shrubs, climbing wisteria, potted plants, and a tree or two. Tiny seedlings into grand gardens grow, but it may take three years for a newly planted property to look lush and leafy. Greenery can always be trimmed back, so don't be afraid of putting in too much—you want it gorgeous *now,* for prospective buyers. And if all you have is a balcony in a condo or co-op, add some big pots and plants. That's one way to green-thumb it eight stories up.

Whether you're renovating to live in or to resell, landscaping is important. You can do it yourself, with a good gardener, or with a landscape architect. If you can't tell a weed from a rosebush and you dislike gardening, you should certainly hire someone to do the job for you. Good gardeners can be found through referrals from neighbors or local nurseries, or by my very scientific approach—driving around town looking for a gardener's truck in front of a house with lovely landscaping. Of all the professionals I consult on my houses, I've always found the gardener to bill the least for what you get.

You can do very well at a discount nursery, particularly if you have a gardener along as your guide. For $100 to $400, depending on which area of the United States you live in, you can buy a whole front yard full of plants and shrubs.

Newly planted gardens need a great deal of love, attention, and water. Get explicit instructions from the nursery or the gardener on particular care and be very conscien-

tious about watering and feeding your new plants—you can
lose them all if you let them languish.

THE ENTRANCE FOYER

*A*fter you've knocked out your buyer with the exterior, hit him again when he walks in the door. Wow him with your entrance and he'll be dying to see the rest.

Flooring

The foyer is generally a small area, so you can afford to go with quality materials for the best visual impact. I like to use a hard surface that's easy to clean, but if wall-to-wall carpeting is your preference, lay an attractive area rug on top of the carpet at the door where there's heavy traffic.

Hard surfaces you might consider are marble, hardwood, tile, travertine (a marblelike surface), brick, slate, stone, and terrazzo.

If you want something unusual, try a painted floor. This is an especially clever treatment for wood floors that aren't good enough to sand, stain, and seal. Putting one color on the floor and adding a coordinated stenciled border for interest is a job you could do yourself. If you want something really exceptional and more formal, hire a professional artist to simulate marble or inlaid wood, or have him paint an original design to fit the space. Any painted floor needs at least three to five coats of polyurethane to seal it. If you're going to walk on the original art you've just spent a fortune to create, you must protect it.

Walls

Mirrors are a wonderful addition to the foyer—as a matter of fact, I'll sometimes do an entire wall in mirrors to increase the size of a small space. As well as giving guests the opportunity to see how they look, a mirror also doubles the impact of a beautiful palm or *objet d'art* that's placed before it.

Soft, warm colors create a welcoming mood in the entry. Avoid bold, flocked, or patterned wallpapers and most foils. They're too strong for a small area.

Lighting

Wall sconces or a chandelier will dress up a foyer and shed enough warm light to welcome a visitor. A strong spotlight on a painting or sculpture is another dramatic way to light an entry.

Decorative Details

Even if you're selling a property unfurnished, you should decorate the entrance foyer. Remember, this is the introduction to a home that says, "Welcome. You've found the property you're looking for." Consider adding:

- Some interior landscaping—good-sized plants or a potted palm

- A table or console, which will be convenient for holding listing statements

- A bowl of fresh flowers—the bigger the better

- A big, framed mirror

- An area rug for warmth and color

If you're in a co-op or condo, you have less flexibility, but you should do whatever you can to make sure that the entryway is attractive. The lobby offers the first impression of what kind of people live in the building—it's evident that they either care or they don't. Mobilize all the owners to agree to remodel the entry if it needs it. After all, they'll be spending just a fraction of the price, since the total costs will be split among all the residents.

If you share a landing with several other apartment owners, you can plan together to decorate the hall on your floor. An addition of a picture, mirror, bench, or palm tree can turn a plain corridor into a decorative entry.

Often the only way to start off the renovation of common areas is to volunteer your time to collect the necessary estimates and samples. I've always offered my help to improve the entrance, because it reflects the tone of the building.

LIVING AND DINING ROOMS

*Y*ou can tell a great deal about a homeowner from the way the living and dining rooms are furnished. These rooms are generally the owner's pride and joy. They are *show*rooms, where the wall treatments, window coverings, furniture, and fabrics clearly indicate the owner's style and taste. The most expensive pieces of furniture are located in the living and dining rooms—even though they're often the least-used rooms of the house. This means that you should attempt to create a feeling of elegance in their floors, walls, and decorative details.

Dressing Them Up

If you have a plain room, one of the best ways to dress it up is by adding woodwork. **Moldings** give walls architectural interest. You can add:

- Wide crown molding at ceiling height and/or rectangles of picture molding for the walls

- Picture molding for dressing up flat doors

- Baseboards, which should be around 6 inches wide to visually support what you create above them.

- A chair rail, a single piece of trim that rims the walls at chair height—one of the simplest details to add (if you're painting your walls, you could use a darker color below the rail, a lighter one above for added interest)

- Wainscoting, a decorative paneling extending from the floor about 30 to 36 inches up the walls will create a formal look

- Decorative Styrofoam moldings at ceiling height when installed and painted can't be distinguished from the real thing

Always keep a fireplace if there is one—a focal point for furniture arrangement, and high on many homebuyers' lists. Built-in bookcases are also wonderful. There's never enough shelving for all the books, family pictures, and bric-a-brac in our lives.

Wallcoverings

Painting is one of the most versatile decorating techniques available. You can choose the guaranteed good looks of a flat latex color on all four walls with white enamel trim—high-gloss or semigloss—on the woodwork. Or you can achieve spectacular effects by texturing paint with **painted finishes.** A sponge, rag, or stippling brush will help you give depth to paint by adding or working off layers of pigment. Painting tricks that suggest marble, burlwood, tortoiseshell, or knotty pine, and a wide range of stenciled patterns will open up a whole new world of decorating with paint.

I used to pay dearly to have an artist turn a boring space into a sophisticated room. Then I started experimenting myself and was amazed at how easy it was to learn the various texturing methods. There are several good, illustrated guides to these painted finishes that are in the recommended reading list at the back of the book.

You need an adventuresome spirit to try one of these

Decorative Moldings

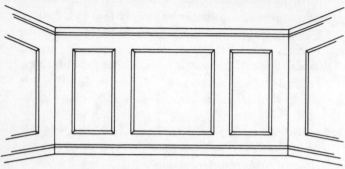

Add picture molding to plain walls.

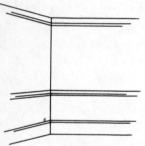

Chair rail

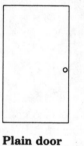

Plain door

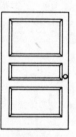

Add decorative molding or even paint it on!

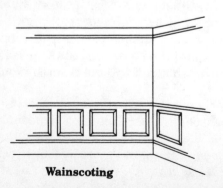

Wainscoting

techniques, but if it turns out well, you have a real selling point when you put your property on the market. Just strive for quality—a professional job, with all the corners, crevices, and moldings finished properly. I painted over my first attempt, wallpapered over my second. But once I got the hang of it, I was putting painted finishes on bedroom, bath, kitchen, and dining-room walls and marbleizing baseboards with a vengeance.

Trompe l'oeil, which means "deceive the eye," is the ultimate achievement of paint magic. This technique yields a three-dimensional painting on a two-dimensional surface. The viewer is tricked into thinking the landscape on the dining-room wall, the books in the formal library, the painted moldings on walls and doors are all real—when they're just an image. It takes a skilled artist to do this work. Don't tackle trompe l'oeil yourself unless you're an accomplished realist painter.

Painted finishes can subtly hide the imperfections of old, cracked walls because of their numerous textures and distressed colors. But wallpaper will do it better; it is now produced to mimic many of these painted finishes and looks lovely in the formal rooms. Stick to the small continuous patterns of strié, ragging, or stippling—don't use rolls of imitation marble. The continuous repetition of the same painted cracks looks fake.

Fabric, either paperbacked, gathered, pasted directly on the walls, or applied over batting for an upholstered look, is the best camouflage of all for cracked or bumpy walls. It's a wonderful decorative look and can also successfully soundproof a noisy room. Again, the proper installation and attention to the finishing details, like hiding staples with a complementary trim, makes a job look professional.

Wall Color

In general, lighter colors are easier to live with, and will probably look more inviting, especially if you're selling a property unfurnished. But strong colors can pull a room together, creating an exciting backdrop for furnishings.

You must know exactly what you're doing when you use strong colors. Once a bold color—burgundy, navy blue, British racing green, deep yellow—moves from the paint sample to the living or dining room wall, its dramatic effect is increased tenfold.

If you don't have decorating experience, but you really want to play out your color fantasies in strawberry or burnt sienna, then get the help of an interior designer. He or she can point out which shade of red works best, or how deep a blue you should select.

Ceilings should be painted a light color, usually white, to keep a room looking open and spacious. If you want to lower a very high ceiling visually, use a darker color. Any desire for blue skies and clouds on the ceiling should be satisfied by looking out the window.

Flooring

The floor covering for your formal rooms should be practical, safe, and comfortable, should wear well, clean easily, and should look great. In addition to the cost of the actual materials, you must also figure in the preparation of old floors, underlaying, and installation, which can take a big chunk out of your renovation budget.

Before you make your selection, you should know whether the rooms will receive heavy or light traffic. You must also consider the transition from one room to the next, both visually and technically. You will need proper thresholds when changing from tile to wood, wood to carpet, or carpet to vinyl.

Hardwood floors are beautiful on their own or with an oriental, Persian, dhurrie, kilim, or any other area rug. Old or new hardwood floors are extremely durable. Hire a professional to do the difficult work of refinishing and sealing them.

Softwood floors were generally installed as underflooring for other floor covering, but when refinished, they can be rustic and lovely. They are usually wide-planked, imperfect floorboards made of pine or fir. With proper sanding and two or three coats of polyurethane, they're very durable, but high-heeled shoes may leave slight indentations.

Wall-to-wall carpet is available in an enormous range of colors, patterns, thicknesses, fiber contents, and costs. Clearly, there's no yardstick to measure how much you should spend per square yard, but don't put out good money for cheap carpet. A reputable carpet manufacturer will show you all the fibers available—from acrylic, nylon, and polyester to sisal and wool—and will price out the samples that interest you at a carpet showroom. Take a floor plan with you so that you can get an estimate on the spot.

Always use a good-quality pad underneath wall-to-wall carpeting and hire a professional to install it. Keep seams out of heavy traffic areas, and roll the carpet at doorways if you don't like metal trim. A runner on stairs is cheaper than fitted carpet, but be sure the exposed staircase is finished well.

Marble, terrazzo, travertine, brick, and slate floors are extremely durable but are not normally laid in large areas because of their weight, expense, and hard surface, though I have seen beautiful homes done in brick, stone, and marble—all in warm-weather climates. They won't be the most popular with the buying audience *or* your wallet.

Linoleum, vinyl, and cork tiles should never be used in the formal rooms.

Ceramic tiles can be smashing in a large room if it fits your motif. I like squares to be 8 × 8 inches or larger, in solid, muted colors.

Six years ago, I got a great deal on some glazed white Mexican tiles, but the estimate to have them laid professionally came out to more than the price of the materials. I figured you have to try everything once, except skydiving and alligator wrestling, so I took a weekend to do the 12 × 15-foot garden room off the entrance foyer by myself.

My professional tilers were working on the master bath, so as they left the house on Friday, I borrowed their tools, mixing buckets, and a grid. I cleared out the garden room, lugged all the tile and cement from the trunk of my car, lined up the tools, and got a good night's sleep, anticipating an early start.

8:00 A.M. Saturday: The first of eighteen buckets of cement stirred by hand. I spread an inch of this mud on the floor, lowered the grid, and dropped nine tiles into the wet cement.

2:00 P.M.: Having crawled on a concrete floor for six hours, I was uncertain that my benumbed knees were still attached to my body. Only half the room was finished; I was exhausted. I wanted to stop at this point but feared the mud would dry hard where I left off, making it impossible to line up the next few tiles properly. Would a coach of the losing team stop a football game at halftime?

6:00 P.M.: My blistered hands felt as if they had just resurfaced the San Diego freeway. I was three-quarters finished.

Midnight: I plopped the last tile in the mud. Bent like Quasimodo, I crawled painfully upstairs to bed.

Sunday: Received breakfast, lunch, dinner, and the Sunday paper in bed. Couldn't move.

Monday: Crept downstairs to admire a most impressive sight. Did I really do all that by myself? Filling in all the spaces with grout was the next phase of the project. I immediately called the tilers to come over and finish the job. It would be months, I suspected, before I could bend to the floor again.

When the tilers arrived, they admitted they had *forgotten* to lend me their giant electric cement mixer and kneepads.

Hiring a professional to tile a floor is expensive, but it's worth it. This is a big job to tackle on your own.

BEDROOMS

*T*here is a house in San Francisco . . . the only property out of the dozens I've bought in that city that I still occupy. Why? Mainly because of the master bedroom.

It's my favorite room in the world.

The bedroom positively radiates self-indulgence. The

bed is located beneath a giant bronzed skylight that opens at the touch of a button. It has a marble fireplace and a huge clawfooted bathtub, positioned before a full view of the San Francisco Bay. On a lazy day, I can soak up some rays in bed or fill the tub and take a sunbath.

When the workmen were gutting the original bathroom, I decided I would not let the tub fall victim to a sledgehammer. I told them to carry it into the bedroom and leave it. They didn't realize, though, that I wanted to *bathe* in it.

"Plumb the tub?" cried my contractor. "In the bedroom? Are you kidding?"

"I'm perfectly serious," I told him, holding my ground. "The tub goes beside the bay window."

Now, thanks to my perseverance, I can sit in a bubble bath and look at the lights over the bay.

After a hard day on-site or after a long plane flight, that bedroom is my landing strip. When I'm alone, I spend most of my time there. I read, relax, work, write, type, and watch Johnny Carson. When I awaken, I open the skylight, stretch my arms toward the sky, and shout, "I love this room!"

Everyone should have a bedroom designed for his or her tastes and fantasies—it should be a personal space that is fun, relaxing, enjoyable, and slightly outrageous.

If you're planning to live in a property before you resell, heed the following rule: *The master bedroom should be romantic first, then functional.* Make the bedroom warm, attractive, interesting, and intimate. A cool, masculine grayflannel or glen-plaid look is great—but in the library.

Creating a Luxury Bedroom

Whether you're renovating a large house with big rooms or a small apartment where each square inch is at a premium, the master bedroom can be your headquarters for work and play.

- Enhance the size. The bigger the better. Enlarge this room by breaking through walls to other bedrooms, and create a master suite that includes a study area, entertainment center, dressing room, and super bath.

- Extend the bedroom with a deck or balcony. French doors can lead to outdoor space or a terrific view.

- Add a loft to the room if you have high ceilings. This gives you extra floor space.

- Add a skylight, lifting your ceiling height to the sun and stars.

- Recess shelving in between the studs inside the walls.

- Utilize attic space for a two-story suite. This is one of the least expensive ways to increase the square footage of a property. By getting rid of the existing bedroom ceiling, you can give yourself a spectacular cathedral ceiling and a whole new room to play in. You need to add a skylight or windows, and then design an office, library, dressing room, or video room on the upper level and connect it to the bedroom with a staircase or ladder.

An attic must be 7 feet 6 inches high or more if you intend to turn it into living space; otherwise, the alteration may not warrant the cost of insulating, sheetrocking, reinforcing the floor, doing the finish work, and painting.

If you're installing a skylight, there are Plexiglas double-domed ones for strength and good insulation, or skylight windows that open for ventilation. You can have a shade or blind custom-fitted so you or your buyer won't wake up with the sun every morning.

A two-story bedroom suite creates a dramatic living area. The visual change is overwhelming, and the extra space is a prime selling point.

Flooring

You want bedroom flooring that looks wonderful and offers maximum comfort.

Wall-to-wall carpeting is the most popular bedroom covering. It looks warm and is easy to maintain, pleasing to the eye, and inviting to bare feet. If you're carpeting all the bedrooms, consider selecting one color that will work in each room and the hallways. With a continuous flow of color, the entire floorspace will appear larger and more harmonious. A different color in each room reminds me of Neapolitan ice cream. If your kids persist in wanting blue and you're decorating in buff, put an area rug over the carpet in their rooms.

I love **wood floors** in bedrooms, with an area rug for warmth. Installing new hardwood floors is costly, but you can always refinish those wide, wonderful floorboards underneath the floor covering that came with the property. Sanding, staining, and polyurethaning existing wood floors would cost less than installing quality carpet over thick padding.

Hard, cold surfaces like **tile, marble, slate, stone, and brick** can look like a page out of a decorating magazine, but they can also make a room feel twenty degrees colder, particularly when you step out of a warm bed on a blustery winter's day.

Color in the Bedroom

Keep the color light, flattering, jolly, and comfortable to the eye in the master bedroom. Warm colors—pastels like peach, pink, or yellow—are flattering to everyone, and those of us over forty need all the help we can get. Save the cool shades—blues, greens, and purples—for the kids. Use neutral colors if you're remodeling for immediate resale.

I rarely paint any wall white. What about black? Well, I really don't like to talk about it, since it's a closed chapter in my life. But I did use black once, in Florida in the late sixties. Black walls, chrome-and-glass furniture, fur bedspread, white carpet, bold fabrics on the windows, and black-and-white nudes on the wallpaper in the bathroom. What can I say? Ghastly. I was young and inexperienced. Forget black in the bedroom.

One color of latex painted on all four walls with white on the ceiling, moldings, baseboards, door, and window frames is as safe as milk and cookies. But bedrooms are excellent places for any of the painted finishes mentioned earlier.

Wallpapers are marvelous in a bedroom, too—small prints, striés, tiny polka dots, or stripes. When you're tempted by a giant bright floral print, stop and ask yourself whether you or your buyer could really face those same damn flowers every morning.

Decorative Details

There are many touches you can add that will enhance the warmth and intimacy of a bedroom:

- *A fireplace* is great. Most bedrooms are near the roofline, so installing a fireplace won't be *that* expensive. Metal flues come in stock lengths and are priced by the foot. A fireplace is a cozy, romantic asset to any bedroom.

- *Wide crown molding* at ceiling height is a dramatic touch for a master bedroom.

- *A chandelier* is more elegant than a flush-mounted ceiling fixture. You might also consider wall sconces for diffused light.

- *Mirrors and a strong light* should be added to the dressing area.

Make the master bedroom exactly what you want it to be: a center of operations, a private place for rest and contemplation, or a grown-up playpen. But whatever you do, make it a *knockout*.

OTHER ROOMS

*I*f your thought is for immediate resale, *make every extra room as adaptable as you can.* The possible buyer for your house may or may not have the same purposes in mind as you for the additional space. It's silly to go overboard with nursery-rhyme wallpaper anticipating a buyer with a baby, when you may turn out to get one with an eight-year-old child who can't live without a complete Cabbage Patch overhaul.

Your particular buyer may want children's rooms, a guest room, an office, a sewing room, a mirrored exercise studio, a study or library, or a music room. He probably will *not* want a rec room in the cellar, so don't bother spending a lot of money to renovate below the first floor. An out-of-the-way playroom for kids might be suitable downstairs, but most people are no longer entertaining in basements without windows.

Until fairly recently, any den in good standing was treated to wood paneling, but unless the paneling is real— lovely walnut or oak—it looks as bad on the interior as aluminum siding does on the exterior.

If you're moving in before resale, and you have a carpenter on-site, be sure to have him build storage into all of the additional rooms. Extra bookshelves and cabinets can work equally well for home entertainment equipment or toy storage. Windowseats are wonderful in any room, and every storage spot adds a few more dollars to your property's value.

If you're living in, the additional rooms will fit the needs of your particular household. You can relegate one to guest use, and when you have no sleep-over guests, it can serve as an office, a TV and music room, a sewing room, or a library. Decorate to coordinate with the rest of the house.

You don't have to do a great deal to the additional rooms to attract a buyer. The very fact that such glorious space exists is enough.

Checkpoints

Your exterior, entrance hall, formal rooms, bedrooms, and family rooms will become major selling points of your house if you:

- ▸ Remember that first impressions often snag a buyer.

- ▸ Keep your decorating simple but elegant.

- ▸ Make the most of all the space you have and try to expand it, particularly in the bedrooms.

- ▸ Use painted finishes and attractive wall coverings.

- ▸ Select floor coverings that are warm and comfortable, but will accommodate traffic.

- ▸ Make extra rooms of the house adaptable.

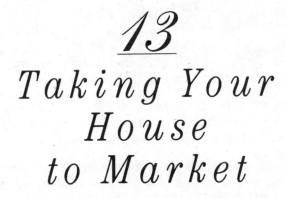

13

Taking Your House to Market

Four months, two weeks, and three days later, you're finished. It's brilliant. The property is immaculate, the windows sparkle, the brass shines, and there are two—yes, *two*—luxury bathrooms off the master bedroom! This was your first homewrecking experience. The plan is to move in, wait a year, and then test the market.

MOVING

Believe it or not, moving day can be tremendously exhilarating, despite the strain. This is the day when everything is put together and a new house—your house—emerges. Yes, you will be living out of boxes for a while, but it's going to be worth it. Honest.

There are many ways to offset or reduce the trauma of moving.

1. PLAN AHEAD. MAKE CERTAIN THAT YOU HAVE a functional kitchen and bathroom as well as a place for each family member to sleep. Get a list of inexpensive local restaurants and go out for dinner at the end of fourteen-hour workdays.

2. TAKE THE SMALL THINGS OVER EVERY DAY before the big move. It's amazing how helpful it is to pack up a boxful of items each time you go over to the new property and unpack them wherever finished space is available. If you take over the small stuff, the movers will only have to handle the heavy furniture and appliances.

3. LABEL BOXES PROPERLY. USE MARKING PENS or colored stickers on boxes and furniture to indicate which floor of the house and which room they go to.

4. PACK ACCORDING TO WEIGHT AND SIZE. Heavy things like books and records should go in small boxes; light things like hangers and shoes can be piled together in large boxes. And, needless to say, you should pack objects inside other objects to save space.

5. TAKE EVERYTHING APART. YOU'LL SAVE time—and breakage—for the movers and for yourself if you remove shelves from bookcases, light bulbs from lamps.

6. BUY MOVERS' CARTONS. REGARDLESS OF HOW many trips you make to the liquor store or supermarket, you'll never find those wonderful, sturdy barrels, boxes, and wardrobes provided by professional movers. These boxes won't fall apart—especially on a rainy moving day. Your mover can drop some off—they're well worth the price.

Adults are generally resistant to change, and moving can be traumatic for them. Men seem to take moving worse than women, perhaps because they aren't as involved in the way everything's going to look when it's finished.

Children, on the other hand, have a marvelous ability to

adapt, and they may actually enjoy a move, seeing it as a fantasy trip into a new world. Make them an integral part of the move and the new house. If things aren't exactly finished, you can turn inconvenience into an adventure by letting them:

- Sleep in sleeping bags on the floor if their beds haven't arrived.

- Brush their teeth by flashlight if you can't get the bathroom light to work.

- Skip their bath for a day if the plumber forgot to connect the hot-water heater.

- Help plan their rooms. Early on, offer them a few choices of color and furnishings and let them pick what they like best within the range you've given them. If they want to paint, let them do their closet.

If possible, try to retain some element of stability in a child's life. You can do this by renovating houses in the same area and having your child continue to attend the same school. My son William moved all over San Francisco with me, but he didn't change his school or his friends. The path to his front door just changed every twelve to eighteen months. I renovated sixteen houses with William in tow. We lived temporarily in one room, cooked meals in a toaster oven, washed dishes in the bathtub. I never stopped being a good mother; I never stopped being a good homewrecker.

Although I'm not in favor of living in a demolition site if you don't have to, it's cheaper than paying rent in one place and shelling out a mortgage payment, especially when finances are tight. Kids think camping out is fun, up to a point. And you can learn to adapt, knowing that it's only temporary.

TIME TO SELL

*Y*ou may not move in at all. You may stay in the residence you've lived in for years and renovate one new place after another, just for the purpose of resale. You think you won't get attached to a property you don't live in? If you're anything like me, you'll find that going through an entire remodeling process is similar to giving birth. And marketing your property after all those broken fingernails, long hours, and endless bags full of dirt and debris is like putting your beloved child up for adoption.

It used to bother me to know that someone else would reap the benefits of my hard labor. But when those full-price offers started rolling in, I got over it. In about twenty minutes.

Marketing your masterpiece will be easy compared to what you've been through, because *people want to buy homes in move-in condition.*

If you sell right after the renovations are finished, your return on money invested will be at its peak. When the systems are brand-new, the paint job is perfect, everything's under warranty, and the whole place sparkles, your property will take its highest profit jump. You have to decide whether to sell now, for a high, quick return on your investment, or wait a while to see if property appreciation surpasses your yearly net operating costs.

SELLING THE PROPERTY YOURSELF

*Y*ou *can* do it yourself, but I never have. I like to avoid the hassles of screening prospective buyers, staying home so I can escort them from room to room, worrying about whether they're qualified to get a mortgage, and dealing with the hundreds of tiny details that arise in every house sale from the first showing through the closing.

But, you may say, a perfectly remodeled house should sell quickly and easily, so why not sell it yourself? If you think you can do as terrific a sales job as the real estate agent who sold *you* the property, then go ahead, but remember these few pointers that may make your sale easier:

- Keep the exterior immaculate: Cut the grass, trim the shrubs, pick up all litter in the driveway and around the grounds.

- Make the porch or entrance inviting: Get a new doormat and a pot of colorful flowers.

- Be sure the lights are on throughout the house or apartment if the day is dark.

- Keep the thermostat at a comfortable temperature.

- During a showing, don't oversell—wait to be asked questions.

If you are selling your property yourself, you must approach it in a systematic and businesslike manner.

1. GET "COMPS" IN YOUR AREA. YOU HAVE THE right to list your property at any price you like, but don't be unreasonable. Check the newspaper's real estate section and the recent sales recorded at city hall to see what comparable houses in your neighborhood have sold for. Put a slightly higher price tag on your home than you really want. A prospective buyer likes to negotiate, so allow a little room for give and take.

2. SET YOURSELF A TIME LIMIT. DECIDE TO place your ads for one or two months—no more—and see who's biting. If you're anxious to sell but haven't received any offers in this time period, approach the experts and see what they can do.

3. PLACE ADS IN SEVERAL PAPERS. AN AD FOR A week in a local paper may run you around $40; in a major

metropolitan daily, just a weekend ad may cost $60 to $80. The ad should be concise and to the point, mentioning the highlights of your property. Stress its good location—be sure to mention the neighborhood, the price, and that the house has been completely renovated.

4. **THINK TWICE BEFORE PUTTING A SIGNBOARD** out front. Whenever I see "For Sale by Owner" signs in front yards, I invariably walk up and ring the bell. I would *never* use this technique for selling my own home because I couldn't stand the traffic, the strangers, or the disruptions in my life. I'd much prefer to do newspaper advertising and make appointments by phone.

5. **PRESENT YOUR HOUSE ON PAPER TO THE** buyers. Gather all the information you have and write it down. You can hand a listing sheet to each interested party who comes through the door. Remember to include:

- Address
- Asking price
- Property taxes
- Approximate size of all the rooms
- Number of bedrooms and bathrooms
- Decks, patio, garage, basement, wine cellar
- Type of heat
- Which appliances are included and which items are not part of the sales price
- Available financing, if any
- Your name and phone number, on the bottom of the sheet

Also write down appealing extras like the location of the nearest supermarket, schools, playgrounds, places of worship, hospital, movie theaters, shops, restaurants, and public transportation. If you want to be particularly helpful, you can even provide maps of the town, courtesy of the local Chamber of Commerce.

Return all phone calls promptly. You could lose a good deal by letting somebody hang on too long. And finally, if you've caught a buyer all by yourself, write down the terms you've agreed to and consult a real estate lawyer, who will draw up a contract for you. This is another time when you *should* seek legal assistance. A lawyer will ensure that negotiations go smoothly, and will be able to guide you through the many steps of a contract and closing.

If you are selling a co-op apartment, you will have to defer to the board in your selection of a prospective buyer. Selling a condominium, however, is just the same as selling a house—you don't need anyone's approval.

Selling the Property
Through a
Real Estate Agent

I strongly recommend that you leave the sale of a property in the capable hands of an experienced agent who makes deals for a living. I always return the listing of a property to the agent who sold it to me. He or she will be familiar with the house and able to explain all the remodeling that was done to it. Also, with this double-commission incentive, I know the agent is going to work hard to sell the property, and, more important, will continue to show me good properties we can both profit from.

Nine out of ten buyers work through a real estate office, which means that agents have an eager and captive audience to parade around your property. What's more, it's wise to stay in the good graces of the real estate community, especially if you are thinking of home renovation as a career.

If you sell your home without the aid of a realtor, you are telling the pros you don't need them. But you do! You need their connections, their expertise, and their direct line to the best properties in town. You should have realtors on your side so that they'll call you first when they find another house or apartment for you to renovate.

Hiring a realtor does not really cost you anything. Together, you set a sales price, figuring in a commission, so it's the buyer who is actually paying the fee. However, if you start turning properties around often—especially big, expensive ones—you might want to try negotiating the percentage of commission down from the standard 6%, especially if you're buying and selling through the same agency. Since you've renovated the property beautifully, it's going to be a snap and a pleasure to sell. So ask whether the agent will take 5% or even 4%, or maybe 6% of the first $100,000 and 5% of the balance. It's worth a shot.

When your property is ready for sale, you will have to sign a **listing agreement** with the agency. This gives it the exclusive sales right to your property for a specified length of time—generally, six months. If you are nervous about tying yourself to one agent, particularly if it's someone you've never worked with before, you can agree to a shorter listing period—say, three months with the option to renew at the end of that time.

Here's how the sales process works:

1. **THE LISTING AGENCY USUALLY HAS AN OPEN** house for its own agents. They spend time examining the property and asking questions of the owner. They decide on a price and write up a listing statement with all the particulars.

2. **FOR THE FIRST WEEK, THE LISTING AGENCY** likes to keep the property in house. This gives the agents of that firm the chance to show it to all their clients and sell it within their office—collecting 100% of the commission. They may have an open house during one weekend of this initial sales period. Open houses, particularly on unfurnished properties, offer wonderful selling opportunities, often snaring people wheeling baby carriages, walking off a

Sunday lunch, or jogging, as well as those who are specifically looking for property on their own. I don't generally
advise having an open house when you're in residence. It
unfortunately provides an excellent opportunity for someone to scout out your possessions and come back later to
relieve you of them.

3. IF THE HOUSE HASN'T SOLD IN A WEEK (THIS
period of time is negotiable—on an expensive property
where time is not only money but very big money, you may
want to limit the exclusive to a few days), the agency will
open the property to other brokers in town. The listing
agency holds a "broker's open"—not a golf tournament, but
an open house for all other agencies to view the property.

4. AT THE SAME TIME, THE LISTING AGENCY MAY
place the property with a multiple listing service. This
means that the listing sheet and photo of the property will
appear in the Multiple Listing Book that circulates to every
member agency in the city. Now, any of these agents can
show the property—and if they sell it, the lister must split
the commission with them, 50-50.

Your listing agent should know everything about the
property, and should *always* accompany a prospective buyer
to answer all his questions and point out the hidden closet
behind the bookshelf, operate the movable skylight, and explain that the chandeliers and appliances stay but the can-
opy bed does not.

What should you expect from your agency?

- Weekly newspaper advertising (the agency
  should give you a written statement confirm-
  ing that it will place the ads and pay for them)

- Magazine ads for higher priced properties

- Good-looking statements with a quality exterior photograph—and possibly a couple of the
  interior

- Distribution of these statements to all other
  agencies

- Placement of your listing—by computer if they have it—in the Multiple Listing Book

- Placing a signboard on your lawn if you want one there (I personally avoid these for aesthetic reasons, but agents claim they are a big selling tool)

- Handling all appointments to show the house (taking care of your keys, making sure to lock up, being careful to keep pets in)

- Conducting an open house if you've agreed to have one

- Helping a buyer to find appropriate financing (many agents are wonderful about explaining interest rates and mortgages and will introduce a buyer to several lenders)

- Giving you a weekly progress report (it's enormously helpful for a seller to know just what's going on, how many prospective buyers have seen the property, and what the response has been, negative as well as positive)

- Presenting all offers, which should always be made in writing

- Negotiating a good deal for you

Should you ever list a property with more than one agency? Generally speaking, I get better performance from a company when it has an exclusive. The bosses will obviously push their agents to sell, because it means a higher commission. Two agencies don't necessarily give you twice the exposure unless the first one is very small and hasn't the huge client list of a larger firm or the money to spend on promotion and advertising. Just avoid having your home look like an overdecorated Christmas tree with four different signboards on the front lawn.

In some cities, like New York, it may be advantageous for the owner to list with several agencies. Occasionally, the exclusive listing means that a house will be shown only to that agency's clients. This cuts down on exposure, which could increase the time it takes to sell.

Should you be present when the agent is leading customers through your house? In most cases, no. The buyers have an easier time of it when the owner's not around. It's hard for them to imagine it could be *their* house when you're physically present. If you do stick around to answer questions, stay calm and uninvolved—and *let the agent do the selling*.

I have one developer friend who insists on being present so that she can set a pan of brownies in the oven. The odor of baking chocolate, she swears, acts like an aphrodisiac on most homebuyers. She tells me that it only takes her six pans of brownies—or six showings—to sell her property.

The real estate agent you select becomes your employee—he or she is working for you for a fee. Don't hesitate to make suggestions if your property isn't moving. You can demand a rethinking of the sales presentation, or some office brainstorming. The agents from the firm can go over the negatives and positives of the property point by point, deciding which elements they should be promoting. Agents earn good money, so you have a right to insist that they do a good job.

A very successful San Francisco agent drove up beside me one day and said, "Thanks, Suzanne, for this new Mercedes!" It didn't bother me at all that she'd earned enough from the sale of one of my properties to buy the car of her choice. Florian has worked nonstop, seven days a week, for over twenty-five years and deserves any car she wants to drive. She's tough and effective.

I did ask her, though, if I could at least drive it on weekends.

TIMING THE SALE

I generally allow four months from the time a property goes on the market to sell it. Most of my places sell within thirty days because they're immaculately renovated and in perfect move-in condition. On average, an attractive, well-located property should take one to three months to find the right buyer.

If your sale is taking longer than it should, ask yourself if there is some selling point you or your agent is not capitalizing on. Is there a way to attract a different kind of buyer? Is there something specific the house lacks that might push it over the edge from interesting to irresistible?

There are lulls in the real estate business, and you want to try to avoid having to sell your property with little or no profit when the market is low. In almost every part of the country, *the low periods are always followed by highs*. This is a volatile business, and sometimes only six months or a year can bring substantial increases in property values.

WHEN TO SIT
AND WHEN TO SELL

*R*emember that you don't have to accept the best offer you get if it's not the offer you had in mind. If you are considering an offer lower than you expected, ask yourself:

- Do you *have* to sell? Are there personal or financial reasons that impel you to move, or to take what you can out of this deal and be satisfied with that?

- Do you feel you've done the very best job you can on this property? Is there anything else you could do that might make a significant difference in its value?

- Have you found another property that you want to buy? If you have your eye on something wonderful that could be snapped up fast, you may feel it's imperative to accept the best offer that comes along.

- Does your real estate agent think that the offers you've been getting are justified in this
market? Maybe you've overpriced the property.

Never sell yourself short. You have slaved over the property, put your blood, sweat, and tears right into the floorboards, and you deserve everything you can get back. If you
don't at the very least break even on your purchase, renovation, and carrying costs for the amount of time you've
owned it, then you're doing yourself a great disservice. If
you give up now, you may never have enough confidence in
your homewrecking abilities to try again.

What are your alternatives?

1. LEASE THE PROPERTY FOR A YEAR, IF YOU
feel its current market evaluation is low. The area you selected may simply not have appreciated at the rate you expected—but it may skyrocket next year. A piece of real
estate is a unique investment—you can get a return on
your purchase while you're sitting on it. Unlike old comic
books, Burma-Shave signs, or Edsels, which, when once out
of vogue, must collect dust for decades before they're valuable again, a property can bring you income while you're
waiting for a slow market to rally.

It's always possible, when you lease, that you will find
the perfect tenant—the one who wants to buy. A beneficial
arrangement for you both, of course, would be the **lease-
option.** Discuss the possibilities with your tenant, and request a 5% nonrefundable deposit in return for a year's option to purchase the property at a set price. At the end of
that time, when the lease is up, you may have a live-in
buyer on your hands—while his monthly rent payments
have covered your carrying costs. If he doesn't buy, you keep
his deposit and you can remarket the property.

2. LIVE IN THE PROPERTY YOURSELF. THE BENE-
fit of renovating a property and residing in it before you sell
is that it buys you time. If the market is not right, you can
simply stay put, enjoying the fruits of your labor, gaining
equity in the property, and deducting the mortgage payments until the world of real estate sees brighter days. This

means that regardless of present market conditions, you're earning money just by staying put.

3. TAKE A SMALLER PROFIT THAN THE ONE YOU expected. You never get hurt taking a profit. So when you planned on making $15,000 but find yourself in a position to make $5,000, you're still doing all right. Maybe you should sell and move on. A $5,000 profit may look okay when you have only one more mortgage payment in the bank.

4. WAIT IT OUT. IT MAY BE WISE TO SIT ON THE property for a while. After all, you've worked long and hard and you don't want the next buyer to reap the rewards a year from now when values go through the roof. If you can afford to carry the property a little longer, it may be the right time to have patience.

5. TAKE THE MONEY AND RUN. THIS IS YOUR last-ditch alternative. When you can't lease the property and you haven't a cent left to make another mortgage payment, you may have to sell, no matter what the price. There is, however, a tax advantage for you here—the government gives a tax break for taking a business loss if you have other income on which to write it off. This is not pleasant, of course, and you wouldn't want to make it a habit.

YOUR FIRST SALE:
THE BEGINNING
OF A CAREER

*O*nce you've found a great house, remodeled it beautifully, sold it, and made a nice profit, you'll have an incredible amount of expertise as a homewrecker. Now you know where the tile companies and wholesale carpet places are; you can tell which wallpapers will work and which colors will not. You understand that buyers get enthusiastic over the tiniest details. You've discovered how effective an agent can be in clinching the deal. And you're probably thinking that the hard part is over—next time will be easier.

You have already started down the road to a safe, tax-deductible, and profitable business. As with any new undertaking, be it selling encyclopedias or acting on the stage, the first experience is the one that teaches you the most and builds your confidence to go on.

When you are starting out, I recommend that you do one property at a time. Live in it after the work is done, and once you're mentally and physically prepared to do another—then sell.

Don't stop now! The first house or apartment is an important lesson—the groundwork for a graduate degree in homewrecking.

Checkpoints

You can sell your remodeled house for a profit if you:

► Attract the right buyers with well-written ads, statements, and photos.

► Are willing to screen all comers when selling the property yourself.

► Hire an experienced, hardworking real estate agent who knows the fine points of your property and is able to communicate them to buyers.

► Set a reasonable price that will still ensure a profit and not impede a quick sale.

► Are willing to lease for a while if your property doesn't sell within half a year.

14

Investing in Rental Property

Once you have bought and sold a few residences for a profit, you may feel ready to venture out into the larger world of real estate. In addition to renovating single-family residences, you can buy other property for investment and earn income by renting it out.

The progression from buying single-family homes to buying properties with rental and investment potential happens differently for different people—some buy a few homes at a time, some purchase new condominiums, some even decide to become high-powered landlords, managing huge multiunit buildings, or converting them into condominiums for sale at a sizable profit.

Income property—houses or apartments bought with the express purpose of leasing to others—has problems and rewards completely unlike those you've already encountered. In your own single-family dwelling, you have 100% control, because you can live in it and sell it when the market's right. But the profits you can earn from owning and operating a multiunit dwelling depend on tenants for cash flow and a guaranteed monthly income. Your property becomes part of a competitive marketplace where you must wait for the potential renters to come to your door.

That's not to say you won't get desirable tenants in your attractively homewrecked property. But there's no guarantee that the units will always be fully occupied, or that all the rents will be in on time, all the time. And in some cities, rent-control regulations make it impossible to get certain tenants *out* of a building you want vacant.

RENTAL PROPERTY
AS A BUSINESS

*M*anaging income property can be a profitable, exciting, and rewarding profession. Many have succeeded at it—others have not. The success stories are those of individuals who learned everything they possibly could about becoming a landlord before they bought their first building.

Residential property can be the home you live in or an income property you've purchased to lease. The two types are definitely related, but they don't feel, look, or perform alike. Your home can be an emotional purchase; investment property cannot. While both should be located in the best neighborhood you can afford, an income property may not necessarily be where you want to live. Your residence requires more attention to detail—more personalization, more creature comforts; income property will be made comfortable by the tenants who live in it. Your home creates a love flow; income property must create a cash flow.

If you think you'd like to invest in income property:

- Be inquisitive. Talk with everyone you know or can meet who has been involved in income property.

- Read, read, read. There are over a hundred

books available for the first-time investor that instruct, educate, and demonstrate the various how-to's of purchasing rental property; several are included in my recommended reading list at the back of this book. These books are invaluable if you intend to make this a profitable business. Some of the rules and tax deductions have changed with the 1986 tax reform bill, but most of the principles are still valid.

- Work out all the numbers—the amount you have in cash, what you can borrow, what all the operating costs are, and what the incoming rents will be.

- Don't give up a full-time job to buy income property until you are certain that the buildings you intend to own can generate enough money to support you.

- Don't become an absentee landlord. When you're just starting out, buy property near where you live.

- Investigate all the properties for sale in your area and inspect them thoroughly. Learn how income property operates with and without a manager, an elevator, a doorman, a security system, and a garage.

- Study the building code in your city to see what multiple-unit dwellings require in the way of sprinklers, fire extinguishers, smoke alarms, escape exits, auxiliary emergency lighting, and general safety.

- Understand that in 1986 all rental real estate assets became "passive investments" for tax purposes. Depending on your taxable income, you may be prohibited from writing off some of the annual costs that have traditionally been deductible.

- Consult your accountant to find out the benefits and drawbacks of owning income property—he will tell you about any deductions, depreciation allowances, improvement write-offs, and trading tax-free into other buildings. Familiarize yourself with all the changes in the 1986 tax reform bill with regard to owning investment property—a lot of the benefits, "the perks," have disappeared.

- Understand what being a landlord means. It can take up a lot of your time.

- Start small, think big. As with your first home purchase, don't jump in over your head. Begin by tackling small, income-producing buildings, not Trump Tower.

Because there are so many people looking for good income property, well-located multiple-unit dwellings that can break even on costs are veritable gold mines in most cities. They're also harder to find than the Loch Ness Monster. If you renovate the units one by one, spiff up the lobby and exterior, and raise the rents yearly, you can take a building with a negative-cash-flow situation and gradually nudge it into the positive-cash-flow column. And when you decide your landlording days are over, or when you want to move on to a new building, you'll see a handsome profit on resale.

There are two questions to ask as you search for the right income property:

- Will the rents I collect on the building cover all my operating expenses?

- If I can afford a short-term negative cash flow, can I raise the rents (through renovation and yearly increases) to cover all my monthly operating costs within a year or two?

Buying income property as a business makes sense only

if the rents collected from the tenants cover all your expenses and the building is in a location where it will climb the ladder of real estate appreciation.

Do You Want to Be a Landlord?

*B*eing a landlord means being a manager, unless you incur the additional expense of hiring one. If you are in charge, you will need to devote a lot of time to dealing with tenants. You have to replace their broken windows, unclog their drains, fix their toilets, and receive their phone calls in the middle of the night.

For me, being a landlord is like eating watermelon: The rewards are delicious, but all those little hassles! I've tried it, I've profitted from it, but it's not my favorite occupation.

Owning a profitable business, for many people, far outweighs the drawbacks of running it. You may choose to be a landlord if:

- You have intentionally bought and renovated a run-down property not to resell, but to lease out for long-term investment.

- Your newly renovated, unoccupied house isn't selling, so you decide to recoup some of your carrying costs by renting it out until the market changes.

- You've bought a brand-new unit in a condominium development to lease now and resell later for a profit.

- You've bought a property with an eye toward retirement. You'll lease it now and move in later.

- You've bought a two-unit building with the in-

tention of living in one unit and renting out
the other.

- You've received permission from the city to
add an income unit to your house.

- You've decided to go on sabbatical, explore a
new city, or go around the world, so you want
to lease your fully furnished home.

- You own two furnished properties in different
cities, or a vacation home as well as a primary
residence, and you want to lease one out while
you're not living in it.

- You've bought a piece of property for your
mother or father to live in; they lease it back
from you.

- You want to start building a real-estate empire, buying one good income property after
another.

- You're ready for a challenge, hard work, and a
lifelong dream—a guesthouse or a bed-and-
breakfast inn.

Residential income property is unique in that you can
get a return on your investment *while* you're holding on to
it. On top of all this, your property is appreciating daily.

How do you find tenants for your income property? You
can advertise in the local newspapers and put a sign outside the property stating that it is for rent.

In most cases, however, it's preferable to use a professional leasing agency. Go with the pros—particularly your
first time out. The agency fee (about 10% of the total lease)
is worth paying for the job they perform.

What will the agency do for you?

- Advertise at their expense for tenants.

- Answer all phone calls of interested parties.

- Show your property to clients.

- Screen prospective tenants, checking their bank and credit references.

- Request information from previous landlords.

- Verify salaries from employers.

After finding a suitable tenant, the agency will deliver to you a signed contract and a security deposit, as well as the money for the first and perhaps the last month's rent. The security deposit serves as a buffer so if there's any damage to your property, the tenants' money covers it when they move out.

The agency will also notify you when a tenant wants to extend his lease or when he gives notice. Thirty days before a tenant leaves the premises, an agent will start showing the apartment again so that you won't have any lapse in rents.

Unfurnished Rentals

*R*enting out a brand-new unfurnished condominium or a house you've remodeled nicely but not elaborately is the most typical method of earning income on investment property. Ideally, you should provide all appliances and make sure the house or apartment is immaculate when you show it. It's best, in this kind of rental, to be conservative in your color scheme.

Your agency will tell you what the going price is for comparable space in your area. Don't expect to charge over market rates unless rental space is at a premium. If you break even the first year on all your carrying costs with an unfurnished property, you're doing well.

Furnished Rentals

*R*esidential investment properties in major metropolitan areas cost considerably more than those in the suburbs or smaller cities. Because you have to spend more, you will have to rent them for more to cover your costs. In cities like New York, Los Angeles, San Francisco, Chicago, Philadelphia, and Washington, D.C., you can furnish your property and lease it for nearly double the unfurnished rate.

These urban areas cater to transient residents who need short-term rentals and are willing to pay for quality housing. The clientele you attract could consist of relocating families, lawyers trying a case, corporations who may want a company apartment, or actors, actresses, or opera stars rehearsing and performing in the city for several months. In cities where hotel prices run from $100 to $200 per night, your lovely apartment, at, let's say, $70 a day or $2,100 a month, will seem like a bargain.

The shorter the term, the higher the rent. The better the location, the higher the rent.

Creating an elegant rental property to lease by the week or month does not mean installing foam-rubber furniture and supplying three glasses, a lamp, and an ashtray. It means the works: lovely furniture, accessories, paintings, plants, a stereo, television, and fully equipped kitchen. This does not have to cost a fortune—you can furnish a one-bedroom apartment for $5,000 to $6,000 if you shop carefully. (Remember, too, that there are separate depreciation schedules for furniture you buy that's used in rental units.)

If you don't feel you can create a smashing apartment on your own, hire a young or new-to-the-trade decorator. Outline your exact budget and pay the decorator 15% to 20% over the cost of all the furnishings.

But if you decide to tackle the decorating yourself, you'll find that it can be fun to put an apartment together from scratch. I always start with a floor plan of the property and arrange the furniture on paper before I do my shopping. That way, I know exactly what size pieces I need to fit in the spaces. You can buy quality furniture inexpensively at department store sales, furniture store clearances, warehouse liquidations, designers' clearance sales, retail and wholesale shops, and country auctions.

Don't forget to look around your own home—there's probably a piece of furniture in every room that you could live without. Older pieces can be fixed, refinished, painted, or reupholstered to look like new. When you're purchasing new furniture, always ask for a discount—particularly if you're buying in quantity. You'll be surprised how often the stores will give you one.

Sometimes just one or two really good-looking items can make a first-class presentation. Then all you need is the design skill to buy other things inexpensively.

On the next page is a floor plan and purchase guide for a one-bedroom, one-bath condominium on San Francisco's Nob Hill that I bought in 1981 for $102,000. The sale price included the kitchen appliances, wall-to-wall carpeting, and draperies—a big savings when it was time to decorate. I furnished the apartment for $5,000 and I've leased it in the range of $1,500 to $1,750 per month.

My monthly costs for an $80,000 mortgage at around 12% interest, homeowners' dues in the condominium, insurance, and property taxes come to $1,270. I certainly could not have leased this place unfurnished and covered my expenses. By furnishing it well, however, I have a monthly income over and above my operating costs.

LEASING YOUR FURNISHED HOME

*I*t may seem anxiety-provoking to let perfect strangers live with your possessions, but if you feel uncomfortable leasing your own home, you can store all items of sentimental value. Recognize that everything in the house is just that—a thing—and things can be replaced. Leasing your own home is a fine idea for those of you who want to take off for a while—to go on a sabbatical, spend a year abroad, or maybe try your hand at home-wrecking in a new city.

Location is of primary importance in the luxury landlord business. People will pay to be in the best neighborhoods; high-paying tenants won't consider anything but.

Floorplan

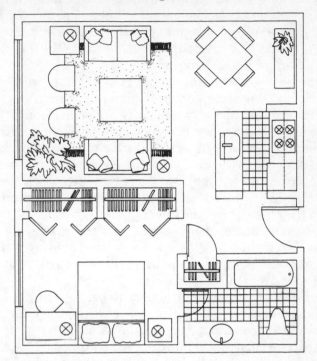

Loveseats (2) on sale, $425 each	$850
Chairs (2), $250 each	500
Coffee table	200
End table	100
Lamps for living room (2)	150
Dining table	300
Dining chairs (4)	600
Sideboard for serving	150
Accessories for living-dining room	350
Kitchen equipment (china, glasses, flatware, pots and pans)	300
Bed, queen-sized	150
Linens and bedcovers	200
Desk	150
Chair for desk	150
Night table	100
Lamps for bedroom (2)	100
Accessories for bedroom	250
Bath towels	50
Color TV	200
Stereo	150
TOTAL:	$5,000

With a well-located, fully furnished house, you can generally write a most attractive lease. I was able to collect enough rent on my house in San Francisco to pay my mortgage, insurance, and property taxes and have money left over to cover my monthly housing costs in London. I couldn't afford *not* to leave town!

I generally use rental agents to select appropriate tenants for my own home, screen them, and collect a whopping security deposit (usually one or two months' rent). If I'm out of town, the agency is responsible for coping with any emergency that might arise. If the tenant informs the rental agent that the dishwasher is no longer functional, he or she can confirm that it died a legitimate death and can authorize (with my consent) the delivery of a new one, for which they'll send me the bill.

For extra peace of mind, you can increase the rental charge and include weekly maid service. This way you have a "chaperone" going into the property on a regular basis to make sure everything is in order.

But don't worry if your housecleaner reports back that the living-room furniture is in the bedroom, the guest room has been turned into a gymnasium, and the tenants have hung all the rugs on the walls. Some changes in your decorating are to be expected, because tenants move furnishings around to suit their own tastes. As long as they don't do any damage, you have nothing to be concerned about. Just be sure your contract states that the house must be returned to you in its original condition.

I once rented out my house to a wonderful "country" couple. The day after they'd moved in I called and asked if I could come over and give them the extra sets of keys I'd promised. I found them surrounded by an aging German shepherd, a Labrador retriever, their mother-in-law's Pekingese, and a tremendous black crow in a giant bird cage in the kitchen where my antique Belgian stove used to be. The furniture had all been reshuffled, two of the beds had been moved into the garage, and the guest bedroom held enough Nautilus machinery to equip a health club.

What did I do? I shot the crow. No. I took a deep breath, handed over the keys, and thanked heaven for security deposits. The couple were high-budget tenants with good references, and I knew they would restore the place to its original splendor before they stepped out the door a year later. And guess what? I was right. The place was immaculate—all ready to rent again. (But my next lease was very specific about pets!)

One way to avoid rental surprises is to rent directly to friends or to friends of friends. This doesn't mean you shouldn't arm yourself with the same kind of ironclad contract you'd sign with strangers, however. That way, everybody *remains* friends.

My home in San Francisco will never officially be mine. Yes, I purchased it, I'm on title, I totally renovated it, and I pay the mortgage every month. Even so, it will always be known as "the Mary Martin House" because Mary leased it from me for two years while she was filming *Over Easy* in the city. Whenever people ask where my house is and I tell them, they invariably say, "Oh, you live in the Mary Martin house." Yep, I do.

REZONING YOUR HOME
TO INCLUDE
A RENTAL UNIT

*Y*our own home is most likely zoned by the city you live in as residential. If you want to convert part of your living space to a rental, you must comply with the city's zoning ordinances. Strictly zoned residential areas do not permit establishments like offices, stores, or restaurants.

Zoning can change, however. Areas of gradual alteration in a city are called T-zones, or transition zones. Previously zoned single-family neighborhoods may open up to include multiple-unit dwellings or even commercial businesses like doctors' and lawyers' offices.

You can apply to the planning commission for a variance to change the zoning of your property if, say, you wish to convert your single-family dwelling into two units. It's a long procedure, permission is not always granted, and neighbors can fight you at a public hearing if they're concerned about the increased number of cars occupying valuable parking places and a general decline in the character of their neighborhood.

If you're successful in obtaining permission to rent out part of your property, you will have to comply with city codes and restrictions, and this may mean incurring some additional expenses. For example, you may have to install a fire escape if you don't already have one (each family must have two means of egress). You'll have to decide whether you want your tenants to have their own utility meters and perhaps their own furnace so that they can pay their bills directly.

Remember that although you will be writing off a portion of your house and its upkeep on your income taxes, you will have to claim the extra income you collect in rent payments. And because you have "improved" your property, your property taxes will probably be adjusted upward.

Being an on-premises landlord is convenient, because you're right there to take care of any and all emergencies. It's inconvenient, because you're readily available when your tenant knocks on your door asking for "just one more favor." Landlording in your own home is not everyone's cup of tea.

For every legal unit in major metropolitan cities in the United States, there is probably at least one illegal apartment conversion. If during a routine city examination for tax adjustments, or because a jealous neighbor complains, you're caught with an illegal apartment, you may be asked to remove the second kitchen or swear on your life that only your mother-in-law will live there. However, inspectors often cast a blind eye on these units because there's such a shortage of good rental space in many cities.

MANSION INVESTMENTS

*O*nce you've moved from condo to cottage to three-bedroom house, you may start looking for an even larger challenge. You suddenly hit upon a veritable mansion that's elegant, enormous, and totally run-down. But with the proper touch, it could become the most magnificent house in town. And maybe the most expensive.

Your friends say you're crazy. Your kids think the place is haunted, but they love ghosts. Your agent is pretty sure he can sell it when it's all done up. Your banker approves the loan request, and your contractor can't wait to get started. Up until the day you sign the final papers, your common sense keeps telling you to pull back, to remember that there simply aren't that many mansion buyers running around with megabucks. Your creative genius is longing to accept the challenge, and the devil in you is saying, "Go ahead!"

Granted, mansion buyers make up a small percentage of the homebuying population. You will not sell this beauty in a week or even six months, but there is always someone around who wants the best property in town, and if you're sitting in it, that person will pay a good deal to get you out. And your potential profit is significant—probably five times what you would make on a smaller house.

Realistically, you should tackle a mansion only after you have a great track record. You will need credibility to be able to borrow the necessary funds for purchase, to do the renovations, and to meet the monthly debt service—which can be staggering. If you are in the market for a mansion, be sure to plan on more monthly payments than you normally would, allowing for the length of time it will take to sell.

You can offset your costs, however, by making the best use of this beauty. Lease it out for weddings, bar mitzvahs, corporate parties, motion-picture shoots, TV-show tapings, or as a background to photograph clothes catalogues. (You can get about $1,000 a day for a big photo session.)

While you're trying to sell your mansion, have fun living in it. Plan on holding a family reunion, a roller-skating derby on the lower level, or weekend sleep-over parties of thirty. Entertain like Gatsby and live like a queen!

INVESTING
IN A GUEST HOUSE

*T*here's another possibility for a mansion with a lot of bedrooms if you can obtain the proper zoning—and that's a bed-and-breakfast inn. Home-cooked breakfasts with linen napkins, freshly squeezed orange juice, delicious coffee, a fire burning in the common area. Ma Innkeeper in the kitchen, Pa Innkeeper chopping wood, and Kid Innkeepers at the front desk. No video games, maybe one television in the parlor; charming bedrooms with calico curtains; loving hands creating a home away from home.

The B&B business is enormous—and enormously profitable—in the United States. Most establishments don't hesitate to charge $50 to $100 per room. But they're so much more comfortable and charming than the big chains with formal dining, valet service, and a telex machine.

I love B&Bs and had a huge success with one I ran in San Francisco in the late 1970s. I started the venture with a good friend and business associate with whom I owned a couple of investment condominiums.

Malin phoned me one day about a lovely mansion that was for sale. The building had been zoned a guest house during the war, and every prospective buyer was trying to figure out how to turn it into a private residence. She believed the place should remain a guest house, and that we should rent out elegant rooms by the month for elegant prices.

The house was a jewel—an early 1900s brick building with a wonderful garden entrance. Inside were ten spacious guest rooms with high ceilings, beautiful moldings, fireplaces, and hardwood floors. The only drawback was that there was an adjoining bathroom for every two bedrooms. Also, the condition of the house was awful. Not only had the building last been zoned during the war, it had also last been cleaned then.

We bought the property for $300,000 and pledged to give the seller a down payment of $60,000 six months after closing, when Malin and I completed the sale on another building we jointly owned. The seller took back 80% financing. This meant we were carrying a $240,000 first mortgage at 10%. We also took out a $60,000 second mortgage to pay for the renovations. Except for the real estate commission and closing costs, this was a no-money-down purchase. With debt services on two mortgages, property taxes, insurance, staff salaries, utilities, and extras, we had a grand monthly expenditure total of $3,800. We planned to rent each of the ten rooms for $380 a month, hoping to break even after the first year.

Three weeks into our renovation, a *hotel* license arrived in the mail for renewal. What did guest-house zoning with a hotel license mean? We discovered we could rent out our rooms by the week, not only by the month as we had thought. If we charged hotel prices of $40 per night or $280 a week, we would bring in a whopping $1,200 a month per room. Not bad, when the break-even figure was $380.

Malin was the manager and I was the renovator. I had a marvelous time, buying linens by the case and beds by the dozen. Chairs, lamps, ten oriental rugs, handmade quilts, the works! And I actually came in under budget because I was buying in quantity. I worried a little about the lack of private baths, so I installed large built-in vanities and sinks in each room. Our guests didn't mind—sharing the facilities was all part of the guest-house charm.

The guest house opened in late 1978. Our week-long tenants loved it; some stayed for months. Thanks to a four-page color spread in *San Francisco Magazine,* the word got out, and suddenly we had no vacancies—bookings months in advance.

Most of our success I credit to Malin's managing. Tom, our resident "Jeeves," got a free apartment in the basement and was paid a minimal salary. He adored the place and played his role to the hilt. In addition to doing the cleaning and laundry and preparing breakfast, he served champagne in his own silver ice bucket and informed the guests that this hotel was so special, he watered the plants with Perrier. (We suspect he occasionally did!)

Proper, constant, and honest management is the key to any small hotel. As manager, you must eat, sleep, and drink your job. It engulfs your life like a new romance, with few of the rewards.

After two years, the work became more than full-time, and both Malin and I were ready to move on. We put the property up for sale. Price tag: $1.4 million.

Yes, that was a lot, even for San Francisco. Our realtor, a crackerjack commercial agent, arrived at the figure by working the numbers—present gross income, vacancy factor, operating costs, property taxes, and available financing. She assured us it would go for full price, and she was right. We sold to a buyer who planned to take our efforts one step further and sell the rooms as timeshares.

So after acquiring the mansion with no money down, financing the purchase and renovation with two loans, and maintaining a positive cash flow each month, we sold our guest house for over four times the original cost. Not bad for two neophytes in the hotel business.

Our B&B was a little more of a challenge than the one you might like to attempt, but it serves as a good example. A large "white elephant" mansion from the ten-to-fifteen-bedroom era offers a wonderful opportunity if you purchase it at the right price, obtain good financing, and have the proper zoning. The rental income on each room can cover the monthly costs of a total renovation and a full-time staff.

These houses are sprinkled all over the United States, from Princeton, New Jersey, to Sonoma, California. They're generally easy to buy because they're hard for an owner to sell—they're costly to heat and to maintain and are surrounded by large grounds that demand constant attention.

You can run a much smaller operation, a "boarding-house" in your own home, by renting out one or two bedrooms on a nightly or weekly basis. This is not a bed-and-breakfast, even if you serve the morning meal, and is possible only in certain states, where zoning permits.

In order to run a B&B, you must apply to the local planning commission for the proper zoning. In some states, if you're going to serve food, you must apply for a restaurant license as well. Once you're set up, the best ways to attract business are by advertising in local magazines and newspapers, by printing business cards for your satisfied customers to distribute, and by word of mouth.

If yours is a first-class operation, with quality furnishings, good service, and a homey but elegant atmosphere, and you commit yourself to becoming a full-time manager or hiring one, you can make a B&B into a flourishing business with lots of earning potential.

INVESTING
IN MULTIPLE-UNIT
DWELLINGS

*J*ust when you've embarked on your third, fourth, or fifth successful residential renovation and are feeling quite proud of yourself, some of your developer colleagues may wander by to watch the proceedings. They'll kick a few two-by-fours, peer at your floor plans, poke around the construction site, and tell you that the house looks great. All your houses look great. Then, in the same breath, they'll remark upon your incredible lack of ambition. They'll want to know why the devil you're still piddling around with *houses*.

"After all, the big money's in development!" they'll say. "Multiunit dwellings. Converting apartment buildings to condos and co-ops. You'll never make a killing if you stick with single-family housing."

Well, I thought, maybe this wasn't the end of the rainbow. It was true, I was making good money. All my renovated houses were selling, and I loved my job and my work crew—but it was possible that I was missing out on something. "Condo" had recently become the hottest buzzword in real estate lingo.

So I finally succumbed. I gave in to temptation and bought a ten-unit apartment building for $1.3 million. It looked as if I had everything going for me—a Pacific Heights location (an excellent residential neighborhood in San Francisco) and an easy condo conversion because the building was in pretty good shape. It just had to be brought up to code. I needed to put in a few more sprinklers, replace some of the electrical work, add restricting showerheads in the bathrooms, and hang fire extinguishers on each floor. I figured on a half-million-dollar profit when I put the units up for sale at the end of my renovation job and conversion, eighteen months hence. It would take me twenty-five houses to make that much!

But things did not proceed as planned. In the early 1980s, with interest rates topping out at 20%, the real estate market was a tricky business—single-family homeowners as well as developers were feeling the pinch. Tenants were also beginning to protest apartment conversions in the city, and as their objections grew stronger, the city began to apply the brakes. Conversion rules changed almost daily in 1981, and red tape was being manufactured as quickly as Rubic's cubes. The number of conversions dwindled. When I started my venture, the city was permitting a thousand units to be converted a year with a minimum of bureaucratic hassles. By the time my renovation was under way, the number of conversions had dropped to two hundred a year. It took me three years, rather than the one and a half I had planned on, to get approval.

In the meantime, I was struggling to pay my monthly carrying costs. Because of the new rent-control laws the city imposed, I was allowed to raise rents only 7% the first year and 4% each of the next three.

After four years of negative cash flow, I sold for exactly the amount that I had put into the building. I received the total of my original purchase price, my carrying costs, and the improvements I'd made on four of the apartments. So I broke even. No profit, no loss.

When money is tight in real estate, it's time to sit tight. To keep hold of your properties, live in them or lease them out—don't try to convert and sell them.

I'm not trying to scare you away from conversions with this less than heartwarming story—I'm only pointing out the problems I encountered. You can still buy apartment buildings in many big cities and turn them into condos or co-ops for a profit—*if*, and this is a big if, you can bankroll a negative cash flow while you're converting and they are located in an area that's not overbuilt.

There is a halfway point between the single-family home and the multiunit apartment house—a two-to-six-unit building. In most cities, buildings with six units or less can be converted into condominiums with a minimum of red tape if they are owner-occupied, because many of the limitations the city imposes on larger buildings don't apply.

The great thing about converting a small property is that you can live in one of the units and rent or sell the others depending on your need for monthly income or cash return on your original purchase. This is such a good investment, in fact, that small multiple-unit buildings priced right in good neighborhoods tend to be as rare as puppy feathers. If you find a great one, don't think twice—buy it!

OWNING A SECOND HOME

A second or vacation home can be a good compromise between a residence and a rental property. You can kill three birds with one stone, buying a nice little retreat for yourself, renting it out if you choose, and upgrading it so that you can sell for a profit in a few years.

Around 5% of the population owns a second home and many have profited from resale when their property is located in a popular and growing area. The government allows you to deduct all the interest you may be paying on a loan plus the real estate property taxes from your taxable income. Just as you do with your primary residence.

A second or vacation home is a pure luxury item—purchased by the majority of Americans for their own personal use and enjoyment. It can be a country hideaway, an hour or two drive out of a major metropolitan area, or a city pied-à-terre for the homeowner who calls his suburban home his primary residence. It can be a condo in Florida when you reside in Ohio or a Colorado ski chalet when you're a resident in Texas.

You must be able to afford the time, money, and energy to keep a second home in the same good shape as your primary residence, for present enjoyment and future resale.

I've been able to reduce the additional monthly outlay of mortgage payments, taxes, insurance, and utilities by having a partner who shares the expenses. One rarely occupies a second home even 50% of the year. Four partners can use a second home one week each month—reducing each partner's cash investment and monthly expenses considerably.

If both the financial and physical obligations of owning a second home have turned your dreamspot into an albatross, you can rent it out to offset some or all of the monthly expenses. You must check with your accountant or tax adviser to see if renting a second home will be a tax advantage for you in your particular income bracket.

You can make excellent profits on the sale of a second or vacation home in a desirable area, but the kind of renovating you do must be carefully thought out. As with other types of properties, over-remodeling is a big mistake. But insulating a summer lakeside cottage so it can be used in the winter, for example, can be a wise investment—as long as the location is right.

PARTNERSHIPS
AND CORPORATIONS

From purchasing to financing, improving, leasing, and managing, income property is a hands-on operation. It requires a thorough education in real estate law, accounting, business, design, and public relations.

If the thought of dealing with tenants, managing monthly cash flow, documenting expenses, handling vacancy factors, and maintaining property other than your own residence doesn't send you into paroxysms of joy, fear not. It could—the idea is to get your income property operating smoothly so that you feel comfortable enjoying time away from it.

Sometimes the best way to do this is to share the responsibility. By going into a joint-venture partnership with someone else, you may acquire the necessary support system to get you moving. I have joint-ventured many real estate deals, dividing the liabilities along with the profits. Especially in a first business venture, a partnership is a wonderful way to get started.

If you intend to buy and sell properties as a business, the time may come when your accountant strongly suggests that you incorporate. There are a variety of tax advantages in doing so.

When you are a corporation instead of an individual, you are allowed to deduct any and all expenses incurred for your business. You may write off a company car, company stationery, company business trips. You are also taxed at a different rate, depending on your individual situation. Discuss the advantages with your accountant or tax adviser.

IS INCOME PROPERTY FOR YOU?

*I*f your homewrecking business really takes off, you may find yourself juggling several properties at once. You may be collecting rent on one property, buying another, and considering a third—all in the same month. It's exhilarating, challenging, and profit-making. The wonderful thing about a real estate career is that it offers you the opportunity to take charge of your investments and make them work for you.

As someone who has owned properties on both sides of the Atlantic, I can attest to the fact that there's nothing at all to equal the sense of accomplishment that comes with the ability to buy and renovate property, and keep rolling the profits from one investment to another. Collecting income from property you own is a double bonus—you are being financially recompensed for spending your money wisely.

Checkpoints

You can earn income on properties you own but don't live in if you:

- ▸ Look for positive cash flow in the properties you purchase.

- ▸ Lease unfurnished or furnished income units.

- ▸ Lease out your own home through a reputable agency.

- ▸ Rezone your house to include a rental unit.

- ▸ Invest in a mansion to realize bigger resale profits or create a zoned guest house.

- ▸ Convert a small multiunit dwelling to condominiums.

- ▸ Buy a vacation home yourself or with partners.

- ▸ Form a partnership or corporation to share the responsibilities of income property.

15

What Do You Really Want from Real Estate?

t was 9:00 P.M. All of Anne Washington's guests moved from the drawing room into the dining room, where dinner was being served. Anne's fiancé, Larry, led the party into the beautifully appointed room.

Henry Schuman leaned toward his wife, Karen, as they took their seats. "Anne really knows how to throw a party. Champagne and caviar to start, hired help, Chef Gregory in the kitchen. She must have made a killing on that last house she sold."

Karen nodded. "I hear the final price was over twice

what she paid for it. When it's public record next month, remind me to look it up."

Anne Washington *did* make a bundle on her last home sale—the third in seven years. She started homewrecking when she decided her office job wasn't terribly exciting or challenging anymore. The first time she sold a house, she doubled the salary she was getting. The second time, she earned so much she quit her job.

Anne smiled graciously across the table at the Jacksons. "Charlie, sweetheart, we're going to miss you, running off to the East Coast with a big company promotion. What are you going to do with your wonderful little house?"

"You wouldn't believe it," Charlie responded, "but we just signed a lease with a lovely couple who are planning to rent it for a year. It'll net me a nice little profit every month."

There were other success stories at the table. Larry, Anne's fiancé, was a true real estate pioneer. He was one of the first two purchasers in the high-rise condominium on Main Street. Everyone made fun of him when he bought— who wanted to live downtown? What a crazy investment! But he earned $20,000 profit on his first condo sale and nearly twice that on his second.

"How's your son doing?" Larry asked Charlie Jackson.

"Splendid," Charlie nodded. "He and Sally just had a baby and they're making money hand over fist renovating old houses in Hoboken, New Jersey.

"And speaking of making money on real estate," Charlie went on, "my brother Josh bought a studio apartment four years ago to use as a small office. He wanted peace and quiet to write the novel of the century. No, he never did sell the book, but he sold the studio this year and netted a $45,000 profit!"

The first wine was served, and Larry stood at the head of the table to salute his hostess and the guests. "It's been a good year for all of us," he said, raising his glass. "May we continue to enjoy our good health and wonderful friends, and live as happily as our mortgages will allow."

The conversation throughout the dinner wove back and forth from politics to theater to local gossip, but it kept returning to recent house and apartment sales as it does at dinner parties everywhere these days. Real estate is a hot topic.

Right now, we're enjoying a buying boom in this country. People aren't fixed to one spot—they're very mobile, with a spirit that encourages change. They don't have to buy just one house in a lifetime; they can buy a new one—a better one—whenever they're ready.

So what are *you* waiting for? The time has come for you to make your move, to put down this book, get out of your chair, and *act*. Often the hardest part of adopting a new profession or moving to a new city or putting a new idea into action is simply having the courage of your convictions—daring to make that difficult leap from paper to practice. Rolling the dice. Overcoming the fear factor.

I was lucky when I began homewrecking. I didn't know I was starting a business, so I had nothing to be afraid of. But you, having made your way through chapters on every aspect of buying, renovating, and reselling property, are clearly aware of what you can do. Or what you'd like to do.

You may be thinking of everything that could go wrong, of all the pitfalls, the mistakes, the sleepless nights. You may say to yourself, "I can't possibly. I'd have an easier time coordinating a royal wedding."

Being prepared is one thing. Overanticipating problems is another. If you keep thinking about what might go wrong, you'll never get started doing things right. And guess what? It's okay to make mistakes. I certainly did—all the way up to Property Number 71. Yes, I spent sleepless nights worrying about what I was going to do about the Wolfe range that wouldn't fit into the house, the contractor who promised he'd finish in May and was still working in July, and the boiler that flooded a condo the day it went on the market. There were times when I went over my renovation budget and a few occasions when I had only enough for two mortgage payments but not an offer in sight. Problems crept up—but so did solutions.

The nice thing about home renovation is that, unlike betting on a losing horse or making an unwise purchase in the stock market, you always have a chance to make a second choice—be it changing the decor or leasing the place out until the market rallies. *You are always in control of your investment.*

Every experience, good and bad, with every house or apartment I sold, taught me how to be a better negotiator, a better designer, a better buyer, a better deal-maker. A better and more capable person. If the picture I paint seems rosy to you, if it sounds as if I tumbled effortlessly into a successful real estate career, it's not because it was a cinch. It's because I loved every minute of it—including the pitfalls and the problem-solving.

What do *you* really want out of real estate? You may not wish to do what I did, to buy and sell properties quickly, juggling the profits for more creative deals. You may simply wish to stop renting and buy a property so that you'll have one appreciating asset in your life. Or move to a better neighborhood. Or create a nice income. Or become an inveterate do-it-yourselfer, renovating one house slowly and carefully over a period of years, then selling it so that you can buy another and begin the process all over again.

You can delve into home renovation just once or twice, or keep trading up into the nicest house in town. After your first experience, when you see the demand for beautifully renovated homes, you may decide to make this a full-time business and buy income property as well.

You can do anything you want. Go fast, go slow. But do it now. Next year will not be too late, but properties will be more expensive. Always remember that you're not alone. If you put yourself in the hands of a good real estate agent, in the office of a top accountant, and into a pair of overalls beside a reputable contractor, you'll learn about every aspect of home renovation from experts.

Being housewise, buying and renovating real estate, means knowing how to work with people—dealing with different personalities, learning from everyone who can help you, and joining the team. Your positive attitude will enable you to handle the problems that arise and make each work day an accomplishment. Once you've built a reputation as a person who treats people fairly and has a good time doing it, you have started down the profitable path to homewrecking success.

Do it. Take a risk. Get up and out. You have places to go, people to contact, questions to ask, and properties to see. You'll find excitement, challenge, hard work, and tremendous satisfaction in becoming housewise. You'll sharpen your old homemaking skills and acquire new ones along the way.

I gambled on real estate and turned up all aces. You can too. The world loves a winner, so act like one. In this business, it's not hard to become one.

Recommended Reading

GENERAL REAL ESTATE BOOKS

All America's Real Estate Book. Carolyn Janik and Ruth Rejnis. Viking Penguin, 1985.

The Complete Book of Homebuying. Michael Sumichrast and Ronald Shafer. Bantam, 1985.

INVESTMENT GUIDES

How to Build a Real Estate Money Machine. Wade Cook. Regency, 1981, rev. 1986

How to Make It in Real Estate When You're Cash Poor. Hollis Norton. Simon and Schuster, 1982.

Inside Real Estate. H. I. Sonny Bloch and Grace Lichtenstein. Weidenfeld & Nicolson, 1987.

Nothing Down. Robert G. Allen. Simon and Schuster, 1980, rev. 1984.

The Smart Investor's Guide to Real Estate. Robert Bruss. Crown, 1985.

Interior Design Books

The Art of Stencilling. Lyn Le Grice. Clarkson N. Potter, 1986.

Attention to Detail. Herbert W. Wise. Putnam, 1982.

Decorating with Paint. Jocasta Innes. Harmony Books, 1986.

Designers Guide to Surfaces and Finishes. Penny Radford. Whitney Library of Design, 1984.

English Style (1984) and *French Style* (1982). Suzanne Slesin and Stafford Cliff. Clarkson N. Potter.

The House Book (1976), *The Kitchen Book* (1977), and *The Bed and Bath Book* (1985). Terence Conran, all published by Crown.

Italian Style. Catherine Sabino and Angelo Tondini. Clarkson N. Potter, 1985.

Pierre Deux's French Country. Pierre Moulin, Pierre LeVec, and Linda Dannenberg. Clarkson N. Potter, 1984.

All *Sunset* and *Ortho* books about specific areas of the house; Mary Gilliat and Laura Ashley decorating books are also recommended.

Index